OWNERSHIP AND CONTROL

Margaret M. Blair

OWNERSHIP
AND
CONTROL

RETHINKING
CORPORATE GOVERNANCE
FOR THE
TWENTY-FIRST CENTURY

The Brookings Institution
WASHINGTON, D.C.

Copyright © 1995
The Brookings Institution
1775 Massachusetts Avenue, N.W., Washington, D.C. 20036

Library of Congress Cataloging-in-Publication data:
Blair, Margaret M., 1950–
  Ownership and control : rethinking corporate governance for the twenty-first
century / Margaret M. Blair
  p. c.m.
  Includes bibliographical references and index.
  ISBN 0-8157-0948-X (acid-free paper). — ISBN 0-8157-0947-1 (acid-free paper : pbk.)
  1. Corporate governance—United States. 2. Corporate governance—Law and
legislation—United States. I. Title
HD2785.B543 1995
658.4—dc20   2095-2435
                                  CIP

The paper used in this publication meets the minimum requirements of the
American National Standard for Information Sciences—Permanence of Paper for
Printed Library Materials, ANSI Z39.48-1984.

Designed by Alan Carter
Composition by AlphaTechnologies/mps, Mechanicsville, Maryland
Printed by R. R. Donnelley and Sons, Co., Harrisonburg, Virginia

FOREWORD

IN THE UNITED STATES, publicly traded companies generate about 58 percent of all national income and employ about a third of all employed people. Thus the health of these institutions and questions about their role in society are matters of perennial interest. With former communist countries looking to the West for models of how to organize their own institutions of capitalism, it is unsettling to see U.S. corporations embroiled in takeovers, boardroom battles for control, downsizings, and restructurings. It is not surprising, therefore, that business leaders and policymakers are asking whether existing forms of corporate governance are working as well as they could. In particular, will they continue to maximize wealth creation in a world where markets for financial capital are increasingly global and where the specialized knowledge of employees is increasingly important?

In this book Margaret Blair reviews how the institutional arrangements for the governance of public corporations in the United States are supposed to work, in theory and in law, and she lays out the economic rationale for these arrangements. She then assesses two partially conflicting arguments as to why the existing system might not be performing as well as it could: 1) that shareholders do not have enough power to control management and prevent misuse of corporate resources; and 2) that pressures from the financial markets cause managerial myopia, which, if true, implies that shareholders should have even less influence than they do. Blair then presents her own view, that exclusive emphasis on the powers and rights of shareholders leads to underinvestment by other stakeholders and thus diminishes potential corporate wealth creation.

Blair argues that corporations should be regarded not just as bundles of physical assets that belong to shareholders, but rather as institutional arrangements for governing the relationships among all of the parties that contribute firm-specific assets. This includes not only shareholders, but also long-term employees who develop specialized skills of value to the corporation, and suppliers, customers, or others who may also make specialized investments. If the job of corporate management is to maximize the total wealth created by the enterprise (as Blair argues it should be), rather than just the value of shareholders' stake, then management must take into account the effect of corporate decisions and actions on all stakeholders in the firm. But, she says, stakeholders must be defined very specifically to mean those who have contributed firm-specific assets that are at risk in the enterprise.

This project was partly funded though the Brookings Center for Law, Economics and Politics, which receives financial support from the AT&T Foundation, the CIGNA Foundation, CSX Corporation, Crum and Forster, Inc., Honeywell, Inc., Reinsurance Association of America, Springs Industries, Inc., Starr Foundation, State Farm Insurance Companies, and Union Carbide Corporation. In addition the project received support directly from the Vanguard Group. All of this financial support is greatly appreciated.

The author would also like to thank the many people who read various drafts of the manuscript as it was being prepared, providing detailed and helpful feedback: Henry Aaron, Bernard Aidinoff, Elizabeth Bailey, David Binns, Sanjai Bhagat, Barry Bosworth, Thomas Cole, Roger Conner, William Dickens, John Friedland, William Gale, Theresa Ghilarducci, Claudia Goldin, Michael Higgins, Lynn Karoly, Margaret Levenstein, Martin Lipton, Ellen Magenheim, George Martin, Martin Mayer, Paul Milgrom, Nell Minow, Adam Posen, Edward Regan, Lois Rice, Mark Roe, Charles Schultze, Daniel Sichel, Donald Stockdale, Timothy Taylor, Andrew Vollmer, Steven Wallman, and Peyton Young. Marc Rysman and Aaron Sparrow provided able and loyal research assistance. The book was verified by Jason Rhoades, Laura Kelly, and Aaron Sparrow. Martha Gottron edited the manuscript, Deborah Patton prepared the index, and Lisa Guillory provided general assistance to the author.

The interpretations and conclusions are those of the author and should not be attributed to any of the groups that provided financial support, to any individuals who provided assistance, or to the trustees, officers, or other staff members of the Brookings Institution.

Bruce K. MacLaury
President

April 1995
Washington, D.C.

CONTENTS

1. Introduction   1
2. A Primer on Corporate Governance   17
3. A Finance Perspective on What's Wrong with the System   94
4. Are Financial Markets Too Short-Sighted?   122
5. Can Institutional Investors Fix the Governance System?   145
6. Whose Interests Should Corporations Serve?   202
7. Toward a New View of Goals and Governance in the
   Corporate Sector   235
8. Governance Structures Designed for Total Wealth
   Creation   275
9. Policy Conclusions and Recommendations   323
References   341
Index   361

1

INTRODUCTION

UNTIL THE 1990S THE PHRASE *corporate governance* was rarely uttered outside the arcane world of law school texts and academic treatises. Since the Great Depression, the basics of corporation and securities law appeared to be well established and settled in practice. The same seemed to be true of most of the other legal, cultural, and institutional arrangements that determine who owns large corporations in the United States, how they are controlled, and how they relate to their various constituents, including shareholders, creditors, employees, customers, suppliers, and the communities where they operate. Not that large corporations have been immune to criticism: consumer advocates, labor leaders, environmentalists, scholars, and policymakers have been concerned for a long time about corporate behavior, including market concentration and

1

oligopoly power and whether corporations can be compelled to behave in socially responsible ways.[1] But few people questioned
whether the rules and customs by which large business corporations
are organized, financed, and governed in this country were fundamentally sound.

Events of the 1980s and early 1990s have broken down that
complacency. Issues of corporate governance—including the power
and responsibilities of boards of directors, the rules governing takeovers, the role and influence of institutional investors, and the pay of
chief executives—have come to dominate the pages of the business
press. Corporate governance issues have also come under scrutiny as
part of the ongoing public policy debates about the ability of U.S.
firms to provide a growing standard of living for U.S. citizens and to
compete effectively in international markets. Dozens of new jour-
nals and newsletters have been started to report on developments in
corporate governance, high level commissions have been established
to consider reforms, numerous new laws and rule changes have been
passed and others have been proposed, and corporate leaders and
Wall Street investors alike are self-consciously examining the formal
and informal rules by which they operate.

Those rules can be enormously complex and varied. Corporations
are legal devices for assembling and organizing capital, labor, and
other resources to produce and sell goods and services. Corporations
are chartered at the state level and are legal entities separate from
any of the individuals or groups who participate in or contribute
resources to them. Although protected and sanctioned by the government, they are generally private enterprises, the product of complex sets of state charters and private contracts and agreements
among their many participants. In the United States the government
has avoided direct involvement in the management of corporations.

---

[1]See, for example, Herman (1981).

Instead, its role is indirect, providing the legal and institutional environment to encourage and support wealth-creating economic activity. To be most effective, that environment should foster the development of efficient corporate governance structures, that is, systems of governance that lead to the most efficient use of resources to create wealth for society as a whole.

Although numerous individuals, from financial investors to suppliers, to employees, may contribute resources to and have a stake in the success of a given corporation, the broad policies, strategic plans, and day-to-day decisions in large publicly traded corporations are largely controlled by professional managers. These are typically individuals whose own at-risk assets are small relative to the assets they administer. Thus the central problem in any corporate governance system is how to make corporate executives accountable to the other contributors to the enterprise whose investments are at risk, while still giving those executives the freedom, the incentives, and the control over resources they need to create and seize investment opportunities and to be tough competitors.

The phrase *corporate governance* is often applied narrowly to questions about the structure and functioning of boards of directors or the rights and prerogatives of shareholders in boardroom decisionmaking. In this book I adopt a much broader view of corporate governance, one that refers to the whole set of legal, cultural, and institutional arrangements that determine what publicly traded corporations can do, who controls them, how that control is exercised, and how the risks and returns from the activities they undertake are allocated. This book is about what constraints and requirements are imposed on those who manage corporations, whose interests managers must serve, what influence and recourse the various constituents have, and what pressures they can bring to see that their interests are served. These arrangements include corporation law and boardroom practices, obviously, but they also include aspects of corporate finance, securities and bankruptcy law, laws

governing the behavior of financial institutions, labor relations practices, contract law and theory, property rights, compensation systems, and internal information and control systems.

Although economists, legal scholars, management specialists,
and organizational theorists often treat each of these subjects as
separate fields of study, a small but growing group of researchers
have come to believe that studying them together is essential to
understanding how they operate as whole systems.[2] A book of this
length obviously cannot treat all of these subjects in full.[3] But I
touch on all of these issues in considering whether the corporate
governance system in the United States, taken as a whole, tends to
assign control rights to the parties that have the incentives and the
information they need to use resources in ways that most efficiently
generate wealth.

The issue of control is extremely important, but this book is also
about ownership, a concept that is fundamental to economic activity
in a free market economy. Ownership of private property is the
central mechanism by which incentives are created for the efficient
use of resources in a free market economy. But, despite its importance, ownership is a complex concept with multiple meanings, and
in the context of corporate governance, it is a particularly slippery
word. Applied to real property or other well-defined physical assets,
ownership normally entails the right to possess or dispose of the
asset, the right to use the asset in any way not specifically prohibited
by law or proscribed by prior contract, the right to claim the proceeds

---

[2] Aoki (1988) and Gerlach (1992) each study the Japanese corporate governance
system in this kind of holistic way. Kester (1991, 1992a, and 1992b) has done
comparative studies of U.S., German, and Japanese corporate governance systems that
take this systemwide approach. Porter (1992) is also in this spirit.

[3] An excellent textbook on the economics of organizations by Paul Milgrom and
John Roberts of Stanford University looks at the economics of many of these issues
(but not the legal aspects) in a fairly comprehensive way. See Milgrom and Roberts
(1992).

from the sale of the asset or the returns generated by the asset, and
the responsibility for bearing certain risks associated with possession and control of the asset. The rights of possession and control of
physical assets are customarily bundled together with the right to
receive benefits from the asset and the responsibility for bearing risk
associated with its misuse or with a decline in its value. But it is
important to realize that this bundling of rights and responsibilities
is a matter of legal and social convention. This book is about those
conventions as they apply to corporations.

In large, publicly traded corporations, the normal rights that con-
stitute ownership of real property have been unbundled and parceled
out to numerous partipants in the enterprise. Many physical assets
may be involved, as well as many intangible assets, and the various
rights and responsibilities associated with those assets are carved up
in many different ways. Thus taking "ownership" as the starting
point in discussions about corporate governance, a point from which
certain rights or claims are supposed to follow, is quite problematic.
Indeed, I argue that the common assertion that "shareholders are the
owners" of large corporations is a highly misleading statement that
often does more to obscure the important issues than to illuminate
them.[4] This book considers what shareholders' claims, rights, and
responsibilities are and should be in the context of a more general
discussion about how all the various rights, claims, and responsibilities for corporate performance are and should be divided among all
the participants in the corporate enterprise.

I begin by explaining in chapter 2 how the existing system of
corporate governance typically works, examining first the basic system as it applies to the small company financed by a small group of

---

[4]Milgrom and Roberts (1992, p. 289) define "owning an asset" to mean "having the
residual rights of control" and distinguish that right from the right to the residual
return. I discuss what these residual rights mean in ch. 2.

investors. Then I show how legal and institutional arrangements have evolved to deal with the problems that arise for large companies, whose investors may be widespread and virtually anonymous to the company and its management. These legal arrangements include securities laws, fiduciary responsibilities of officers and directors, laws governing mergers and takeovers, and laws governing shareholder voice. Other, less formal institutional arrangements include the customs and practices of boards of directors and the internal systems for measurement, control, and compensation. These various arrangements set some basic ground rules—some legally enforceable, some merely customary—that help determine what information is disclosed to whom, who has what claims against the firm and what mechanisms to enforce those claims, and who has what other rights and responsibilities.

Each of these clusters of legal and institutional arrangements forms the basis for an entire field of study, and generally, each developed separately, without a unified goal of trying to make corporations more efficient or productive. Some were put into place, for example, to prevent outright fraud or abuse by management or by some group of security holders, while others evolved more or less by historical accident. All have been the subject of controversy and of reform proposals in recent years. No one subfield is examined here in enough detail to satisfy the experts, but I have set out to show how all of the parts work together and to consider various reform proposals in this larger context.

At least five developments are responsible for the intense business, media, academic, and policy focus on corporate governance issues. The first was the perception in the mid-1980s that many U.S. companies were falling behind their Japanese and German counterparts in the rate at which they were investing in new plant and equipment, introducing new products, or pursuing new markets. U.S. corporations were accused of abandoning markets to Japanese and German rivals rather than committing themselves to staying in the game and competing harder for market share. In autos, consumer electronics, machine tools, semiconductors, computers, copiers, steel, and textiles, U.S. companies seemed unable to hold their own against foreign competitors in the 1980s.[5]

Macroeconomic evidence that U.S. corporations were not competing effectively against foreign companies in the 1980s included low rates of investment in long-lived assets and in research and development relative to rates in other industrial countries. Aggregate U.S. productivity growth also lagged behind that in other countries from the mid-1970s, and wages and living standards for most working people in the United States virtually stopped growing.[6] Scholars and policymakers began asking whether these outcomes were a consequence, at least in part, of the way corporations are owned and controlled and how they are influenced by the financial markets.

In the early 1980s articles began to appear arguing that U.S. corporate managers had a "time horizon" problem. The culprits were variously said to be an uncompetitively high cost of capital, poor or misleading internal measurement systems, compensation systems that provided the wrong incentives, or financial market pressures that compelled corporate executives to focus on next quarter's earnings, even at the expense of long-run performance.

---

[5]Brief case studies of each of these industries are provided in Dertouzos, Lester, and Solow (1989), reporting the findings of the MIT Commission on Industrial Productivity. Other major commissions that have studied the competitiveness problem include the Competitiveness Policy Council, set up by Congress; the Council on Competitiveness, a privately sponsored nonprofit research organization; the National Academy of Engineering; and the Cuomo Commission on Competitiveness, appointed by then-governor of New York Mario Cuomo in 1987. The Brookings Institution also sponsored several separate studies whose conclusions are summarized in Baily, Burtless, and Litan (1993).

[6]Dertouzos, Lester, and Solow (1989, pp. 57–58).

In the early 1990s both Japan and Germany sank into serious recessions, and by mid-decade, with the United States in the full flower of recovery, U.S. productivity numbers were looking relatively good. In 1992 and 1993 the U.S. rate of productivity growth was faster than that of any other member of the "Group of Seven" industrial countries except the United Kingdom.[7] Improved productivity led some business leaders and policymakers to argue that the U.S. system of corporate governance was not broken after all. Why U.S. companies had lost so much ground relative to these other countries in the previous few decades remained unclear, however, as did the question of whether the turnaround was sustainable.

A second development that helped thrust corporate governance issues into the headlines and onto the agendas of policymakers was the wave of hostile takeovers, leveraged buyouts, and corporate restructurings of the 1980s.[8] Critics said takeovers were evidence of short-term pressures by the financial markets that made corporate executives paranoid about maximizing short-term returns, even at the cost of long-term performance. Takeover advocates argued the opposite—that takeovers were the financial market's way of disciplining lazy or ineffective management. Numerous takeover strategies and defenses were developed, and they in turn raised all kinds of legal and policy questions about the rights of shareholders, the appropriateness of certain takeover defenses, the role of directors, and their responsibilities to various corporate constituents. Although takeovers and leveraged buyouts slowed considerably after 1989, they picked up again in 1993 and 1994, renewing debate about some of the same issues that had been debated in the 1980s.

---

[7]See International Monetary Fund (1994, table A10, p. 121). The Group of Seven countries are Canada, France, Germany, Italy, Japan, the United Kingdom, and the United States.

[8]See Blair and Uppal (1993) for extensive summary data on the corporate merger and restructuring wave of the 1980s.

A third development was a huge increase in typical compensation packages for corporate executives. In 1983 the median annual pay package for chief executive officers was valued at $1.06 million in 1993 dollars, according to an annual survey of public companies conducted by *Business Week*. By 1993 the median pay package was worth $1.82 million—more than a 70 percent increase in real terms in a decade when employment by the largest companies declined and when median compensation for nearly all other categories of workers and professionals was at best flat in real terms.[9] Individual pay packages exceeding $10 million a year have become almost commonplace in the executive suites of large corportions. Some of the largest pay packages have gone to executives who were presiding over firms that were slashing payrolls or slipping badly in their returns to investors, a fact accentuating the impression of gross excess. W. A. Anders, chief executive officer (CEO) at General Dynamics, for example, was paid $37.6 million in salary, bonus, and long-term compensation between 1990 and 1992. During these three years General Dynamics cut almost 73,000 jobs from its corporate payrolls. Stephen M. Wolf, CEO at UAL was paid $17 million during these same years, while shareholders lost an average of 26 percent a year on their UAL shares.[10]

Some of the largest pay packages are a result of compensation plans put in place in the early to mid-1980s that tied executive pay more tightly to the performance of share prices. Some defenders of

[9]The surge in the average pay package in the *Business Week* sample was even larger than the rise in the median pay package, pushed up by the impact of a few truly stunning outliers. For example, Thomas F. Frist Jr. of HCA-Hospital Corp. of America was paid $127 million in 1992, of which only $1 million was salary and bonus and the rest was the profit on stock options cashed in that year. See Blair (1994).

[10]Compensation data and shareholder return data are from "Executive Compensation Scoreboard," *Business Week*, various issues. *Business Week* surveys about 325 to 350 firms each year, but I eliminated financial firms from the sample before calculating the medians. Employment data are from Compustat.

the high levels of pay argue that these pay packages should be taken as evidence that executives are doing a good job for shareholders. But other participants in the corporate governance debates argue that, on the contrary, the ballooning pay packages are evidence that executives are out of control, that the systems that are supposed to make them accountable to investors and other participants in the corporate enterprises have broken down.

A fourth development is the continual process of restructuring, boardroom shakeup, and "downsizing" at many of the largest U.S. corporations. Massive layoffs, which began in the early 1980s in smaller companies and in "rust belt" industries, are working their way through virtually every sector of the economy. Between January 1, 1980, and December 31, 1993, more than one million jobs were lost at just nine of the largest companies (Exxon, Ford, GE, GM, IBM, Mobil, Sears, USX, and Westinghouse).[11] These companies had been renowned for providing secure, high-paying jobs with good benefits. The process of downsizing shows no signs of abating but, rather, has been spreading even to financially healthy companies such as Procter and Gamble, Xerox, the large telecommunications companies, and, more recently, hospitals and health care companies. Meanwhile, top corporate officers are being turned out of their executive suites with increasing speed if they fail to lay off workers fast enough to keep their company's stock prices growing at an adequate rate. In one brief period, from late 1992 through the end of 1993, chief executives at American Express, Borden, GM, IBM, Kodak, and Westinghouse were all dismissed by directors unhappy with the rate at which these executives were cutting costs. One effect of these changes has been to make large corporations vastly riskier places to work, at all levels in the organizations.

[11]Data are from Compustat.

A final development that has brought corporate governance issues to the forefront is the dramatic breakdown of the socialist economies of Eastern Europe and the former Soviet Union. In Czechoslovakia, Estonia, Latvia, Lithuania, Poland, Russia, and the Ukraine, politicians and their advisers from the West have been frantically trying to create from scratch both the governance systems that can manage and control the newly privatized industries and the legal and institutional infrastructures needed to support these governance systems and to protect and encourage further investment. The immense task is especially difficult because the existing models in the United States, Western Europe, and Asia are so poorly understood.

If corporate governance questions were merely zero-sum power games (for example, does the chief executive get a larger bonus or do the shareholders get a larger dividend?), the public policy questions would be interesting but not terribly compelling. But the experiences of the former socialist countries make clear that the ability of corporations to generate wealth in a sustainable way depends crucially on who has what ownership and control rights over corporate resources, how decisions get made, and what pressures, terms, and conditions come into play. The U.S. system performs vastly better than the systems in most other countries of the world, but important questions remain about why it performs as well as it does and whether it performs as well as it should or could.

The debate about corporate governance is shaped by three very different clusters of views about how governance arrangements affect the performance of corporations and their ability to generate wealth and about how corporate governance rules should be reformed. Each view starts from a different set of assumptions about whether and how U.S. corporations might be performing suboptimally. Because these underlying assumptions are fundamentally at odds with each other, the debate has been confusing and not very productive. But these critical assumptions are rarely examined, and, consequently, the advocates of various reforms often talk past each other.

The first view, which I call the "finance model," holds that corporations are owned by shareholders and should therefore be managed in the interest of shareholders. But because the shares of large companies are held by tens of thousands of individuals and institutions, each holding only a tiny percentage of the total outstanding equity, shareholders are too dispersed to exercise tight control over managers. Corporate managers, therefore, often waste resources by managing companies in ways that serve their own interests, sometimes to the detriment of their "shareholder-owners." This view goes back to legal scholar A. A. Berle and economist Gardiner C. Means, who in 1932 first documented what they called the "separation of ownership from control."[12] Reform measures that start from the finance model premise generally attempt to make managers more responsive to shareholder interests.

An opposing view is that managers are too attentive to the interests of shareholders. According to this view, financial markets are impatient and shortsighted, and shareholders do not understand what is in their own long-term interests. They prefer short-run gains to larger, but deferred, payouts and thus tend to sell out or underprice the shares of companies that emphasize sustained investments in research and development or costly market expansion strategies. Proponents of this "market myopia" point of view argue that companies underperform in some sense because management is too responsive to the short-term pressures coming from the financial markets. The reform measures they advocate focus on insulating management from this short-term pressure or, alternately, attempting to realign the interests of shareholders by discouraging trading and encouraging long-term shareholding.

The third view is that shareholders understand fully what is in their own financial self-interest (both in the short run and in the long

[12]Berle and Means (1932, p. 71).

run), but what is optimal for shareholders often is not optimal for the rest of society. That is, the corporate policies that generate the most wealth for shareholders may not be the policies that generate the greatest total social wealth.

This last argument is very controversial. Although some corporate critics have always railed against the evils of the profit motive, the position of finance model advocates—that shareholders own corporations and that maximizing the value of shares is equivalent to maximizing the wealth created by corporations—has come to dominate the policy debates. Scholars and policymakers rarely challenge this core belief, and even corporate executives, policy analysts, management specialists, and legal scholars who are sympathetic to the proposition that other goals might sometimes be as or more important than maximizing shareholder value do not usually make their arguments directly. Instead, they often join forces with advocates of the market myopia position to argue that financial markets have failed to send the right signals about how to maximize true long-term shareholder wealth.

Nonetheless, the suspicion that shareholder interests may, at times, be at odds with important social goals lurks behind some of the more heated corporate governance debates. Those who believe that firms have a social purpose beyond maximizing value for shareholders tend to oppose reforms that would put more power and control in the hands of shareholders. Instead, they favor reforms that insulate managers from shareholder pressures, that impose more restrictions and regulations on corporate behavior, or that give more power to other stakeholders, such as employees, lenders, or, in some cases, suppliers, customers, or the communities where companies operate.

Thus the debate about whether corporate performance can be improved by reforming the ways corporations are controlled and managed has been pulled in disparate directions. The debate runs deep, touching on such fundamental questions as the appropriate social role of corporations, and whose interests they should serve.

The third and fourth chapters explore the intellectual, empirical, and political foundations for the finance model and the market myopia arguments outlined above. They also examine several reforms proposed by advocates of each of these two views. The fifth chapter examines changes taking place in the ownership of large corporations that some believe could help resolve the problems identified by both the finance model proponents and the market myopia advocates. The most important of these changes is the expansion of equity ownership by large financial institutions, which now own about half of all publicly traded equity in U.S. corporations. Some participants in the corporate governance debates have argued that large financial institutions, especially pension funds and mutual funds, should engage in "relationship investing," thereby playing the monitoring role in large corporations that was originally envisioned for shareholders. Relationship investing involves buying significant blocks of stock, holding these stocks for a long time, and actively monitoring management. This is a role that most shareholders still play in small, closely held companies but that has been neglected in large, publicly traded corporations. This chapter also considers various reform proposals advocated by those who believe that relationship investing by financial institutions can help improve corporate performance.

Both the finance and market myopia models have at their core a belief that society is best served if corporations are run for shareholders. In the final chapters of this book, I develop a variant on the third view discussed above, that society as a whole may not be best served if corporations are run solely for shareholders. Clearly, trying to run corporations in the interest of "society at large," whatever that may mean, is an impossible and, in practice, a vacuous objective. But the goals of corporations should at least be congruent with the interests of the larger society. The question then becomes whether maximizing value for shareholders is consistent with the interests of society at large. I argue that, in a very important set of cases, it may not be. This argument is developed in three chapters, as follows:

In chapter 6, I examine the history—in the law and in practice—of the view that corporations should be run for broader social purposes, and explain why it has largely been rejected in the law and by most economists, other scholars, and policymakers. In doing so, I review the arguments supporting the position that the goal of corporations should be to maximize value for shareholders. The analysis shows that, ultimately, the legitimacy of the finance model position rests on a series of assumptions that it is shareholders who receive the "residual return" and bear the "residual risk" in the typical firm. These assumptions are necessary if maximizing shareholder value is to be equivalent to maximizing social value. Implicitly, these assumptions also form the basis for the corollary argument that corporate governance reforms should focus on making managers more responsive to shareholder demands. I argue that these assumptions are empirically doubtful on their face and are certainly not typical of large business enterprises in the late twentieth century.

In chapter 7, I argue that, in most modern corporations, some of the residual risk is borne by long-tenured employees, who, over the years, build up firm-specific skills that are an important part of the firm's valuable assets, but which the employees cannot market elsewhere, precisely because they are specific to the firm. These employees have contributed capital to the firm, and that capital is at risk to the extent that the employees' productivity and the wages they could command at other firms are significantly lower than what they earn in that specific firm. The more skill-intensive a given firm is, the more likely it is that such firm-specific skills are critical to the wealth-creating activity of the firm. The presence of firm-specific human capital alters the conclusion, but not the logic, of the finance model, by generalizing it to apply to a broader range of assumptions about how wealth is created, captured, and distributed in a business enterprise. When shareholders do not bear all the residual risk, the logic behind the finance model argument points in a very different direction from that typically assumed to be the case by most of the participants in the corporate governance debates. I call my own model the "wealth maximization" model.

In the eighth chapter, I examine several important trends that are altering the way work is done and the sources of wealth creation in business enterprises. In particular, these trends are making the management of human capital much more important relative to the management of physical assets. I consider several existing alternative governance arrangements that can be viewed as adaptations to these developments and several new arrangements that are being tried in some corporations.

An important lesson of this chapter is that the institutional and legal environment should be flexible enough to accommodate a variety of corporate governance arrangements. One of the great strengths of the free enterprise economy in general, and of the version that has evolved in the United States in particular, is its flexibility, its capacity for innovative responses to changing environments. That seems like a simple and obvious observation, but the corporate governance debates often proceed as if the participants thought there were only one right answer, one holy grail. In particular, the debate seems to be fixated on the relationship between corporate managements and shareholders. I argue that this fixation is misplaced. Shareholders, particularly scattered and passive shareholders, are generally in a poor position to exercise all the responsibilities of ownership in large corporations. Meanwhile, other stakeholders, especially employees, may often be in a very good position to exercise the rights and responsibilities associated with ownership. In such corporations, I argue, employees should be given an explicit ownership claim commensurate with their contribution to wealth creation, perhaps by compensating those employees in part with equity shares. In the final chapter I propose a few reforms that would make corporate governance institutions and practices more open to such changes.

2

A PRIMER ON

CORPORATE GOVERNANCE

A SUBSTANTIAL PART OF ECONOMIC ACTIVITY in this country is organized and carried out through corporations. Corporations are peculiar creatures. They are legal structures through which raw materials, capital, labor, and ingenuity can be brought together to produce and distribute goods and services. Their existence is not limited in time or space, and, as separate legal entities, they are distinct from any of the individuals who participate in them. They can own property; collectively, they own 59 percent of all business assets in this country—land, buildings, equipment, and intangible assets such as patents or brand names.[1] And they hire or contract for

[1]Board of Governors of the Federal Reserve System (1994).

17

the work of millions of individuals and thousands of other corporations to create more wealth. They obviously can confer great power on the individuals who control them.

Since Adam Smith wrote *The Wealth of Nations* in 1776, political economists have argued that the workings of a free market with private property would keep businesses and the individuals who control them from abusing their power and would promote the most efficient use of the productive resources they control. If companies make shoddy goods or charge too much for them, their customers will buy from someone else, and they will soon be out of business. If they fail to operate efficiently, their costs will be too high, and, again, they will soon be out of business, freeing up the resources they had commanded so that some other, more efficient producer can use them. If they default on their debts, they will be unable to get new credit or will have to pay very high rates to compensate a lender for the risk.

Market pressure—in the product markets or in the input markets—is thus the most fundamental mechanism in a free market economy preventing business corporations from abusing their power, and the one with the longest pedigree. Whether this mechanism is functioning well or whether it works for a particular problem has been the central question in every public policy debate about the regulation of corporations in the last century. Was market pressure sufficient to keep companies from taking advantage of consumers, or did the government need to step in and break up monopolies? Was competition in financial markets sufficient to keep firms from issuing fraudulent securities or otherwise manipulating the trading of those securities, or must securities markets be regulated to ensure that all parties have the information they need to make informed investment decisions? Were market pressures strong enough to keep companies from abusing workers, or must the government facilitate and protect labor unions? Could market pressures compel corporations to adopt environmentally benign technology, or did markets fail at this task, requiring government pollution control regulation?

When economists, business people, or politicians assert that a capitalist economy with competitive markets will lead to the efficient use of society's resources for total wealth creation, they are making two grand sets of assumptions. The first is that the sort of problems just mentioned can be satisfactorily solved. These problems have to do with what economists call "market failures," including "monopoly power," "externalities," "information assymetries," and "transactions costs." A whole subfield of economics is devoted to the study of these problems and the various regulatory approaches to solving them.

The second grand set of assumptions, which is not nearly so well understood, involves the internal functioning of the organizations through which economic activity is conducted. This book is about that second set of assumptions. Market pressures are less relevant to the internal functioning of organizations, because the central issues have to do with transactions and relationships that take place within the firm itself and not in markets. These issues include who among the various participants in the corporate enterprise controls what, who makes what decisions, and who has what responsibilities for and what claims against the revenues and assets of the company. These issues affect not only the distribution of wealth created by corporations, but also the incentives that all the participants in a corporate enterprise have to invest and engage in wealth-creating activity. Corporate governance is about setting up rules that determine these things in business corporations. And, as stated in the first chapter, the central economic and policy problem to be solved is to allocate decision and control rights to parties who have the incentive and the information they need to use resources efficiently to create wealth, while, at the same time, ensuring that the controlling parties are accountable to all of the other participants who have investments at risk. Meanwhile, the mechanisms that ensure accountability must not be so cumbersome that the company bogs down in procedural hassles.

How Corporate Governance Works in Principle

To understand how these issues have been dealt with in the U.S. system of corporate governance, it is helpful to start with the organization and governance of the simplest corporations.

The Basic Model

Figure 2-1 illustrates the basic model of a corporation. Corporations are organized and run by an entrepreneur or a management team that raises funds to acquire physical capital and to finance initial operations by borrowing from banks or other lenders (debt) or by issuing and selling "equity" shares. In exchange for the equity funds, the corporation gives investors securities ("stock") that are claims on a proportionate share of the net proceeds of any activity undertaken by the corporation, after all obligations to management, labor, suppliers, and other creditors have been paid. Technically, these securities can take a variety of forms, but for now they will be referred to as "common stock" or "common shares" and the investors who hold them as "stockholders" or "shareholders."

Lenders also provide funds. In exchange, lenders get a promise of repayment that has priority over any payments made to stockholders and that is sometimes secured by the assets of the company. Lenders generally charge some rate of interest for the use of their funds, but their claim against the company is limited to the outstanding principal and interest on the loan.

Because payments to shareholders are paid last, shareholders are said to have a "residual" claim. They may get nothing if the revenues of the business are not sufficient to pay lenders, suppliers, and employees and still have funds left over. But if the business is profitable, all of those profits go to shareholders, either as dividends paid to the shareholders or as reinvestment in the business. If invested in projects that have a high enough return, the

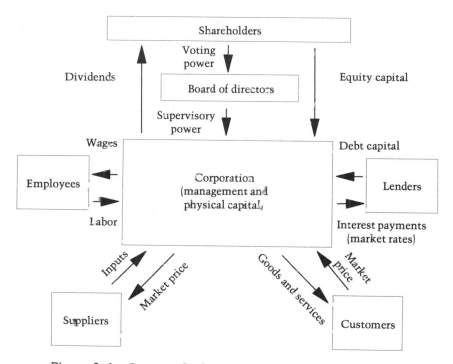

Figure 2–1. *Basic "Black Box" Model of the Corporation*

latter use of profits will increase the value of the company's stock, and shareholders will receive their return in the form of capital gains.

Because shareholders are in this residual claim position, most economists argue that they have the greatest incentive to see that the company makes good business decisions and uses its assets wisely to earn profits. Although shareholders do not directly run the company, they can have a strong influence on its day-to-day management because they are entitled by law to elect the board of directors. The board of directors, in turn, has the power to hire and fire the chief executive officer and other top-level members of the management team and is responsible for monitoring the company's accounts and approving its strategic plans and all of its other important decisions and actions.

One of the most significant advantages to investors of organizing a business through a corporation is that shareholders are granted "limited liability." This means that, if the business activity undertaken by the corporation loses money and the company cannot pay all of its debts, the creditors cannot go after the shareholders to compel them to pay up. Another advantage is that the corporation has a "perpetual" existence independent of any particular officer, director, shareholder, or other participant. But to obtain these organizational advantages, the business must be incorporated, a legal process that in the United States happens at the state level.

Introduction to Corporation Law

Corporation law in the United States consists of statutory provisions and judicial interpretations from statutory and common law. Corporations may be formed for "any lawful business purpose" simply by filing the appropriate documents with the appropriate state officials and paying the relevant fees. As mentioned above, once formed, corporations are legal entities separate from the individuals who formed them, and they may exist "in perpetuity" (unless formally dissolved), regardless of who owns their equity. Moreover, their shareholders enjoy limited liability as well as the right to sell, assign, or otherwise dispose of their shares of the company.[2]

Companies may incorporate in any state they choose, without regard to where their operations are. Since early in the twentieth century, however, Delaware has been an especially attractive state for incorporations, and now more than half of all large companies (those traded on the New York Stock Exchange, for example) are

---

[2]Shareholders in small, closely held companies may face some legal restrictions on their ability to sell and, in any case, may have trouble finding a willing buyer. This issue is discussed later in the chapter.

incorporated in Delaware. Some scholars argue that Delaware achieved this position by winning the "race to the bottom," that is, by making the law increasingly permissive in order to attract corporations.[3] Other explanations for Delaware's dominance of corporation law are more charitable, suggesting, for example, that the Delaware bar works to provide an effective and flexible body of corporate law that is consistent and easy to apply. In any case, the Delaware legislature and Delaware Supreme Court are extremely influential in formulating corporation law.

All corporations are governed by the terms of their articles of incorporation (or charters) and their bylaws. The articles of incorporation must include information about the types of equity securities the corporation is authorized to issue to raise funds; they may include other restrictions or specify governance rules in more detail, but, generally, they are so broadly written that they impose little practical restrictions on what the company can do. The bylaws define the rights and obligations of various officers or groups within the corporate structure and set rules for routine matters such as calling meetings. The articles of incorporation and the bylaws, taken together, can be regarded as the basic architecture for a complex contract among the the corporation, its management and board, and its shareholders.[4]

A Few Words on Bankruptcy

Although not usually thought of in this sense, bankruptcy rules are an important aspect of corporate governance. These rules help determine how a company is to be controlled and managed and whose

---

[3]Cary (1974).

[4]The bylaws and even some minor "housekeeping" details of the articles of incorporation can be amended without the approval of shareholders. A useful introduction to corporation law for the novice is Hamilton (1987).

claims have priority when and if it faces financial difficulties and especially if it seeks the protection of the bankruptcy courts. Creditors such as banks who lend a company money do not have the right to elect directors and normally do not have the right to interfere in the day-to-day business decisions of a company. But if a company fails to make its loan payments or satisfy other terms of a loan, the creditors may then have the power to seize assets or freeze funds in a company's accounts or otherwise exercise some control over the company. If the company seeks protection of the bankruptcy courts or if creditors force a company into bankruptcy proceedings, creditors gain other powers over the company, and managers and shareholders correspondingly lose power. Moreover, the power and rights of various claimants in a distress situation affect their bargaining position even when the company is not in distress.

The Constitution gives the federal government the authority to establish uniform national bankruptcy laws, and the current version of these laws was put in place with the Bankruptcy Reform Act of 1978.[5] Any company may seek protection from creditors by filing a petition with the bankruptcy courts under the provisions of Chapter 11 of that law, even if the company is not insolvent. (Before the 1978 Act, a company had to be insolvent before it could file for bankruptcy protection.) Creditors may force a firm into bankruptcy proceedings only if it is not meeting its debt service obligations.[6] Once a company has filed a bankruptcy petition under Chapter 11, creditors are prohibited from trying to collect on their claims. Existing

[5]Minor amendments to this law have since been enacted, most recently in 1994, but these have not altered the basic framework laid out in 1978.

[6]Creditors can also force a firm into bankruptcy if some receiver, assignee, or custodian takes possession of a substantial portion of a firm's assets. Creditors generally would not want to initiate bankruptcy proceedings unless they felt that other creditors or stakeholders were being given certain advantages or that their own interests were threatened by continuing operations. See Epstein (1991).

management generally remains in control as a "debtor in possession" and is given at least 120 days to file a reorganization plan. The exception is if the court finds fraud, dishonesty, mismanagement, or incompetence, in which case it may appoint a disinterested trustee.

Thus, under Chapter 11, existing management is generally allowed to draw up a new plan for paying off the debts of the corporation over a longer period of time and is allowed to maintain control over essential assets. Reorganization plans nearly always alter the rights of various creditors such as lenders, bondholders, and suppliers. Although creditors and shareholders generally must vote to approve a reorganization plan, the plan that is ultimately accepted by a majority of each class of creditors (accounting for at least two-thirds of the value of claims by that class against the company) will be imposed on all creditors and shareholders. In some cases the courts may even confirm a plan that has not been accepted by all classes of creditors if at least one class of creditors whose claims have been reduced accepts the plan and the court finds the plan fair and equitable. (Such an action is called a "cram down.")

The reasoning behind Chapter 11 is that most corporations—including companies that cannot currently pay their bills—are worth more as going concerns than they are if their assets are sold off to pay their debts. By that logic, troubled companies should be given another chance to succeed. Another principle behind the Chapter 11 process is that, when the ability of a company to generate revenues falls to the point that it can pay its debts but no more, neither creditors nor shareholders have incentives that are consistent with the long-term health and survival of the firm. On one hand, creditors will want to liquidate early to protect their interests if there is any risk that continued operations will further reduce the value of the going concern. Shareholders, on the other hand, will have everything to gain and very little to lose by keeping the firm going and pursuing very risky strategies to try to increase the value of the firm. Thus Chapter 11 leaves control in the hands of management in the hope that management will come closest to having the right incentives to serve all of the stakeholders. But it imposes a new and stricter set of constraints on management by giving veto power over management's plan to creditors and to the court itself.

By giving veto power to creditors, bankruptcy laws shift important aspects of the control of a firm to creditors roughly at the point at which creditors become the residual claimants. This is a subtle point, but one worth understanding because the links among residual claims, residual risks, and control are a recurring theme in this book. The basic model of a corporation assigns control rights to the shareholders on the unspoken assumption that they are the residual claimants. But because shareholders enjoy limited liability, they are not always the *only* residual claimants. Limited liability means that shareholders cannot lose more than they have invested in a company. If the total value of the company declines below the point where the value of shareholders' equity is zero, then, by definition, the value of creditors' claims against the company begins shrinking, and the creditors become the residual claimants. This is the economic rationale for shifting some important piece of control to creditors in bankruptcy.[7]

Assumptions behind the Basic Model

Several other features of the basic model should be noted. The model assumes that the other participants in the enterprise—the employees, lenders, suppliers, and customers—all interact with the firm on the basis of clear contracts, set in advance, on terms independent of the success of the enterprise as a whole. Employees get fixed wages, for example, and lenders get a fixed interest rate. (Lenders may in fact get a variable interest rate. But the variation is usually a func-

---

[7]Easterbrook and Fischel (1991, p. 68).

tion of macroeconomic factors driving interest rates, not a function of the specific performance of the firm. In the basic model, only shareholders—not employees or lenders or any other participants in the firm—contract for a share in the net proceeds of the enterprise. This role is reserved for shareholders, and it is what is meant when shareholders, and not other participants, are said to be the residual claimants. As noted already, the fact that shareholders play this role provides the economic rationale for giving shareholders important control rights and for running corporations in the interest of shareholders. If all other parties were paid at a fixed rate, maximizing the return to shareholders would be the same as maximizing the total wealth created by the firm.

Limited liability for shareholders, however, contradicts the assumption that shareholders are the only residual claimants and, therefore, the residual risk bearers. The limited liability exception is noteworthy because an explicit institutional and legal arrangement (bankruptcy) has been devised to deal with the exception.

Most analyses of corporate governance issues simply take it for granted that shareholders "should," in some sense, be the residual claimants. They are, after all, the "owners." But recall from chapter 1 that being an owner means having the residual claim and residual control rights. Thus, to argue that shareholders should have a residual claim because they are the owners is circular logic. The deeper questions are: does making the suppliers of one class of capital the residual claimants and giving them residual control rights promote economic efficiency, and, if so, why? If not, under what circumstances might other arrangements better promote economic efficiency and wealth creation? These questions are taken up much later in this book, but for now I accept the standard wisdom, which is that shareholders are, and should be, the residual claimants and that they should therefore have residual control rights.

As a practical matter, professional managers, who are not necessarily shareholders, will likely run the day-to-day operations of companies. The basic model recognizes that those managers may be in a position to engage in self-dealing behavior that harms the interests of shareholders. But it also envisions that the shareholders can influence management strongly, that they act more or less as a unified block, and that they have the information they need to understand what running the company in their interest means.

In small, closely held companies, where the basic model comes nearest to matching reality, the shareholders are often intimately involved with the business as friends, family members, and close business associates of the founding entrepreneur, and consequently they are often well positioned to monitor management to see that the company is run for their benefit. This situation is not characteristic of most large corporations in the United States, however. The image of shareholders as a unified interest block closely involved with management is, for most large companies, inaccurate.

Ownership Structure Matters

Since the origin of corporations as major engines of economic activity, two great transformations have occurred in the typical distribution of equity ownership of large companies in the United States. From the middle of the nineteenth century through the 1930s, promoters and industrialists moved away from dependence on wealthy individuals, bankers, and financial institutions for a supply of capital. Securities markets developed initially to support trading in railroads and canals. Efforts to finance the Civil War then greatly expanded trading in debt securities.[8] After the war utilities and ultimately corporations engaged in other forms of heavy industry, began

---

[8]Carosso (1970, pp. 13–15).

raising funds by selling stocks and bonds to anonymous individual investors in these new securities markets. The investors who bought corporate securities thus became increasingly dispersed and distant from management, and large banks and other financial institutions became less influential in corporate boardrooms.

How Ownership Varies from the Basic Model

A landmark study published in 1932 by Adolf Berle and Gardiner Means noted that by the end of 1929 the dispersion of share ownership of large corporations was so great that an identifiable individual or compact group of individuals held a majority of the equity in only 11 percent (only 6 percent by value) of the 200 largest industrial corporations. A dominant minority shareholder or unusual securities structure gave a majority stake to an individual or small group in another 44 percent (36 percent by value) of the companies. But for about half the companies (44 percent by count, 58 percent by value), securities ownership was so dispersed that the managements of these companies were deemed to be in control themselves and not truly answerable to any particular owners or other stakeholders. In the Pennsylvania Railroad Co., for example, the twenty largest shareholders together accounted for only 2.7 percent of total common shares.[9]

Changes in the regulation of securities markets, banks, insurance companies, and investment companies that were initiated in the 1930s carried this trend toward dispersion of equity ownership another step forward. These laws were designed not only to increase the security and safety of the financial system in the United States, but also expressly to curtail the influence of financial institutions on

[9]Berle and Means (1932, pp. 85, 94, 114).

the management of industrial corporations.[10] In particular, these laws prohibited banks from owning corporate equities for their own accounts and sharply limited the proportions of their portfolios that life insurance companies could put into stocks. The laws also imposed tax penalties on mutual funds that invested more than 5 percent of their portfolios in the stock of any one company or held more than 10 percent of the outstanding stock of any one company. Subsequent laws and court rulings supported and augmented the impact of these regulations.

Since the 1930s the dispersion of share ownership has increased markedly. Edward S. Herman repeated the Berle and Means analysis in the late 1970s and concluded that, by 1975, 82.5 percent of the 200 largest nonfinancial corporations (and 85.4 percent of the value of assets of these firms) were under "management" control, as opposed to being controlled by a significant shareholder or other financial interest.[11]

This dispersion of equity ownership means that large companies whose stocks are traded in public securities markets actually look more like the model illustrated in figure 2-2, which I call the "Berle-Means" model of the corporation. The key difference from the basic model is that shareholders are no longer regarded as a monolithic entity, but as separate investors, whose individual holdings in the company are typically tiny compared with the value of the whole company. In this model, the voting power of any individual shareholder is much less influential. Moreover, shareholders find it diffi-

---

[10]Roe (1990) has extensively documented the impact that regulation of financial institutions has had on reducing concentrations of share ownership and thereby inhibiting the role of financial institutions in the governance of U.S. corporations. Table 1 of Roe's article summarizes the laws and court rulings that impose portfolio restrictions on financial institutions. See also Roe (1993d) and Roe (1994).

[11]Herman (1981, pp. 65–66 and table 3.2).

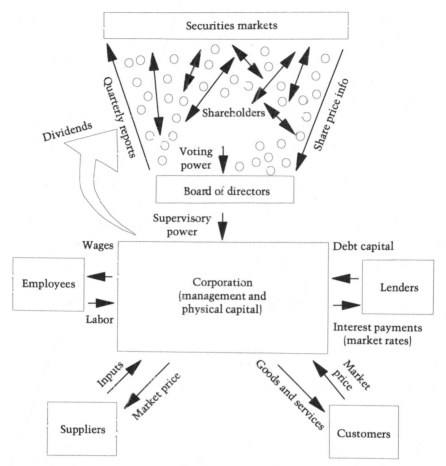

Figure 2–2. Basic "Berle-Means" Model of the Corporation

cult and costly to form groups or to otherwise enhance their collective influence on management.

In this model, however, shareholders have a much more viable and effective option of selling their shares if they do not like the way the company is being run. If many shareholders try to sell their shares at the same time, and few people are willing to buy them, the price at which the shares change hands will fall. The movement of share prices, then, provides a mechanism by which shareholders collectively signal management about how happy or unhappy they are with the way management is running the company. The transition of a company from closely held to widely held and actively traded therefore gives shareholders the benefits of liquidity for their investments and some information about what other investors think about how much the company is worth. But the need for each individual shareholder to know or understand the details of the company's business becomes much less pressing, and it is much harder for shareholders to have any direct influence over the company if they do not like the way the company is being run. This separation of share ownership from control, with all its ramifications, has been a much debated issue of corporate governance.

In general, separating equity holders from management through the financial markets raises four types of governance problems:

- For firms to operate efficiently, management must have enough leeway to take risks, make strategic decisions, and take advantage of investment opportunities as they arise. Management cannot submit every decision to a shareholder vote, and, even if it could, shareholders who are not close to the operations of the company probably would not be able to make informed decisions. Nonetheless, management must be prevented from abusing its power and position by spending resources or undertaking investments that benefit management at the expense of the shareholders. Hence, shareholders need mechanisms for effectively monitoring and restraining management.
- A small, close-knit group of shareholders with a large total share of equity might be quite effective at monitoring management, but, if they are given enhanced control rights, then their power must also be restrained to prevent them from taking unfair advantage of other shareholders.

- A major commitment of time and resources is necessary for investors (or anyone else) to act as effective monitors. But many investors prefer the advantages of liquidity and diversity in their portfolios—advantages that may not be consistent with the time and resource commitment involved in monitoring.
- Investors need reliable and accurate information, developed using consistent measuring and accounting procedures. But any measure of performance can provide misleading information or distorted incentives by encouraging management to focus attention on inappropriate or partial goals. Moreover, releasing certain kinds of information to the public can sometimes weaken a company's competitive position.

Most of the rest of this chapter is devoted to explaining the mechanisms and institutions that have been devised to balance these competing needs. First, however, several other important ways that large corporations differ from the basic model of figure 2-1 are considered.

More on the Role of Debt and Equity

In both the basic model and the Berle-Means model, the distinction between debt and equity is fundamental to the way corporate governance works. As noted above, debt claims in general provide the holders a fixed repayment schedule but little in the way of rights to control the company as long as that repayment schedule (and sometimes certain other terms) is met. Creditors can have a strong influence over a company if it gets in financial trouble, however, and even if a company is financially sound, creditors can influence whether it can obtain additional funding for proposed new projects. A bank that loaned a company the money for a factory expansion, for example, can make it easy or hard for the company to borrow more money for a new office building.

Conversely, equity claims—in particular, common stock—give shareholders the right to vote for boards of directors and on other important corporate issues such as a major merger or any plan that would dispose of a substantial portion of the company's assets. Shareholders are also entitled to receive dividends or other distributions whenever the corporation pays them or, if the company is liquidated, to receive the net assets of the company after paying all debts and any securities, such as preferred stock, that rank ahead of common stocks. These two features, the right to vote and the right to receive dividends and other distributions, are the defining characteristics of common stock, according to the Revised Model Business Corporation Act (RMBCA).[12] Under the terms of the RMBCA, companies must have some outstanding stock with each characteristic, but these two characteristics may be split between two or more classes of stock, so that no one class of stock must necessarily have both voting rights and residual claim rights.[13]

Equity holders receive dividends only at the discretion of management, however, and, except in liquidations, have no direct claim on any of the underlying assets of the company. In large, widely traded companies they have only a nominal amount of control in ordinary times. Owning shares of stock in a company does not mean shareholders can move themselves into a corner office, take the corporate jet out for a test flight, or order the company to hire their children. In

---

[12]The RMBCA is the 1984 revision of the Model Business Corporation Act, which was developed by the American Bar Association in 1954 and revised several times thereafter. Many states have followed these models in developing their own corporation laws.

[13]American Bar Association (1985, p. 85). An investor might be willing to buy shares of stock that offer voting rights but no residual claim rights if he is trying to assemble a large enough voting block to elect his own slate of directors.

principle, equity holders are given important tools to control the company in exchange for accepting more of the ordinary risk associated with the enterprise than creditors must accept. But in practice their ability to control the firm may be quite limited.

Another traditional difference between debt and equity is that companies are often able to repay bank loans at their will or to "call" debt issued to the public at any time after a specified period, but before the maturity date, by repaying and retiring all the bonds in a given issue. (Early repayment is not an automatic right, but many debt contracts permit it.) Thus, if they have the resources to do so, companies can, at their own option, sever their relationships with particular creditors or groups of creditors. Creditors, on the other hand, may not be able to get their money back early unless the borrowing company violates some aspect of the lending agreement. Although some debt claims are traded in liquid securities markets— small investors who own the bonds of a major company such as Exxon or GM, for example, can resell them as easily as they bought them—many of a corporation's liabilities, such as bank loans, payables (funds owed to suppliers), or unfunded pension fund obligations, cannot be easily traded away by the bank, supplier, or pension fund to whom the corporation owes money.[14]

Companies cannot readily call in their equity or sever their relationships with particular shareholders. Shareholders, on the other hand, can get out at any time, as long as they can find someone to buy their shares, which is easy to do in widely traded companies. This ability to sell out at any time is sometimes called the "Wall Street Walk" and, as noted above, is one way that shareholders can signal their dissatisfaction with the way a company is being run.

---

[14]Since the early 1980s, financial institutions have devised numerous ways to "securitize" various kinds of corporate debt, so creditors may find it easier to recover their funds before the corporation pays off the loan.

Although public companies can go into the open market and buy back their own equity, under most circumstances they cannot, unilaterally, decide to buy out the shares of any particular shareholder.[15] Thus equity holders typically have much more control over how long they want to stay invested in a given company than do debt holders.[16] Moreover, a publicly traded company can often control who its creditors are but has very little control over who its shareholders are.

The Mix of Debt and Equity Matters

Does it matter to a company whether the majority of its financing is debt or equity? In an important paper in finance theory written in the late 1950s, Franco Modigliani and Merton H. Miller argued that the value of a firm should depend on its real assets, not on whether the stream of cash flows from those assets are assigned to debt or to equity.[17] This proposition holds, however, only if financial markets are "perfect," if the tax treatment of debt and equity is the same, and if no costs are associated with financial distress or bankruptcy. Of course, the latter two conditions are not met in the real world. Corporate profits, calculated net of debt payments, are taxed. This means that income to a taxable investor holding a company's debt securities is taxed only once (when it is paid to the investor in the

[15]Companies occasionally bought out the shares held by individual raiders during the 1980s to prevent them from taking over the whole company. These selective buybacks were termed "greenmail." But they were accomplished with the consent and participation of the raider, who was a willing seller.

[16]Shareholders do not always have complete control over how long they hold a stock. Minority shareholders, for example, can sometimes be compelled to sell their shares in a "freeze-out" merger, in which the majority shareholder buys all remaining outstanding shares. Hamilton (1987, p. 447).

[17]Modigliani and Miller (1958). Miller was awarded the Nobel Prize in Economics in 1990 in part for this contribution, while Modigliani won the Nobel in 1985.

form of interest), but income from equity is taxed twice—once at the corporate level as profits to the firm, and again when the investor receives it in the form of dividends or capital gains.

Likewise, financial distress is not costless. If a company fails to make full and prompt payments on its debts, it may have trouble getting further credit or may be forced into bankruptcy, which is disruptive and imposes significant restrictions. By contrast, a company cannot be forced into bankruptcy for not paying dividends, because it is under no obligation to make any payments at all to shareholders. The first condition—that markets are "perfect"—is probably not met either, but that is harder to prove one way or the other because it is not a very well-defined condition.[18]

Hence, for decades, standard corporate finance theory argued that the optimal capital structure was neither all debt nor all equity, but some mix that represented a trade-off between the generally lower tax cost of debt and the higher risk of financial distress or bankruptcy associated with high debt levels. The "optimal" balance point is partly a matter of taste for risk. Many older corporate executives, whose families may have had experience with widespread corporate failures in the Depression, for example, fear the risks associated with high leverage more than younger executives typically do and thus tend to think the appropriate balance point is one that involves lower levels of debt. "I grew up in business being taught that anything over a 30 percent debt-equity ratio was risky," Donald S. Perkins told a forum on corporate governance at the Wharton School at the University of Pennsylvania. "I've lived to see most business leaders today feel

---

[18]Brealey and Myers (1991, p. 412) quote Ezra Solomon as saying that "a perfect capital market should be *defined* as one in which the Modigliani-Miller theory holds."

that anything less than a 30 percent ratio under-utilizes a company's borrowing power."[19]

In practice, companies have a third source of financing, at least for new investment: retained earnings. Technically, retained earnings (profits that are not paid out as dividends) are the same as equity, but management often prefers to use retained earnings, rather than new stock issues, because no transactions costs are involved. For example, suppose a company has $150 million in profits but needs to spend $100 million to finance an expansion of its factory. The company can pay out $50 million in dividends and spend the other $100 million on the factory, or it can pay out $150 million in dividends and float another issue of stock to raise the $100 million it needs for the factory. The latter option would probably cost the company several million dollars in lawyers' and investment bankers' fees.

Moreover, the tax treatment of the two options differs in a way that generally makes it advantageous to shareholders for the company to finance investment with retained earnings rather than new issues of equity: dividends are taxable income to the equity holder at the time they are paid out, whereas increases in the value of equity are not taxed until the shares are sold and the gain is "realized" by the investor, which may be many years later. If the company pays out $150 million in dividends, investors would have to pay, say, 30 percent of that, or $45 million, in income taxes on the payments. If, instead, the company pays out $50 million in dividends, investors would have to pay only $15 million in taxes now. The other $100 million would, shareholders hope, add at least $100 million to the value of their equity holdings. Eventually they would have to pay taxes on that gain, but perhaps at a lower "capital gains" rate, and not until they sold. If they died before they sold and left their shares

[19]Donald S. Perkins, "20 Questions of Corporate Governance." Speech delivered at the Wharton School, University of Pennsulvania, September 9, 1990.

to their children, the tax basis for the recipients of the stock would be "stepped up" to incorporate the $100 million, and for all practical purposes, no one would ever have to pay taxes on that gain.

Thus, before the 1980s, corporate managers generally believed that retained earnings were the preferred source of financing for new investment. They kept dividends low, and typically financed new investment first with retained earnings. Then they issued debt, and only rarely (except in the case of start-up ventures that had no retained earnings) did they raise new financing by issuing new equity.[20]

In the 1980s that wisdom began to give way to the view that the key difference between debt and equity to the company is the amount of control these securities give to investors or, conversely, the amount of discretion they give to managers.[21] This theory, if it is right, makes the choice of capital structure for a firm (the mix of debt and equity) an important matter of corporate governance. If interest payments are high relative to cash flows, corporate executives have very little discretion about what to do with cash flows. In particular, they may be prevented from financing new investment with retained earnings because little or no earnings may be left after the interest has been paid. Firms in this situation must borrow from banks, issue new bonds, or float additional stock whenever they want to make new investments, all of which require persuading new investors to commit their money to the company. According to proponents of this new view, the continual need to go to the markets for funds is a useful disciplining device. Critics of large, widely traded companies have often argued that managers are too free to build empires with fancy office buildings and corporate jets or to buy out other companies that they do not know how to run well. The

---

[20]Myers (1984a) labeled the argument that firms behaved this way the "pecking-order theory" of corporate capital structure.

[21]Hart (1993, pp. 19–20) assesses the theory behind this view.

process of having to seek out new funding every time they want to make such investments should help keep this tendency in check. In other words, debt can be a means by which investors exercise some control over corporate decisionmaking because each time a company wants to spend money on major new investments, investors have an opportunity to evaluate what the company is doing and decide whether to invest more money in the company. Under this view, the optimal financial structure for a firm depends partly on how much leeway investors believe managers should have.

This new interpretation of the role of debt and equity offered a theoretical justification for the wave of highly leveraged private buyouts and other debt-driven corporate restructurings of the 1980s. In a private buyout an investor or group of investors buys out all of the outstanding publicly traded equity of a firm, in effect taking the firm private again. Investors who did this in the 1980s often financed the buyouts with large amounts of debt, including loans from banks, insurance companies, and other financial institutions, and "junk bonds," which are high-risk, high-yield bonds sold to financial institutions or to the public. After the buyouts the acquiring companies were usually very highly leveraged, meaning they had high ratios of debt to equity. Hence these transactions were often called "leveraged buyouts" (LBOs). When RJR Nabisco was taken private in an LBO in 1989, for example, its ratio of debt to total assets went from about 0.67 in 1988 to 0.97 by the end of 1989. During this period many other companies financed acquisitions with debt, and still other companies bought back their own stock with funds they raised by issuing debt. FMC Corp., for example, "recapitalized" itself in 1986, taking its debt-to-assets ratio from 0.58 at the end of 1985 to 1.19 at the end of 1986.[22]

[22]Author's calculations from Compustat data.

From 1983 through the end of 1990, public companies collectively bought back $632 billion more than they issued in equity through such transactions, replacing much of what had been equity with debt instruments.[23] These transactions were often explained as mechanisms for compelling firms to pay out cash flow.[24]

Indeed, Harvard professor Michael Jensen, a leading proponent of this point of view and an advocate of takeovers and leveraged buyouts, noted that in a typical LBO, not only is the capital structure of the target firm altered dramatically, but the ownership of the remaining outstanding equity is typically concentrated in the hands of a much smaller group of individuals. Thus, in a sense, once a firm has been bought out and taken private, it looks more like the basic model discussed at the beginning of this chapter. Shareholders in the firm end up with much more control because there are only a few of them, they each hold a large percentage of the outstanding equity, they are typically well represented on the board of directors, and most top executives are also shareholders.

Even creditors have much more control over LBO firms than is typical in traditional, widely traded corporations because the firms are so highly leveraged that they often operate right at the limits of their loan covenants, frequently have to seek additional funding, and, with disconcerting regularity, fall behind on their loan payments and must restructure their loans either privately or through the bankruptcy courts. In April of 1988, for example, Campeau Corp. acquired Federated Department Stores in a highly leveraged transaction. Campeau quickly developed severe liquidity problems. By September 1989 the problems had became so severe that Campeau was forced to sell off Bloomingdale's, a key member of the Federated group. Campeau also had to give up control of Federated to secure a

---

[23]Blair and Uppal (1993, pp. 8–9).

[24]Jensen (1986). This hypothesis is examined in detail in Blair (1993).

loan to buy inventories for the Christmas shopping season, and by January 1990 Campeau had filed bankruptcy petitions.

Undaunted by such stories, Jensen regarded LBOs as a major advantageous innovation in corporate governance. In 1989 he went so far as to predict that highly leveraged firms with concentrated equity holdings would perform so much better than traditional firms that the old style would soon give way to this new form.[25]

In practice, takeovers, leveraged buyouts, and massive financial restructuring as a means of altering the control mechanisms of corporations have proved to be very blunt instruments that present their own serious problems. As former Securities and Exchange Commissioner A. A. Sommer, Jr., put it: "Whatever the diseases that afflicted American business, tender offers in treating them were more like the bloodsucking leeches and the other medical remedies of the eighteenth century than the modern scalpel. They were violent, untidy, occasionally irrational, increasingly undiscriminating, and often the fate of an enterprise depended more upon the skills of investment bankers and lawyers (and their success in enlisting others such as state legislators) than upon the quality of the target or the merits of the transaction."[26] (Tender offers were the legal mechanism by which most takeovers and LBOs were affected.)

Moreover, managers of large companies complain that the high leverage that gives investors more control is a kind of straitjacket that forces managers to focus on short-term earnings performance and can make it difficult for them to respond quickly to attractive investment opportunities. For this reason, the recent focus on finan-

---

[25]Jensen (1989). Jensen has since conceded that takeover activity was subject to excesses. See Jensen (1993).

[26]Sommer (1991, p. 697).

cial structure as a device for corporate governance has been a controversial part of the current debates.

How Real Is the Distinction between Debt and Equity?

Up to now, this discussion has regarded the distinction between debt and equity as being perfectly clear and has treated lenders and shareholders as if they were completely separate and distinct participants in the typical corporation. Once again, however, the real world is not so simple. A variety of complex securities such as preferred shares, deferred payment instruments, perpetuities, and convertible subordinated debentures blur the distinction between debt and equity.[27] Under certain market conditions, for example, junk bonds have risk and reward characteristics that are much more like equity than traditional "investment-grade" debt, although these securities do not carry any voting rights.[28] The use of these innovative financial instruments, combined with limited liability for common shareholders (which by definition limits their risk), raises questions about which security holders are bearing what mix of risk and rewards associated with the enterprise. More important, these innovative financial instruments undermine one of the fundamental assumptions of both the basic model and the Berle-Means model: that common stockholders earn the residual gains from the activities of the company and bear the associated residual risk. If share-

---

[27]See Brealey and Myers (1991, ch. 14) for an accessible description of some complex hybrid financial instruments used in corporate finance. See also Kopcke and Rosengren (1990).

[28]Bond rating agencies such as Moody's and Standard and Poor's estimate the riskiness of publicly traded bonds and the corporations who issue them and assign the bonds a risk rating. Ratings below "Baa" by Moody's or below "BBB" by Standard and Poor's are considered below "investment grade." Junk bonds are usually defined as bonds that are rated below investment grade.

holders do not bear all of the residual risk, it is not necessarily true that maximizing the value of common stock is equivalent to maximizing the total wealth created by the corporation.[29]

In the real world, too, investors who buy the stocks and bonds of widely traded companies usually hold them as part of a portfolio of investments. According to modern finance theory, a properly structured portfolio can protect the investor from bearing any of the firm-specific risk associated with the individual investments in that portfolio.[30] Moreover, investors with widely diversified portfolios lose much of the incentive they might have had to pay close attention to the individual firms represented in their portfolios. Thus a second assumption of the basic model—that of all the various participants in the firm, shareholders have the information they need and the best incentive to monitor management and see that the firm's resources are used efficiently—probably does not hold in the Berle-Means model.

Further Changes in Ownership Structure

Even within the Berle-Means model of the widely traded company, it is important to distinguish between the mechanisms of control (such as the debt or equity instruments, or the mix of these in the

---

[29]It is possible, for example, without any change in the fundamentals of a company, to reorganize a company's financial structure to raise the value of the common stock by shifting additional risk onto creditors. Some critics argue that this was one effect of LBOs. Corporate governance structures that make it easy for one constituent group (in this case, the shareholders) to enrich themselves at the expense of other constituents (in this case, the bondholders) in the long run reduce the willingness of the other constituents to invest in the firm and may lead to less total wealth creation than governance structures that provide more protection for parties whose assets are at risk. See ch. 6, 7, and 8.

[30]See Mishkin (1992, Mathematical Appendix to ch. 5. MA1-MA9) for a clear discussion of the way in which portfolio investing reduces idiosyncratic risk.

financial structure) and the people who exercise control.[31] Although the instrument of control and the legal rights and responsibilities connected with a company's shares of common stock might technically be the same whether the shares are held by thousands of individual investors or are instead concentrated in the portfolios of a few pension funds, effective shareholder power is likely to be much different in each of these scenarios.

Since the 1940s and especially in the last two decades, large financial institutions have collectively come to hold almost half of all corporate equities. The holdings of pension funds (both state and local employee funds and corporate funds) and mutual funds in particular have grown very rapidly—these two classes of financial institutions now control almost nine times as much in total corporate equities as do insurance companies. Although individual institutions rarely hold more than 1 or 2 percent of a given large company, as a group institutional investors may often hold as much as 60 percent of outstanding shares of the largest companies. Table 2-1 shows the change in ownership of corporate equities by financial institutions since 1952. To reflect this transition, the Berle-Means model depicted in figure 2-2 must be amended (see figure 2-3).

The role played by institutional investors is the subject of much controversy in the corporate governance debates. Institutional investors contributed to the takeover wave in three ways, for example. They were major buyers of the junk bonds used to finance some of the deals. They were major investors in leveraged buyout funds, which financed the small buyouts as large firms were broken up in the wake of takeovers. And, often because their trustees believed that their fiduciary duties to their beneficiaries required it, institutional investors readily sold their shares in target companies to the bidders who offered the highest price.

---

[31] Herman (1981) stresses this distinction.

Table 2–1. Holdings of Corporate Equities by Type of Institution, Selected Years

Billions of current dollars

Year	Holdings at market value	Households	Foreign	Financial Groups Commercial banks	Savings institutions	Life insurance companies	Other insurance companies	Private pension funds	State, local pension funds	Mutual funds	Closed-end funds	Brokers & dealers	Bank personal trusts	Total financial groups
1952	170.1	152.5	3.7	0.0	0.3	2.5	3.3	1.8	0.1	3.3	2.0	0.6	0.0	13.9
1955	294.2	260.7	6.6	0.0	1.0	3.6	5.4	6.1	0.2	6.9	2.8	0.9	0.0	27.0
1960	424.9	364.4	9.3	0.0	1.3	5.0	7.5	16.6	0.6	14.8	5.0	0.5	0.0	51.2
1965	734.9	616.1	14.6	0.0	2.3	9.0	12.0	40.8	2.5	30.9	5.6	1.2	0.0	104.2
1970	841.4	572.5	27.2	0.1	2.8	14.6	13.2	67.1	10.1	39.7	4.3	2.0	87.9	241.7
1975	800.2	453.5	33.4	0.2	4.4	27.5	14.2	108.0	24.3	33.7	5.8	3.4	91.9	313.3
1980	1,534.7	933.9	64.6	0.1	4.2	46.3	32.3	223.5	44.3	42.5	4.9	3.3	135.0	536.3
1985	2,360.0	1,210.3	125.9	0.1	5.2	74.0	57.0	464.4	120.1	113.7	4.2	14.1	171.4	1,024.1
1990	3,530.2	1,716.7	221.7	2.2	8.8	97.9	79.9	657.6	296.1	233.2	16.3	9.6	190.1	1,591.8
1991	4,863.6	2,468.6	271.9	4.5	10.3	117.9	94.1	888.5	386.7	351.1	21.8	14.3	234.2	2,123.1
1992	5,462.9	2,810.0	300.2	4.9	11.2	121.7	97.3	962.1	448.9	451.7	23.3	14.8	216.9	2,352.8
1993	6,186.5	3,094.4	340.0	7.0	12.5	139.6	103.4	1,079.5	506.7	668.9	29.3	24.3	181.0	2,752.1
1994	5,877.7	2,817.0	343.4	6.8	11.6	146.7	106.0	1,028.6	495.8	697.2	31.5	18.3	175.0	2,717.3

Note: All data refer to the fourth quarter of that year, except for 1994, where only second quarter data were available.
Source: Board of Governors, Federal Reserve, Flow of Funds accounts, Flows and Outstandings, Washington, various years.

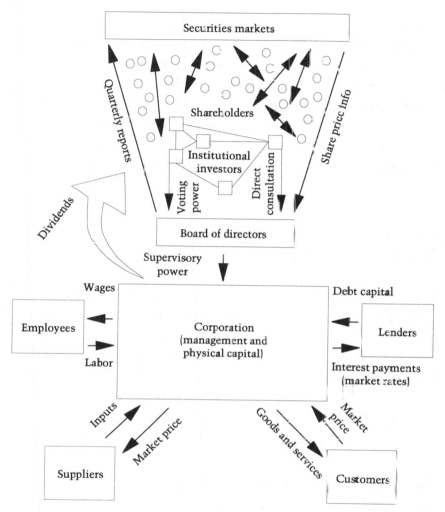

Figure 2–3. *Revised "Berle-Means" Model, with Institutional Investors*

More generally, portfolio managers have been accused of churning their investments, pursuing faddish investment strategies, and being much too quick to buy and sell stocks on relatively insignificant news. This behavior is said to lead to increased price volatility and short-term pressure on corporate management. At the same time, a few financial institutions—especially large pension funds such as California Public Employees Retirement System (CalPERS) and TIAA-CREF—have become very active in trying to influence corporate behavior. Although corporate executives initially resisted this development (and many still do), numerous scholars, shareholder rights advocates, and some policymakers have hailed it because, they argue, institutional investors represent a force strong enough to serve as an adequate check on the power of management.

How the Law Deals with the Widely Traded Corporation

Four clusters of legal arrangements have been developed to respond to these complicated corporate governance problems. These are securities market regulations, the fiduciary responsibilities of directors and officers, laws governing takeovers, and rules governing shareholder voice.

Securities Market Regulations

Before the 1930s the trading of corporate stocks and bonds in large, anonymous markets was left largely to self-regulation. But after the stock market crash of 1929 and the subsequent collapse of economic activity, political pressures to find a scapegoat for the Depression led to Wall Street. A series of federal laws regulating the issuance and trading of corporate securities was a direct response to perceived abuses by issuers, underwriters, and traders during the market boom of the 1920s and Depression of the 1930s.[32] But they also addressed

---

[32]See Galambos and Pratt (1988, pp. 102–05) for a concise history of the politics of securities market regulations of the 1930s. Roe (1994) provides a much more detailed history.

the more general problems of corporate control that are raised any time potential investors are unable to examine directly the books of a company or personally measure the character of its managers.

The major purpose of these laws was to require regular, accurate, and timely public disclosure of financial information by any company that issued publicly traded securities. The two most important laws were the Securities Act of 1933, which regulated all new public offerings of securities, and the Securities Exchange Act of 1934, which created the Securities and Exchange Commission (SEC), gave it the authority to administer the 1933 act, and extended regulation to securities that were already issued and outstanding. The SEC is a bipartisan body, consisting of five commissioners who are appointed by the president and confirmed by Congress for staggered five-year terms.

From the outset, federal securities regulations have avoided interfering directly in the market's judgment about whether any given security is worth investing in; the regulations have instead attempted to ensure that material information about the issuer is accurate and disclosed in a timely manner. The laws make the accounting profession the independent arbiter of how this information is to be collected, tabulated, and reported, and issuing companies are required to have an annual audit conducted by an independent accounting firm.[33] "The primary purpose of the Federal Securities laws is to instill public confidence in the reliability and accuracy of information reported by publicly owned corporations," according to a Senate subcommittee study of the accounting industry's role in fulfilling this purpose.[34]

The 1933 securities act required that all new securities offered or sold to the public be registered, initially with the Federal Trade

---

[33]The SEC can set accounting rules but generally defers to the Financial Accounting Standards Board; the professional organization that determines "generally accepted accounting rules" for the profession. See Hill (1987).

[34]U.S. Senate Committee on Government Operations (1977, p. 1).

Commission.[35] The registration process consists of filing a "prospectus," making a copy of that prospectus available to all purchasers of the securities, and providing additional information and exhibits to the SEC to be made available for public inspection.[36] A prospectus must contain the issuer's name and address and the names and addresses of all directors and officers and owners of 10 percent or more of all classes of the company's common stock, a statement of the issuer's existing capital structure and capital structure after the new issue, a description of how the new funds will be used, and detailed balance sheet and profit and loss statements.[37] The SEC is authorized to seek civil and criminal penalties for false and misleading statements contained in a registration statement or prospectus; a private right of action was also created, so that investors could recover losses suffered as a result of incomplete or inaccurate disclosure. In 1972 registration requirements were extended to solicitation of shareholder votes for approval of mergers and sales of assets.

In addition to regulating securities issuances, securities laws directly regulate the companies themselves through the filing requirements of the 1934 act and subsequent amendments. Under Section 12 all companies that have any securities registered for public trading on a national securities exchange (or that have assets of more than $5 million and at least 500 shareholders) must register with the SEC, and under Section 13, these companies must file various periodic reports. These include an annual "10-K" statement with an audited balance sheet and income statement and an analysis of this

---

[35]The 1934 act amended the 1933 securities act to require that all new public securities be registered with the newly created SEC.

[36]Private placements of securities to institutional investors or small groups of individuals are exempt from the registration requirements if the investors are a small enough group or are believed to have enough sophistication or bargaining power with the issuer or are deemed to have adequate access to inside information.

[37]Hazen (1990, pp. 94–97).

financial information by management, quarterly "10-Q" statements that provide an abbreviated update of the issuing company's balance sheet and income statement figures between 10-K filings, and an "8-K" report whenever any event or change occurs between regular filing periods that could materially affect the market for the company's securities. Independent auditors must certify the 10-Ks, and the chief executive, senior finance and accounting officers, and a majority of directors must sign them.

Securities regulation also affects corporate governance indirectly by influencing who is allowed to trade in a corporation's securities on what information. For example, trading of equity securities by "insiders" (defined as corporate directors and officers and any individual or institutional investor holding 10 percent or more of the outstanding equity) is restricted. Insiders must report all purchases and sales of the company's securities, and if they profit by buying a company's securities and then reselling them within six months or by selling and rebuying within six months, they may be required to forfeit those profits to the company. The SEC has further indicated in recent years that groups of investors acting together as a "voting" group may be required to meet the disclosure rules and be subject to forfeiture of trading profits if the members of this group collectively hold 10 percent or more of a class of equity securities.[38] These restrictions are designed to discourage directors, officers, and major investors in a company from taking advantage of their positions to the detriment of other investors with smaller, more anonymous positions.

Among the most important features of federal securities laws are the generalized prohibitions against "fraud or deceit" or "manipulative or deceptive devices or contrivances." These provide for redress if share-

---

[38]The group must forfeit trading profits only if it is found to have "deputized" someone—to have put a representative on the board, for example. See Black (1990, pp. 545–48).

holders or others believe that the company failed to disclose relevant or important information, provided misleading information, or engaged in transactions that had the effect of deceiving or coercing shareholders. These antifraud provisions are written very broadly, applying to any person or institution that issues, purchases, or sells any kind of a security. Although they have been important in protecting small investors, in recent years they have become controversial because they have provided the basis for hundreds of class-action lawsuits filed by shareholders against companies whose stock price fluctuates unexpectedly. Apple Computer's stock price fell 25 percent in July 1993, for example, when the company announced a loss of $188 million for the third quarter of its fiscal year. A group of sixteen shareholders promptly filed a lawsuit claiming that Apple and its top executives had misled investors by releasing earnings forecasts that were too optimistic.

Such lawsuits have become common, particularly against small, high-tech companies whose stock prices tend to be volatile. Lawyers who specialize in such suits argue that they are an appropriate part of the system of enforcing full disclosure and therefore important in maintaining investor confidence. But executives and other critics of these suits claim that many of them are frivolous, that the litigants simply hope to harass the companies into settling, and that they particularly hurt high-risk, high-tech companies and discourage them from raising funds in the public equity markets. The Senate Banking Committee held hearings in 1993 on whether new laws were needed to limit the circumstances in which companies and executives may be sued, but no further action occurred. The Republican-led Congress has vowed to pursue reform more vigorously in 1995, and in March the House passed a bill making such suits more difficult to initiate.[39]

---

[39]See Ross Kerber, "Shareholder Suits Prompt Reform Push," *Washington Post*, August 8, 1993, p. H1; David S. Hilzenrath, "House Approves Curbs on Shareholders' Suits," *Washington Post*, March 9, 1995, p. B10.

Another controversial application of the generalized prohibitions on fraud, deceipt, and manipulative practices has been their use to prohibit trading on "inside" information or on information that has been "misappropriated" by the person involved in the trading. In the late 1980s, for example, the SEC charged investment banker Dennis Levine at Drexel Burnham Lambert, corporate raider Ivan Boesky, and others with violations of securities laws. Neither Boesky nor Levine were officers or directors in the companies they were trading in, but Levine was deemed to have "inside information" about takeover negotiations under way at various firms, to have passed that information on to Boesky, and to have traded on that information.[40] For example, in April and May of 1985, Levine learned of merger talks between Nabisco Brands and R.J. Reynolds through a friend at Nabisco's investment bank and later learned of a pending takeover of Houston Natural Gas from another friend at the gas company's investment bank. He passed this information on to Boesky, who bought 337,000 shares of Nabisco and 301,800 shares of Houston Natural Gas in advance of public announcements. Boesky made $8.1 million on these two deals in just a few weeks.[41] Levine was ultimately fined $362,000, sentenced to two years in jail, and ordered to forfeit $11.6 million of $12.6 million in profits he had earned in these and other activities.[42] Boesky pleaded guilty to one count of conspiracy to file false documents with the federal government in a related case, was sentenced to three years in jail, and paid a $100 million fine.[43]

---

[40]Although there is no reason to believe that all, or even most, takeovers are tainted by trading on inside information, the controversy over the activities of Levine, Boesky, and others helped fuel the public outcry against takeovers in the mid-1980s.

[41]William B. Glaberson, "Who'll Be the Next to Fall?" *Business Week*, December 1, 1986, p. 28.

[42]Thomas J. Lueck, "Levine Gets 2-Year Jail Term," *New York Times*, February 21, 1987, p. 33.

[43]James B. Stewart and Daniel Hertzberg, "Boesky Admits to Conspiracy Charges: Link, Sources Say, to Drexel Inquiry," *Wall Street Journal*, April 24, 1987, p. 3.

A few years earlier, a *Wall Street Journal* reporter, R. Foster Winans, was convicted of securities fraud for providing stockbrokers with information about forthcoming articles in the *Journal's* "Heard on Wall Street" column. Although the information Winans passed on was obtained by legal research methods, the courts ruled that the information belonged to Winans' employer, not to Winans, and that Winans had misappropriated it. The underlying information itself was technically already public, but because publication of columns about a company can cause market prices to move, Winans was deemed to have inside information because he knew when the columns were going to be published.

Questions have been raised about what clause of the securities laws is violated by trading on inside information, about whether the party accused of violating the prohibition had a duty to disclose the information, about what constitutes material information, and about when information can no longer be considered "nonpublic." Moreover, some finance and legal scholars have argued that neither insider trading nor trading on inside information should be prohibited at all because, they argue, if such trading were permitted, stock prices would more efficiently embody all information about a company.[44] Trading by insiders and trading on inside information have historically been common practices in other countries. But arguments in favor of liberalized insider trading have never garnered much political support because they are regarded as putting small investors at a severe disadvantage. And, in fact, Europe and Japan are moving toward the more restrictive approach used in the United States.[45]

---

[44]Manne (1966). See also Netter, Poulsen, and Hersch (1988, pp. 1–13) for a concise and accessible discussion of the economic benefits and costs of insider trading.

[45]See Council Directive of November 13, 1989, "Coordinating Regulations on Insider Dealing," *Official Journal of the European Communities*, November 18, 1989. See also Friedland (1994) on recent changes in Japan and Japanese attitudes toward

The SEC has recently liberalized some of its rules to facilitate better communications between management and large shareholders and among groups of large shareholders. But some institutional investors still believe that the prohibitions against insider trading and trading on inside information make it risky to hold large blocks of stock in companies or to attempt to engage more actively in oversight. They fear that they will be deemed to be insiders or to possess inside information and therefore be ineligible to trade.

Federal securities laws also regulate investment companies and other institutional investors. As discussed briefly above, these regulations, together with banking, insurance, and pension fund regulation, also tend to discourage financial institutions from owning large blocks of corporate equities and from becoming actively involved in corporate affairs.

Collectively, these restrictions help make large shareholdings much less liquid than small shareholdings and are believed to discourage large institutional investors from taking positions in companies that put them over the legal thresholds for shares owned that cause them to be subjected to the reporting requirements or restrictions on sales. Some argue that these restrictions have also discouraged officers and directors from holding stock in their own companies. Thus these restrictions have implications for who owns corporate equities and for what can be done with them. In recent years, several reform advocates have been reexamining some of these rules to see whether they go too far in inhibiting active investing by institutional shareholders and whether some of them should be relaxed.

---

capital markets; and "Insider Dealing: Balancing Act," *Economist*, May 22, 1993, pp. 22–28, which suggests that Germany is dragging its feet on implementing the insider trading rules. See also Glenn Whitney, "International: Europe Moves to Curb Insider Trading," *Wall Street Journal*, November 4, 1993, p. A 11.

The SEC also establishes the ground rules for "proxy solicitations," which are the means by which management seeks the votes of shareholders in electing directors and approving other corporate changes, and for tender offers, in which an investor or group of investors makes a general and public offer to buy shares held by the public. These are discussed further in the sections below on shareholder voice and the market for corporate control.

Finally, rules of the stock exchanges and membership requirements of associations of securities dealers are also important facets of securities regulation. The New York Stock Exchange, for example, requires listed companies to have an audit committee with a majority of outside directors and to send shareholders quarterly reports.

Fiduciary Responsibilities of Officers and Directors

It is clearly impractical for the shareholders of a large company, as a group, actually to run a company or even to exercise close supervision over managers hired to run the company. Thus, the laws of every state make managers "fiduciaries" for the corporation and require that corporations have a board of directors who also have fiduciary responsibilities and are charged with overseeing management. A fiduciary is someone who has legal responsibility to care for something held in trust for someone else. Boards of directors are expected to formulate corporate policy, approve strategic plans, authorize major transactions, declare dividends, and authorize the sale of additional securities (subject to any limits that might be in the articles of incorporation). They are also expected to hire, advise, compensate, and, if necessary, remove management; to arrange for succession; and to determine the size of the board and nominate new members, subject to approval by shareholders.

Fiduciary duties impose the duties of loyalty and care on managers and directors in carrying out these responsibilities. The duty of loyalty requires the manager or director to avoid conflicts of interest and refrain from self-dealing transactions at the expense of the corporation. If an officer or director engages the corporation in a transaction that benefits that officer or director, the transaction may be subjected to a legal test of fairness that would focus on the merits of the transaction to the corporation, the procedures surrounding its approval, or both. Generally, the courts assume fairness if the transaction has been approved by disinterested directors or shareholders.[46]

The duty of care requires each director and officer to act "(1) in good faith; (2) with the care an ordinarily prudent person in a like position would exercise under similar circumstances; and (3) in a manner he reasonably believes to be in the best interests of the corporation."[47] In cases questioning whether an officer or director has acted with care, the courts have applied a "reasonable man standard," which basically requires "a director in performing his functions to act in good faith, in a manner that he reasonably believes to be in the best interests of the corporation, and with the skill, diligence, and care of a reasonably prudent person."[48]

Treating managers and directors as fiduciaries provides a mechanism for imposing sanctions if they fail to exercise their responsibilities to the corporation, without necessarily requiring that all of those responsibilities be spelled out in precise detail in advance. "The fiduciary principle is an alternative to elaborate promises and extra monitoring," according to legal scholars Frank H. Easterbrook and Daniel R. Fischel. "It replaces prior supervision with deterrence, much as criminal law uses penalties for bank robbery rather than pat-down searches of everyone entering banks."[49]

---

[46]Hamilton (1987, pp. 304–24).
[47]American Bar Association (1985, pp. 219–20).
[48]Palmiter (1989, p. 1359).
[49]Easterbrook and Fischel (1991, p. 92).

The fiduciary responsibilities of managers and directors are broader and more complex than are those of other fiduciaries, such as trustees of personal estates. This is because, under the laws of most states, managers and directors owe their fiduciary duties to the corporation as a whole, rather than to individual shareholders or to individual classes of shareholders.[50] Thus the fiduciary principle by itself does not address, let alone resolve, the question of what a corporation's goals should be or whose interests corporations should serve, nor does it ultimately provide much guidance as to what managers and directors must do to fulfill their responsibilities.

Technically directors may be held personally liable to the corporation for losses that result from breaches of loyalty to the corporation or failure to exercise proper care in managing the corporation's affairs. But the courts have been very reluctant to second-guess boards or management unless gross negligence or self-dealing was involved in the decision or action being challenged. Instead, the courts have generally relied on the so-called "business judgment rule." Although statements of this rule vary, the idea behind it is that routinely subjecting managers' decisions to judicial scrutiny would probably cost more in the long run than would tolerating some bad judgments and minor malfeasances.[51] Thus, as a general rule, the courts have given managers broad discretion.

In recent years the business judgment rule has been applied to protect directors who adopt antitakeover provisions such as poison pills or selective stock repurchase plans. Poison pills are devices intended to make a takeover less attractive to an acquirer by making the shares of the target company worth less after a takeover. An example would be a special series of preferred shares issued to

---

[50]Hamilton (1987, pp. 302–03). Wallmar (1991, p. 192) emphasizes this point: "Allowing directors to act in the best interests of the corporation promotes the interests of all stakeholders."

[51]Easterbrook and Fischel (1991, p. 93).

existing shareholders that gives those shareholders expanded voting rights or the right to redeem their preferred shares at an inflated price in the event of a takeover. In 1984, for example, Household International adopted a complex poison pill to head off a leveraged buyout by John A. Moran and his company Dysner-Kissner-Moran (DKM). Moran and DKM sued, claiming that poison pills unduly restricted shareholders' rights, but in *Moran v. Household International*, the Delaware courts upheld the plan under the business judgment rule.[52] Another takeover defense is known as a selective stock repurchase plan; this is the tactic Unocal used to keep T. Boone Pickens from taking over the company. Unocal offered to buy back shares of its own stock at an especially high price but excluded those shares held by Picken's company, Mesa Petroleum, from the offer. In this case too, the Delaware courts ruled that the tactic was a legitimate matter of business judgment and refused to overturn it.[53] In both cases the courts said the defensive tactics forced an acquirer to negotiate a fair price with the board, although critics of both decisions argued that the tactics helped entrench management.

Nonetheless, although the courts have interpreted the business judgment rule liberally to give managers and directors broad latitude, the courts have also subjected certain decisions of directors to rather intense (and devastating) review. In particular, they have ruled that, once a company is for sale, directors must try to get the best price rather than deal exclusively with one bidder. In *Smith v. Van Gorkom*, a 1985 Delaware case, for example, directors of Trans Union Corp. were found personally liable for losses to shareholders because, the state supreme court concluded, directors had not adequately informed themselves about the value of the company at the

---

[52]*Moran v. Household International Inc.*, 500 A.2d 1346 (Delaware 1985). See also Hamilton (1987, p. 312).

[53]*Unocal v. Mesa Petroleum Co.*, 493 A.2d 946 (Delaware 1985).

time of the proposed sale and therefore were not entitled to the protection of the business judgment rule regarding the agreed price.[54] In a bid negotiated privately by Jerome W. Van Gorkom, Trans Union's chief executive officer, the price offered for Trans Union was about 50 percent above the price at which the company's stock had been trading, but a few executives of the company thought even that bid might be too low. Directors, however, failed to challenge the plan and in fact approved the proposal without the advice of outside consultants in a meeting that lasted only two hours. The company's investment bank was later unable to find a higher bid, but the Delaware Supreme Court said directors breached their fiduciary duties in accepting the original bid, and the subsequent effort to solicit other bids did not cure the initial breach.[55] Some legal scholars have suggested that, after the Van Gorkom decision, the courts have used an "informed business judgment" standard that requires directors, under certain circumstances, to exercise appropriate diligence in ensuring that they have all the relevant information they need to make an informed decision.

The total judgment against the directors in Van Gorkom was $100 million, but the case was settled for $22 million, provided in part by the purchaser in the transaction under attack and in part by the directors and officers (D&O) liability insurance. In the wake of the Van Gorkom decision, D&O liability insurance rates increased dramatically and directors at several corporations resigned. In response, the state of Delaware and several other states altered their corporate codes to prevent or reduce the chances of liability damages being awarded for cases involving a breach of duty of care.[56] Nonetheless,

---

[54]*Smith v. Van Gorkom*, 488 A.2d 858 (Delaware 1985). See also *Revlon, Inc. v. McAndrews & Forbes Holdings, Inc.*, 506 A.2d 173 (Delaware 1986). Both cases are described succinctly in Hamilton (1987, pp. 314–15).

[55]Fischel (1985, pp. 37–38; 1445–47).

[56]Hamilton (1987, p. 314); Monks and Minow (1991, p. 108).

directors and officers were, in effect, put on notice that their positions entailed certain risks unless they exercised appropriate diligence, especially regarding major transactions. Thus, the ruling in this case is one of several factors that have encouraged directors as a group to become much more diligent and assertive in the boardroom in recent years.

Other recent court decisions have also influenced board room behavior. The courts, for example, have tended to defer to the judgment of directors if the board is dominated by "outside" (non-management) directors, and this deference has led to changes in the composition of boards. These factors and others have encouraged reformers to look more closely at the other informal rules and customs by which boards operate.

The "Market for Corporate Control"

For several decades after Berle and Means documented the separation of equity ownership from control in modern large corporations, organizational and legal scholars wondered how this separation would affect the behavior of companies. Would widely traded companies still try to maximize profits for shareholders even if shareholders did not have effective control? Or would managers pursue other goals?

Working the problem from different angles in the 1960s, Robin Marris, an economist, and Henry Manne, a legal scholar, arrived at the same theory about the resolution to this dilemma at about the same time. They posited that public corporations would not stray too far from profit-maximizing behavior because market forces would restrain management from using corporate resources in ways that do not advance the interests of shareholders. The market they had in mind was the market for the shares of the company's stock (which Manne referred to as the "market for corporate control"). If management failed to make investments or take actions that would maximize the value of those shares (by maximizing the stream of future profits those shares would earn), they argued, an opportunity would be created for a more skilled or more scrupulous management team to take control of the company. The usurping team would remove the poorly performing management and capture the gains from improved management through the higher stock prices.[57] Competition in the market for corporate control would thus give shareholders ultimate control and compel firms to engage in profit-maximizing behavior, just as economic models of the firm assumed.

These insights were widely appreciated by theorists, but made little practical difference in corporate governance at the time. In the 1980s, however, the Marris and Manne hypotheses suddenly became more than academic. During that decade, a wave of leveraged buyouts, in which even some very large companies were bought out by investors and taken private, and "hostile takeovers," in which investors bought out companies through unsolicited tender offers that management opposed, turned the market for corporate control into a real threat hanging over the heads of management, and its impact on corporate governance and performance has since been an extremely controversial topic. This controversy is explored in much more detail in the next two chapters, but for now I make only a few points about the legal and institutional environment in which this corporate governance mechanism has operated.

There are two ways to gain control of a company without management approval. The first is a "proxy fight," in which an outsider challenges existing management by proposing an alternative slate of directors and attempting to win support from shareholders (see the next section). The second possibility is a "tender offer," in which the would-be acquirer (usually another company or consortium of investors) gives public notice that it will buy shares of stock at a

---

[57]Marris (1964, pp. 29–40); Manne (1965).

certain price. This price is typically set well above the current market price to encourage shareholders to tender their shares. Tender offers thus bypass management. To win control, of course, the acquirer must buy a majority of the outstanding shares, which means that a significant number of shareholders must "vote with their dollars" and accept the offer. But no shareholder meeting and no formal vote are required for the transaction to proceed.

For more than thirty years, the only significant regulations on tender offers were those sections of the Securities Exchange Act of 1934 that governed the issuance of the securities used to finance the offer. In 1968 Congress passed the Williams Act, amending the 1934 law to extend regulation of tender offers to offers for cash. As with other federal securities laws, these laws rely primarily on disclosure of material information for their effectiveness, rather than on letting a government agency or the courts rule on the merits of individual transactions. They require any person or investing group that acquires 5 percent or more of a corporation's voting stock to file a disclosure statement with the SEC within ten days of crossing the threshold; supplementary disclosure statements must be filed if the acquirer makes further purchases of stock that exceed other thresholds. In addition, offerors must disclose takeover plans, and any tender offer must be held open for at least twenty business days. The regulations also prohibit "fraudulent, deceptive, or manipulative acts or practices in connection with any tender offer."[58]

---

[58]The question of what practices are "manipulative" has provided fodder for many court cases. As discussed earlier, the courts have decided that poison pills, discriminatory self-tender offers, and "two-tier" tender offers are not manipulative as long as they satisfy full disclosure requirements. Two-tier tender offers are those in which the acquirer offers to pay a high price for, say, 55 percent of the outstanding shares in order to gain control, but then a lower price for the remaining 45 percent. The idea is to encourage shareholders to tender in the first round of the offer. See *Schreiber v. Burlington Northern, Inc.*, 105 S.Ct. 2458 (1985), in which the Supreme Court limited the interpretation of "manipulative" to refer only to cases that involve misrepresen-

Between 1968 and 1982, several states also passed so-called "first-generation state antitakeover statutes." According to Mark Roe, a Columbia Law School professor, these "require offerors to file with the state, require bidders to wait before commencing offers, sometimes allow the state administrator to determine the fairness of offers and stop them if they are unfair."[59] Contested tender offers were extremely rare during the early part of this period, and the few raiders that attempted them were regarded as renegades and outlaws by the establishment business and investment community.

In 1982, however, the Supreme Court made takeovers easier by striking down the first generation antitakeover laws. The test case was an Illinois law that called for any tender offer to be registered with the secretary of state and to go through a twenty-day waiting period. During that time the secretary of state would review the offer to determine whether it met all disclosure requirements. MITE Corp., which made a cash tender offer for all outstanding shares of Chicago Rivet and Machine Co., met all SEC filing requirements, but instead of complying with the Illinois law, filed suit to have the statute invalidated. In *Edgar v. MITE*, the Supreme Court found that the twenty-day waiting period undermined shareholders' rights to accept a tender offer within a reasonable period of time and ruled that other terms of the Illinois law imposed "a substantial burden on interstate commerce which outweighs its putative local benefits." Justices wrote six separate opinions in the case, which in general held that the Williams Act appropriately balanced the interests of

---

tation or nondisclosure. The courts have ruled that "parking" securities, in which the true identity of the holder is disguised, is manipulative. See *SEC v. Jeffries*, consent order, Federal Section, Commerce Clearinghouse Law Reports, 93, 171 (S.D.N.Y. 1987). These cases are discussed in Hazen (1990).

[59]Roe (1993d, table 3-2) provides a helpful summary of takeover laws and court rulings as they evolved in the 1980s. The rest of this section draws heavily from information in this table.

offerors, target companies, and shareholders and that state takeover regulations could not upset this balance.[60]

Around the same time, whatever social, moral, or professional inhibitions had discouraged establishment investment bankers and other financiers from backing hostile takeovers were rapidly breaking down. Drexel Burnham Lambert succeeded in creating an active market in high-risk, high-yield junk bonds. And the number of original-issue junk bonds issued rose from twenty-six in 1980, with a face value of approximately $873 million, to ninety-four by 1985, with a face value of more than $8 billion.[61] By the mid-1980s major investment banks had begun providing financial backing for hostile takeovers. By 1983, when T. Boone Pickens made a serious run at acquiring Gulf Oil Co., which had approximately $7 billion in assets at the time, the idea that hostile takeovers were a threat hanging over the heads of management moved out of the realm of theory and became tangible and real, even to executives of very large companies.

Corporate executives and their lawyers responded by developing some ingenious new protections. In 1983 the Lenox Corp. rejected a partial $413 million bid by Brown-Forman Distillers Corp. and instead issued a special class of preferred stock to its existing shareholders that would convert to preferred stock of the acquiring company in the event of a takeover. Moreover, the preferred stock was further convertible into a special class of voting stock of the acquiring company. The Brown family held a 62 percent interest in Brown-Forman at the time. Lenox's maneuver discouraged a partial bid by Brown-Forman because any shares of Lenox that were left outstanding would dilute the controlling position of the Brown family.

---

[60]*Edgar v. MITE Corp.*, 457 U.S. 624 at 643–46 (1982). See also Snipes (1983).
[61]Blair and Uppal (1993, table 2-5). Data above are reported in nominal dollars; data in Blair and Uppal are reported in real (inflation-adjusted) dollars.

Numerous other companies followed suit, creating their own poison pills, and in 1985 the Delaware Supreme Court validated this maneuver in the *Moran v. Household International* decision. Corporations also amended their charters to require "supermajorities" to oust current board members and instituted "staggered" boards, in which terms of only one-third of the board members expired each year.[62] Both of these tactics make it harder for an acquirer to gain actual control of the board even after the acquirer owns a majority of the stock.

Also in the mid-1980s, states passed another round of antitakeover laws under pressure from managers of threatened companies and often with the support of workers who believed their jobs were threatened. These laws provide that when a shareholder obtains a large proportion of the outstanding shares, that shareholder can be prevented from voting shares in excess of some threshold level, such as 20 percent, unless the remaining shareholders vote to restore voting rights to those shares.[63] "Control share laws," as they are called, were upheld by the Supreme Court in 1987.[64] In the late 1980s states passed yet another round of antitakeover laws (again, usually under pressure from management of a specific company targeted for takeover). These expand the constituencies directors can or, in some cases, must consider—such as employees or communities—in deciding whether to accept a takeover proposal. These laws help protect executives who resist a takeover offer—even at a price

---

[62]Many such charter amendments predated the widespread use of the poison pill. Once the pill became an option, many companies elected to use it rather than charter amendments "in part because it was more effective, and in part because institutional investors and pension funds would not vote for charter amendments after 1984," according to Martin Lipton, the attorney with Wachtel, Lipton, Rosen & Katz who is credited with inventing the poison pill strategy. Private correspondence from Lipton to the author, spring 1994.

[63]Black (1990, p. 556).

[64]*CTS Corp. v. Dynamics Corp. of America*, 481 U.S. 69 (1987).

that includes a substantial premium—by giving them a broader range of rationales for their resistance that the courts must accept as legitimate.

Takeover activity slowed down considerably after 1989 and then picked up again in mid-1993 with a series of announced mergers in the telecommunications, entertainment, health care, and transportation industries. Most of these recent deals do not seem to be driven by charges of lackadaisical management at the target companies, however. Nonetheless, some of the legal questions debated in the 1980s have resurfaced. In 1993, for example, shareholders wanted the board of directors of Paramount Communications to accept an offer from QVC, which the shareholders believed would give them the best upfront payoff. But Paramount's management and board wanted to accept an offer from Viacom, which directors argued would be in the "long-run" best interest of the company. In December 1993 the Delaware courts ruled that directors must at least agree to give equal consideration to the QVC offer. A fair bidding contest was set up, which Viacom ultimately won.[65]

This decision seemed to weaken a decision by the same courts several years earlier in a case also involving Paramount Communications. Then, Paramount was the spurned would-be acquirer, attempting to take over Time Inc. In an effort to ward off the Paramount offer, Time quickly completed a previously discussed but unconsummated deal to merge with Warner Communications.[66] Paramount sued, along with Time shareholders who believed they would have been better off if Time were sold to Paramount. In that case, the Delaware courts ruled that Time's board had not violated their fiduciary duties in rejecting the Paramount deal and pursuing

[65]Geraldine Fabrikant, "The Paramount Deal," *New York Times*, December 23, 1993, p. A1.

[66]Time did this by initiating a tender offer for Warner, an action that, unlike a merger agreement, did not require shareholder approval.

the deal with Warner because the latter had been undertaken pursuant to Time's carefully developed long-range strategy.[67]

Rules Governing Shareholder "Voice"

Short of trying to take a company over and run it themselves, shareholders have two different mechanisms for influencing the way a corporation is run. They may "exit" by selling their shares, which, if enough shareholders do it, tends to drive the price of the company's stock downward, signaling management that shareholders are dissatisfied. Or shareholders may try to communicate their views directly to management. The latter approach has been called "voice," following the lead of Albert O Hirschman who in 1970 distinguished the two approaches in a wonderfully insightful book entitled *Exit, Voice, and Loyalty: Responses to Declines in Firms, Organizations, and States.* Hirschman argued that, if participants in an enterprise were able to exit freely, they would not be very motivated to use voice to try to reform the enterprise, whereas, if they were unable or constrained in their ability to exit, they would be more likely to find effective ways to use voice. And, indeed, shareholder voice can be quite effective in small, closely held corporations where, not coincidentally, investors may find it hard to sell their shares. In large corporations with widely traded and very liquid securities, the ability and willingness of shareholders to exercise effective voice is greatly weakened. This section looks at the legal and institutional tools for exercising voice that are available to shareholders in widely traded corporations.

Corporation law is based on a model that is sometimes referred to as "shareholder democracy" or "corporate democracy." Edward Jay

---

[67]*Paramount Communications, Inc. v. Time, Inc.*, 571 A.2d 1140 (Delaware 1990), pp. 39–40.

Epstein argued that this political model of corporate governance emerged in response to concerns during the Depression that corporations were performing very poorly and managers were not accountable to anyone. Mechanisms of shareholder democracy were instituted to head off the threat of government intervention in the actual control of corporations. "Managers would be made responsible to share owners through a democratic process of voting, just as representatives are responsible to citizens," Epstein wrote. "To make this linkage more credible, the Securities and Exchange Commission (SEC) . . . imposed administrative rules on corporations that were designed to assure fair and timely elections for directors, as well as to make sure that the corporations disclosed all pertinent information to dissident shareholders."[68]

In principle, the law is intended to give shareholders a significant amount of control. In pratice, it does not always work out that way. Technically, shareholders must regularly elect or reelect the board of directors, but shareholders cannot easily remove a director whose term has not expired, and shareholders do not, typically, participate in the nomination process for new directors.

Apart from the election of directors, the number of matters that must be submitted to shareholder vote is limited. Under most state laws, these include substantive amendments to the articles of incorporation and fundamental changes that are not part of the ordinary business of the company, such as merger, dissolution, or disposition of a substantial part of corporate assets. In the latter case, however, many state laws give directors "gatekeeping" authority by requiring that proposed transactions be submitted to shareholders only if the directors have already approved them. In most states shareholders also have the right to file derivative suits on behalf of the corpora-

[68]Epstein (1986, pp. 5–6).

tion and to adopt resolutions making recommendations to the board of directors.[69]

Shareholders vote on directors and other matters at annual meetings, which all state corporation laws require, or at special meetings called to consider specific issues. Because most shareholders do not actually attend these shareholder meetings, votes are usually cast by proxy. That is, shareholders designate some agent to vote their shares for them. In large public companies, management usually asks shareholders for the right to vote their shares when it submits a slate of candidates for election to the board and mails out notices of the annual meetings; shareholders routinely grant this authority.

The proxy process is regulated at the federal level under Section 14 of the Securities Exchange Act of 1934. As already mentioned, this law requires that public companies furnish shareholders with certain information when they announce an annual meeting and solicit proxies.[70] Until recently companies were always required to file these "proxy statements" with the SEC ten days before sending them to shareholders. New rules promulgated in the fall of 1992 streamlined proxy filing rules, and the prefiling requirement was waved for many situations. Proxy statements must include details about each of the directors up for election.

Anyone may challenge existing management by engaging in a "proxy contest," that is, by soliciting from shareholders the right to vote shares against management proposals or for a competing slate of directors. Such dissidents must meet many of the same filing requirements that management must satisfy. But the rules governing the proxy process, many critics charge, have traditionally tilted

[69]Hamilton (1987, pp. 156–57, 160).

[70]Companies are also required to provide certain information to shareholders if a majority of the board of directors is replaced without a shareholders' meeting in connection with a transfer of controlling interest.

the balance of power strongly toward existing management and against dissidents.[71]

Historically proxy filing requirements have been interpreted very strictly, making it difficult for shareholders to communicate with each other at all—even if they are not soliciting proxies—without the approval and support of management. Large shareholders who wanted to find out whether other shareholders were dissatisfied and might be willing to support some sort of amendment to the bylaws or other challenge to management, for example, were deemed to be engaging in a proxy solicitation and required to meet all of the associated public notice and advance filing requirements. Legal scholar Bernard S. Black noted that "a communication that doesn't solicit anything can still be a 'solicitation'! The test is whether the communication is 'part of a continuous plan ending in solicitation and which prepare[s] the way for its success.'. . . Advertisements urging state takeover of a public utility and story ideas given to the financial press can qualify."[72] Moreover, companies are not required to supply lists of shareholders of record to dissidents, unless they have met the official proxy solicitation requirements. Even then, management can choose to mail out the dissidents' proxy material instead of turning over the list of shareholders to the dissident—in which case management controls the timing of the mailing.

In the fall of 1992, the SEC relaxed some of these rules, making it somewhat easier for shareholders to communicate with each other. The rule changes exempted from all proxy requirements persons who have no special relationship to the company (that is, who are

---

[71]In separate articles Edward Jay Epstein and Nell Minow complained about the old preclearance requirement for proxy soliciters, for example. See Epstein (1986, p. 15) and Minow (1991). Epstein concluded that "the costs of hurdling all the legal barriers and mounting a full-scale proxy battle in a major campaign can run into the millions of dollars."

[72]Black (1990, pp. 537–38).

not officers or directors or major investors seeking control), who are not seeking proxy authority, and who do not have a special interest (other than as a shareholder) in the question being put before the shareholders. Shareholders who own more than $5 million in a company's securities must notify the SEC if they communicate in private with other shareholders about an upcoming voting matter, but they do not have to obtain prior approval. And they may publish their views or announce their own voting intentions without meeting the proxy filing requirements. The new rules also guarantee that shareholders have a chance to vote on each proposal separately by making it illegal for management to "bundle" together several proposals in an effort to force shareholders to vote for or against the whole package.[73] These rule changes obviously weaken the position of management and were thus opposed by such groups as the Business Roundtable.

By the fall of 1993, there was growing evidence that institutional shareholders and other investors were taking advantage of the new rules to communicate with each other and to put pressure on management. When Medical Care America initially rebuffed a merger proposal by Surgical Care Affiliates, for example, a group of seven major investors in Medical Care America convened a meeting in New York to discuss the situation. They then mobilized a lobbying campaign in which, over the course of a few weeks, institutional shareholders accounting for more than 40 percent of Medical Care's stock expressed their concerns directly to Medical Care's directors.[74] Before October 1992 these actions would have violated securities laws.

The original rationale for the strict rules inhibiting shareholder communications was to prevent groups of shareholders from engag-

---

[73]SEC (1992).

[74]John Pound, "Where Shareholder Activism Is Paramount," *Wall Street Journal*, December 7, 1993, p. A16.

ing in manipulative practices that put small shareholders at a disadvantage. But many individual investors as well as institutional shareholders supported these recent reforms. The United Shareholders Association, a lobbying group formed by T. Boone Pickens in 1986 ostensibly to represent the interests of individual investors, for example, cited reform of proxy voting rules as one of its three original missions.[75] Although no serious abuses by large shareholders had occurred during the first two years the new proxy rules were in force, it remains to be seen whether the new, more relaxed rules will work to the disadvantage of small shareholders in the long run.

SEC rules also allow shareholders meeting certain conditions to present proposals for action to management, and, if the proposals and the shareholders submitting them meet certain tests, management must include these proposals in the proxy statements and give other shareholders a chance to vote on these proposals. If management opposes a proposal, it must include in the proxy a brief statement by the proponent in support of it. These provisions were used extensively in the 1960s and 1970s to introduce certain political or "social responsibility" proposals, such as attempts to compel companies to adopt the "Sullivan principles," which prescribed a set of operating rules for companies with investments in South Africa to eliminate segregation and unequal treatment of blacks in the workplace.[76] Social activists still use these provisions, but shareholder rights activists are now also using them to oppose takeover defenses (such as poison pills) in corporate charters or to try to force compa-

---

[75]Shortly after the new SEC rules had been put in place, the association declared victory and announced that it was disbanding. See Ralph V. Whitworth, "United Shareholders Association: Mission Accomplished," Remarks to Investor Responsibility Research Center Conference on Shareholder Management and Cooperation, October 27, 1993.

[76]Civil rights activist Reverend Leon H. Sullivan developed the Sullivan Principles while serving as a director of General Motors in 1976. "Sullivan Redux," *New Yorker*, October 7, 1985, pp. 31–32.

nies to rescind them. Shareholder groups generally oppose these defenses because the stock prices of companies that are protected from takeovers tend to be lower than they would otherwise be.[77]

Management is not required to submit to shareholder vote all proposals put forward, however. The rules about what managers are entitled to omit are constantly being reviewed, challenged, and revised. Until recently, for example, the SEC upheld managements that refused to submit proposals regarding executive compensation to shareholders on the grounds that this issue was not a proper matter for shareholder action (because it relates to "the conduct of the company's ordinary business"). In 1991, however, the SEC changed its interpretation and now requires management to include proposals having to do with executive compensation in the proxy statements.

The bylaws of individual companies also govern the ability of shareholders to influence management, and in recent years CalPERS and other large institutional investors have submitted proposals to many companies designed to change bylaws in ways that enhance shareholder voice and influence. For example, the largest increases in proxy proposal activity from the 1990 to the 1991 proxy season, according to the American Society of Corporate Secretaries, were in proposals to eliminate staggered board terms, to allow confidential voting, and to provide for cumulative voting.[78] Cumulative voting procedures would give shareholders the right to cast multiple votes for a single director so that a director could be elected by a minority of shares. For example, suppose a company had submitted a slate of ten directors. Shareholders would have ten votes for each share they held, and under cumulative voting, a shareholder with ten shares

---

[77]Easterbrook and Fischel (1991, pp. 196–98) summarize the empirical evidence that takeover defenses depress stock prices.

[78]American Society of Corporate Secretaries, Inc. (1991, pp. 2–3).

could cast all one hundred votes for a single director. All of these changes would give minority shareholders more influence over the outcome of an election.

In recent years shareholder rights advocates have explored other ways to increase shareholder influence. Joseph Grundfest of Stanford's Law School, for example, has advocated that shareholders engage in what he calls "just vote no" campaigns if they are dissatisfied with the performance of management or directors. These are efforts to encourage shareholders of a given corporation to withhold their proxies for management's slate of directors or for any management proposals they oppose. Withholding a vote, he argues, "signals a lack of confidence" but is much less costly than a proxy contest.[79] Grundfest further suggests that shareholders should explain to management and the board why they are unhappy.

Similarly, Harvard Professor John Pound, executives of CalPERS, and several institutional shareholder groups have advocated more formal and informal governance roles for large institutional shareholders.[80] Proposals include holding regular meetings between directors and institutional shareholders (outside of annual meetings), setting up special committees on boards to deal directly with shareholder groups, and allowing institutional shareholders to nominate directors. These advocates have also used an informal mechanism for exercising shareholder voice: jawboning incumbent management and directors in the media.[81]

---

[79]Grundfest (1993).

[80]See, for example, Pound (1992a).

[81]Several recent studies have credited such shareholder activism with improved returns for shareholders of the targeted companies. See, for example, Gordon and Pound (1993) and Nesbitt (1994). Because most of the examples of shareholder activism cited in these studies involved considerable media attention, however, it is not clear whether the changed performance is attributable to activism through the traditional mechanisms of shareholder voice or to the pressures produced by the media spotlight.

Despite recent and proposed changes in law and practice that have tended to strengthen the mechanisms of shareholder voice in corporate governance, many corporate law scholars and others interested in these matters still doubt the usefulness of the corporate democracy model. Epstein calls corporate democracy a "myth" and a "fallacy."[82] Similarly, Columbia University law professor John C. Coffee Jr. says that, even if the rules of voting were not stacked against them, shareholders would (and perhaps should) be passive because of the time and money it would cost them to involve themselves in the governance of the companies in which they invest. They would also have to give up too many of the benefits of liquidity, he says. Liquidity is important to many shareholders, he argues, especially some financial institutions, and they should not be too quick to compromise it.[83] Finally, Jensen argues that the large publicly traded corporation is so hopelessly inefficient, and the idea of shareholder democracy so inadequate to the task of reforming it, that this organizational form will inevitably be replaced, under market pressure, by closely held corporations. Only in closely held firms, he believes, can shareholders, in fact, exercise the control they were intended to exercise.[84] Thus these scholars and advocates, each for somewhat different reasons, believe that the corporate democracy model is unrealistic and that the primary source of power for most shareholders in public corporations continues to be their ability to sell their shares.

---

[82]"The reason that this approach is doomed to fail is that the electoral model of politics, which depends on political parties, competing candidates, newspaper coverage, and symbolic issues, is not applicable to the governing of corporations," wrote Epstein (1986, p. 43).

[83]Coffee (1991).

[84]Jensen (1989).

Institutional Arrangements for Dealing with the Separation of Equity Ownership from Control

Although the law sets the broad rules of engagement, a large part of the actual governance and control of corporations occurs through a myriad of customs, cultural norms, and institutional arrangements that are not written into law but that may be heavily influenced by it. This section examines the effect on governance of two clusters of such arrangements: the operating procedures, customs and norms of boards of directors; and internal systems of measurement, control, and compensation.

The Culture in the Boardroom

In principle, the board of directors is the single most important corporate governance mechanism. It is "the institution to which managers are accountable, and the institution which is accountable before the law for the company's activities."[85] Directors have the legal authority to perform almost every function that even the most strident advocates of corporate governance reform would like to see. The problem is that, in practice, they often do not have the appropriate incentives or the procedural mechanisms in place to elicit the most effective oversight. Paul G. Stern, nonexecutive chairman of Northern Telecom Ltd., writes that "boards have the power to govern, but they do not have the process."[86] Accordingly, much of the corporate governance debate revolves around questions about what boards of directors should do, whose interests they should serve, and

[85]Oxford Analytica Limited (1992, p. 7).
[86]Stern (1993, p. 8).

how they can best be organized to ensure that they carry out their duties.

Boards have most often been criticized for being "rubber stamps" for the CEO. In U.S. companies the CEO very often also serves as the chairman of the board; only about 20 percent of the S&P 500 companies have separated the office of CEO from that of chairman. In contrast, publicly traded corporations in Great Britain commonly have outside (nonmanagement) chairmen.[87]

In U.S. corporations board members other than the chairman are typically either part of the management team, in which case they report to the CEO and are unlikely to be strong critics, or they are outsiders (nonmanagement) who were selected by the CEO or by a nominating committee strongly influenced by the CEO. "Independent" in principle, these outsiders may in fact know little about the business of the firm and are therefore very dependent on the CEO and other senior officers of the company to tell them what is going on. In the recent battle for control of Paramount Communications, for example, Paramount's board was criticized for not challenging or questioning the sparse information provided by Paramount CEO Martin Davis. "In memos and statements filed in a suit QVC brought against Paramount in Delaware Chancery Court, a picture emerges of a chief executive so determined to ward off QVC's overtures that he sometimes withheld crucial information. On numerous occasions, the board wasn't given a chance to weigh information that would have put preferred suitor Viacom in an unflattering light—or made archfoe QVC's bid look more attractive" according to a story in the *Wall Street Journal*.[88]

---

[87]Jacobs (1993, p. 120).

[88]Johnnie L. Roberts and Randall Smith, "The Plot Thickens: Who Gets the Blame for Paramount Gaffes? Big Cast of Characters," *Wall Street Journal*, December 31, 1993, p. A1.

Although in principle directors serve at the discretion of share-holders, it is extremely difficult for shareholders to remove a board member and impossible in most instances (outside of a proxy fight) for shareholders to nominate a new director; shareholders can do little more than vote for the directors selected by the directors themselves (with strong influence from management) or choose not to vote.

Another problem that weakens the effectiveness of boards as monitors of management is that being a board member is not considered a full-time job. Outside directors frequently are senior officers of other companies or accomplished professionals from other fields who may serve on numerous other boards. They often do not (and cannot) take the time to understand fully the industries and the companies on whose boards they serve. In 1983 Korn/Ferry International reported that the average director devoted only about 123 hours a year to board duties. By 1991 that had declined to 94 hours a year.[89]

One of the most important problems impairing the function of boards is the lack of consensus not only about their goals, but also about whose interests they should serve. In a study based on surveys and interviews of board members, Jay W. Lorsch concluded that directors themselves are not sure what their goals should be and are troubled by the lack of consensus on this question.[90] This lack of consensus stems in large part from a lack of social consensus about the goals, obligations, and priorities of public corporations in general. This confusion about corporate priorities and director duties now thoroughly infects corporation law at the state level and is a central element in the debates on corporate governance.

---

[89]Korn/Ferry International, *Board of Directors, Tenth Annual Survey, 1983*, and *Board of Directors, Nineteenth Annual Survey, 1992*, New York, pp. 9, 12.
    [90]Lorsch and MacIver (1989).

In sum, many critics have charged that the institutional design of boards of directors in the United States discourages effective and critical oversight.[91] More fundamentally, some critics have questioned whether boards of directors, no matter how constituted or motivated, can ever do any more than react to management's decisions.[92] To the surprise of many of these skeptics, however, boards of directors appear to be assuming more power in practice. From mid-1992 to the end of 1993, boards ousted the CEOs of poorly performing companies in numerous well-publicized cases.[93] Such actions are "evidence of a seismic shift" in the independence and effectiveness of corporate boards, according to shareholder advocate and board critic Nell Minow.[94]

Beyond the headlines, scholars, professional associations, and special commissions have been studying the structure, culture, and incentives of directors to try to design better systems, and many boards of directors have been actively trying to restructure and reform themselves. One nearly universal proposal is that boards include a majority of outside directors. Many reformers argue that directors should not only be "outsiders," but should also be "independent," although the definition of independent varies somewhat depending on who is advocating this reform. Roughly, though, these proposals define "outsiders" as directors who are not employees, former employees, former officers, or persons who receive or have received compensation from the

---

[91]Numerous books and articles have been written harshly criticizing boards of directors for their ineffectiveness. See, for example, Monks and Minow (1991, especially ch. 3).

[92]Oxford Analytica Limited (1992).

[93]Examples include Robert Stempel at General Motors in October 1992, Paul E. Lego at Westinghouse and John F. Akers at IBM in January 1993, James Robinson at American Express in February 1993, Kay R. Whitmore at Kodak in August 1993, and Anthony D'Amato at Borden in December 1993.

[94]Nell Minow, "Revolt of the Corporate Boards," *Legal Times*, May 18, 1992, p. 22.

company for any services other than their service as a director, while "independent" directors are defined as outsiders who have no other affiliation or link to the company other than as shareholders and board members. The latter definition would exclude union representatives, executives of banks that supply significant credit, or executives or directors of companies that are major suppliers or customers. By some definitions, if the CEO of company A serves as a director for company B, any executive of company B would not be considered an "independent" director at company A.

The idea behind adding more outside and independent directors is that they are likely to be relatively objective critics of management. Although nearly all reformers agree that boards should include more outside directors, they disagree about whether those directors should also be independent and whether they should or should not represent specific constituencies.

The pressure to add more outside directors dates back to the 1970s, when several corporations were involved in scandals and misconduct such as bribing of foreign officials. As part of the settlements of the resulting shareholder lawsuits, the courts required companies such as Northrup and Phillips Petroleum to shift their board composition to majority outside directors.[95] By the late 1980s most large companies had outside majorities, and there were indications that board selection processes were changing in ways that seemed likely to bring in more "independent" directors.[96]

---

[95]Jones (1986, p. 346).

[96]The 1993 Korn/Ferry survey reported that 1992 was the first year that board vacancies were filled more often through recommendations of other board members (74 percent) than through recommendations of the chairman (72 percent). Recommendations from institutional investors and the use of nominating committees and executive search firms were also increasing. Korn/Ferry International, *Board of Directors, Twentieth Annual Survey, 1993*, New York, pp. 11–12.

A second common reform proposal is to reduce the size of boards, and boards in fact appear to be shrinking. The average board of large U.S. companies had fourteen members in 1987 but only twelve in 1992.[97]

Another increasingly common reform is the establishment of special committees within boards to perform certain functions. Special committees allow directors to develop certain areas of expertise and focus the responsibility for decisions in those areas on a smaller number of people. This process, it is believed, shifts power, at least in those areas, away from the CEO toward the committee members.

In addition to executive committees that are empowered to take actions for the whole board on routine matters, public companies are increasingly forming other standing committees, particularly audit, nominating, and compensation committees. A few companies have also formed special social responsibility, environmental, corporate ethics, or corporate governance committees. Until recently, most such committees were optional. But since 1978 the New York Stock Exchange has required audit committees with a majority of outside directors for listed companies and since late 1992 the SEC has required firms to have compensation committees. Firms must also include in their annual filings a report from the compensation committee justifying the compensation packages awarded to CEOs. Congress reinforced the latter requirement in the summer of 1993 when it included a section in its budget bill eliminating the corporate tax deduction for executive compensation packages that exceed $1 million a year, unless those packages tie compensation tightly to performance and meet certain other requirements. One of these stipulates that the com-

[97]Korn/Ferry International, *Board of Directors, Twentieth Annual Survey*, 1993, New York.

pensation package be determined by a compensation committee composed entirely of outside directors.[98]

Whether these reforms make a signficant difference in the performance of companies is a largely unanswered empirical question. Nonetheless, pressure from shareholder activists and the media are pushing public companies to create such committees, to fill them with outside directors, and to undertake yet other reforms.

Internal Measurement Systems and Controls

Because the major thrust of financial regulation has to do with requiring disclosure of relevant information, it is not surprising that an important component of the extralegal institutional arrangements of corporate governance is the set of rules and measurement and reporting systems that determine what information gets collected, how it is assembled and reported, and who has access to it. These systems vary widely from company to company, ranging from the most primitive double-entry bookkeeping systems to sophisticated cost accounting systems and specialized measures of performance for analyzing, evaluating, and decisionmaking with regard to quality control, capital budgeting, inventory control, and personnel evaluation and compensation.

Internal controls and information systems are obviously critical to the day-to-day management processes in companies. They are linked to corporate governance questions by several issues. The first is the legal question of what information must or should be disclosed in the public documents of a firm. A second is more subtle. Beyond the legally required disclosure, policymakers and other par-

---

[98]John Balkcom, "Viewpoints: Coming Clean on Compensation," *New York Times*, November 1, 1992, p. 3–11; and Timothy D. Schellhardt, "Passing of Perks," *Wall Street Journal*, April 13, 1994, p. R4.

ticipants in the corporate governance debate are asking whether companies can explain to their investors what they are trying to accomplish in ways that allow investors to do more than simply react to quarterly earnings reports.[99] A third issue concerns whether the internal systems are measuring the right things. Are the long-term goals and objectives of the owners of the company being translated adequately into internal performance measures? Or are the short-term performance metrics used internally by management to set goals and measure progress distorting the long-term goals?

Accounting rules are determined by a private-sector organization, the Financial Accounting Standards Board (FASB), with input from the professional and trade associations that sponsor the FASB. Although accounting methods and rules are modified often in an attempt to reflect changing business realities and the need for more relevant information, they have been criticized from all sides in the corporate governance debates. A major complaint is that accounting procedures are too flexible and permit companies to hide problems far too long. The major accounting firms, which handle the bulk of the auditing work for publicly traded companies, have also been criticized for being too cozy with their clients, for not flagging potential problems, and for glossing over actual problems.[100] In a recent example, the accounting profession was blamed for failing to provide regulators with better information about the rapidly deteriorating financial condition of many savings and loans. In particular, savings and loans were carrying assets on their books at their original cost, instead of their fair market value, which was often much lower. In response to this criticism, the FASB issued new rules in

---

[99]A key argument made by those who believe investors are "myopic" is that they do not have access to information that could help them make better judgments about a company's long-term prospects.

[100]See U.S. Senate Committee on Government Operations (1977) for examples of accounting abuses of both types.

1990 and 1991 requiring public companies to disclose more information about the fair market value of all financial assets or liabilities.[101]

Some critics have also argued that public companies should be required to report a much wider variety of information, and the SEC and several members of the accounting profession have been considering proposals to expand reporting requirements. But such proposals have proved extremely controversial. In late 1994 the American Institute of Certified Public Accountants (AICPA) issued results of a multiyear study of ways to expand and improve disclosure in financial reports to provide more useful information for investors and financial analysts. In the end, the AICPA backed away from the most ambitious proposals, arguing that "undisciplined expansion of mandated reporting could result in large and needless costs" and that "companies should not have to expand the reporting of such information until there are more effective deterrents to unwarranted litigation."[102]

The AICPA recommended only that companies be required to break out earnings into those attributable to "core" continuing operations and those attributable to the earnings from gains or losses on financial assets (even if those have not yet been realized through a sale of the asset) and that companies be required to provide a more extensive breakout of information by line of business. They also recommended, in special cases and by agreement between the company and its investors and analysts, a much more detailed auditors' statement that would discuss the company's problems and potential problems. The AICPA's recommendations are not binding on the

---

[101]See "Company News: Accounting Rule for Assets," *New York Times*, December 17, 1991, D3. See also Financial Accounting Standards Board, "Statement of Financial Accounting Standards No. 105: Disclosure of Information about Financial Instruments with Off-Balance-Sheet Risk and Financial Instruments with Concentrations of Credit Risk," Publication 089, Norwalk, Conn., March 1990; and "Statement of Financial Accounting Standards No. 107: Disclosures about Fair Value of Financial Instruments," Publication 110-A, Norwalk Conn., December 1991.

[102]Jenkins (1994, p. 4C).

industry, but they are likely to have a strong influence on the future direction of mandatory reporting requirements.[103]

Accounting methods have also been criticized for providing irrelevant and unhelpful information. Two leading critics are H. Thomas Johnson and Robert S. Kaplan. They argue that accounting information was originally developed to help plan the financing of a firm and was not intended to be used to direct production units and workers. But since World War II, they say, "financial accounting information [has] intruded upon and distorted the financial and other information companies had used for decades to manage not only operating activities at the worker and business unit levels, but also strategic product choices at the enterprise level."[104] The problem with using financial accounting information to manage production, the authors argue, is that it does not "provid[e] timely and detailed information on process inefficiencies" and focuses too much attention on "inputs such as direct labor that are relatively insignificant in today's production environment."[105]

More generally, accounting information provides only an after-the-fact tabulation of actual dollars received, paid out, billed, owed, written off, or set aside for special purposes. Johnson and Kaplan suggest that auditors and regulators, "mindful of their responsibility to users of financial statements, [prefer] conservative accounting practices based on objective, verifiable, and realized financial transactions." This practice leads to a focus on reporting actual expenditures rather than attempting to measure opportunity cost or value created.[106] Information only on actual expenditures may be a mis-

---

[103]AICPA (1994).

[104]Johnson and Kaplan (1991, p. 43).

[105]Total labor costs are important, but direct labor costs are often quite small. See Johnson and Kaplan (1991, p. 2).

[106]Johnson and Kaplan (1991, p. 13).

leading measure of a company's performance as a whole and provides a poor guide to decisions about future investments.

The other internal control systems, such as capital budgeting systems, quality control systems, and personnel evaluation and compensation systems range from formal to informal and tend to be quite idiosyncratic from one company to the next. Typically, they are developed internally (often based on models developed and taught in business schools) to help management predict, measure, control, and reward those aspects of performance deemed most important by the management of that particular company.

A major criticism of these other internal measurement and control systems is that they sometimes measure, control, or reward the wrong thing. Some critics have charged, for example, that capital budgeting procedures are typically based on calculations of return on investment, or return on equity, when they should be based on estimates of how the investment will affect shareholder value.[107] Other critics have charged that capital budgeting systems focus too intently on quantifiable predictions about financial performance and fail to take into account the cost of not making an investment or the unquantifiable value of the experience and "organizational capabilities" that may come from making an investment.[108]

---

[107]Rappaport (1986). Although Rappaport and others are critical of using return on invested capital as a decision-tool in business, the idea of measuring profits as a percentage of the value of invested capital (rather than as a percentage of sales) was a major breakthrough in business management in the early 1900s. Chandler (1977, pp. 445–48) gives an interesting account of this development, credited to the DuPont Company. This technique was widely adopted after World War II.

[108]Baldwin and Clark (1992) define organizational capabilities as "combinations of human skills, organizational procedures and routines, physical assets, and systems of information and incentives, that enhance performance along a particular dimension." Myers (1984b, p. 134) has argued in a similar vein that proceeding with certain investments often provides firms with the option of making further investments that they would be unable to make if they had not made the first investment. Although

Although the subtleties and uncertainties in the use of any measure of performance are primarily management issues, they have entered the governance debate because corporate executives have argued that investors tend to be too "numbers driven" and not sensitive enough to unquantifiable or soft factors or gut-level judgment calls. Shareholders and other stakeholders want to hold management to performance standards, but managers want to be protected from what they experience as financial market meddling and second-guessing of their judgment based on poor information.

Compensation Systems

Questions about what should be measured in a company are closely tied to questions about what should be rewarded. The recent flap over executive compensation dramatizes this issue. The controversy stems partly from the sheer size of executive pay packages. Before the mid-1980s executives of nonfinancial, publicly traded companies were rarely paid more than $5 million in a single year. Since the late 1980s, however, annual compensation packages of $5 million to $10 million have become so commonplace that they no longer make headlines. From 1987 through 1993, there were at least 275 instances of an individual corporate executive making more than $5 million in a given year and at least 94 of these involved an executive making more than $10 million. Total annual compensation topped $20 million for sixteen executives in 1992 and 1993. In each of those years, at least one executive was paid more than $100 million.[109]

---

the value of such an option is difficult to measure, it is probably not zero. But leaving this option value out of the decision process implicitly treats its value as zero.

[109]Data from *Business Week* surveys, various years. These large compensation packages often reflect gains on stock options that the CEO exercised during the previous year; such gains are reported as income. Those options may have been awarded over several years, and so it is somewhat misleading to treat the entire gain

The growth in compensation has not been isolated to a few "jack-pot" winners. According to an annual survey conducted by *Business Week*, real median pay among executives of some 250 large firms rose 68 percent from 1983 through 1993, a period when real wages for average working people were stagnant.[110]

The high level and rapid growth in executive pay has raised questions about what executives are being rewarded for and whether existing corporate governance systems provide appropriate incentives for and adequate monitoring of executives. In years past, for example, compensation schemes were criticized for rewarding managers who increased total sales revenue or total profit, instead of improving productivity or return to shareholders. In a widespread effort to tie executive pay more strongly to long-term stock price performance, corporations in the 1980s increased their use of compensation schemes that include "stock options." These options give the executive the right to buy the company's stock at a given "strike" price at some point in the future. Suppose a company whose stock was selling for $50 in 1990 granted its CEO an option that year on 100,000 shares of the company stock with a strike price of $50 and an exercise date in 1994. If the stock price of the company rises to $75 by the exercise date, the corporate executive could at that time exercise his option and realize an immediate gain of $2.5 million. If the company's stock price is only $45 by the exercise date, however, the executive has no gain. But he also has no loss since he does not actually own the stock. Stock option awards provide somewhat skewed incentives because they can give executives a virtually unlimited potential for gain if stock prices rise but may inflict no penalty if stock prices fall. Nonetheless, their use in compensation packages has expanded rap-

---

on those options as compensation in the exercise year. Nonetheless, that is what current accounting rules require.

[110]Blair (1994) and *Business Week* surveys, various years.

idly—executives favor them for tax reasons—and they provide the potential for linking pay to at least one measure of performance.

Still, the use of stock options has not eliminated outright abusive practices in compensation awards. In some cases, for example, company directors have "reset" the option by giving it a lower strike price so that the executive has made money even when the price of his company's stock has fallen. After the stock market fell suddenly in the fall of 1989, for example, directors of Northrop allowed CEO Thomas Jones to swap 1.2 million options to buy Northrop stock at $45.88 for 1.2 million options with a strike price of $29.88, for an immediate gain of $4.5 million.[111]

And in 1993 Anthony D'Amato negotiated a new contract as CEO of Borden that guaranteed him a base pay of $900,000 a year, plus homes in New York and Columbus, Ohio, where Borden has offices, plus 100,000 new stock options. These were to help replace 400,000 options D'Amato held that were worthless given the price of Borden's stock in late 1993. D'Amato's contract further provided that if the shareholders failed to approve the stock options, Borden would be obliged to give him something of "equivalent" value. Abuses such as these have led critics to charge that existing governance systems often permit executives to set their own pay, with little or no real evaluation and oversight by directors and little connection to any measures of performance. In just the last few years, shareholders have won a greater say in how executives are paid. Under pressure from shareholder activists, D'Amato was fired at Borden in December 1993, for example. Although shareholders complained most about the company's lackluster performance, they cited D'Amato's pay package among their grievances.[112]

---

[111]Crystal (1992, p. 4).

[112]Alison Leigh Cowan, "Borden's Board Ousts Chief to Calm Investors," *New York Times*, December 10, 1993, D1.

More generally, most large companies have created compensation committees with a majority of outside directors to determine executive pay.[113] And, as noted above, the SEC made it easier for shareholders to get involved in executive pay issues when it ruled in 1991 that executive compensation was an appropriate matter for shareholder proposals and, in 1992, that companies must disclose much more information than they had previously been reporting about how executive pay is determined and how it compares with compensation of executives of other similar companies. Congress gave further impetus to these trends when it passed a budget bill in 1993 that limited the corporate tax deduction for executive pay that does not meet certain guidelines.[114] Among the guidelines are a requirement that any pay in excess of $1 million a year be based strictly on the achievement of predetermined performance goals set by a compensation committee of outside directors and approved by shareholders.

The rules for accounting for stock options have also come under review. Under current FASB accounting rules, stock options do not have to be reported as income to the executive until they are exercised, and they never have to be reported as an expense to the company (although they may be deducted for tax purposes at the time the options are exercised). The FASB reviewed these rules and in 1992 proposed changes that would require firms to assign a value to options at the time they are issued and deduct from shareholder earnings the value of options granted to executives or other employees. Under a blizzard of opposition, especially from small, high-

---

[113]The Korn/Ferry survey for 1993 reported that 95.2 percent of companies had separate compensation committees and that these committees had an average of four outside members and no inside members.

[114]The rules apply to the CEO and the next four top executives. See Joann S. Lublin, "Firms Forfeit Tax Break to Pay Top Brass $1 Million-Plus," *Wall Street Journal*, April 21, 1994, p. B1; and Timothy D. Schellhardt, "Passing of Perks," *Wall Street Journal*, April 13, 1994, p. R4.

technology companies that use options extensively in compensation packages, the FASB dropped the proposal in late 1994. Instead, it proposed that firms merely note in footnotes the impact of options granted on net profit and earnings per share.[115]

These changes are helping to realign executive compensation systems so that executive pay is tied much more tightly to returns to shareholders. But the reforms are unlikely to drive down the levels of executive pay and may lead to further increases. That is because the large pay increases of the last ten years were driven by the shift toward the use of stock options. The share of CEO pay that comes from "long-term compensation" rather than "salary and bonus" grew from 34 percent on average in 1983 to 68 percent on average in 1992.[116] Stock options are the largest component of long-term compensation, and in nearly every case where total compensation exceeded $5 million, the largest part of those pay packages was attributable to the exercise of stock options.

What All This Means for Corporate Governance

By necessity, these brief accounts of the mechanisms by which corporations are governed and controlled are cursory and vastly oversimplified. Volumes have been written on each of these mechanisms, and whole careers devoted to their study. But because each cluster of laws and institutional arrangements was developed independently in response to particular problems, the resulting system is rarely examined as a whole to see how these mechanisms work together and what their collective effect might be on the ability of

[115]Lee Burton, "FASB Softens Plan on Deducting Costs of Stock Options," *Wall Street Journal*, December 15, 1994, p. A2.
[116]Blair (1994).

companies to operate efficiently, to produce products that can compete, to provide good jobs with good benefits, and to provide profits for shareholders—in other words, to create wealth for society as a whole.

Large corporations with widely traded securities are fundamentally different from small, closely held companies and raise a number of complex corporate governance problems. Yet the belief commonly held by business leaders, policymakers, and economists that the best way to create wealth for society as a whole is to maximize value for shareholders is based on an implicit assumption that large, widely traded corporations behave like the basic model presented at the beginning of this chapter. The facts of how large corporations are structured and governed cast serious doubt on that proposition.

3

A FINANCE PERSPECTIVE

ON WHAT IS WRONG WITH

THE SYSTEM

THE BURGEONING INTEREST in corporate governance issues is spurred in part by concerns about whether the system of governance in the United States provides sufficient incentive for investment, adequately monitors and restrains managers, or otherwise promotes the optimal use of resources for wealth creation. Three clusters of arguments have been made about how and why the existing governance system may be producing less than optimal outcomes, and three corresponding sets of reforms have been proposed to counteract or correct these failures of the system. This chapter examines a critique of the corporate governance system that arises from finance theory and that has dominated the political and academic debate in recent years. The other two clusters of arguments will be examined in subsequent chapters.

The finance view of what is wrong with the governance system holds that shareholders do not have enough control or influence over management and that companies therefore too often get away with lackluster performance, while executives enjoy lavish perks. This view of the flaws of corporate governance dates back at least to Berle and Means, who, in 1932, were the first to document and analyze the shift from an economy based on relatively small enterprises, owned and managed by individuals or small groups of individuals, to one dominated by large, multiunit enterprises whose shareholdings were widely dispersed and whose shareholders were no longer likely to be in control. This separation of equity holding from control, they noted, raised questions about whether corporations would be managed optimally from the shareholders' viewpoint. Berle and Means' concerns were not new. A century and a half earlier, Adam Smith had anticipated that corporations would exhibit this sort of problem. "The directors of such companies, however, being the managers rather of other people's money than of their own, it cannot well be expected that they should watch over it with the same anxious vigilance with which the partners in a private copartnery frequently watch over their own," he argued in *The Wealth of Nations*.[1]

Although poor business performance was a serious concern during the Depression, when Berle and Means wrote, it was not a leading concern for most of the next half century, particularly during the prosperous decades following World War II. Instead, critics worried that corporate executives could get away with engaging in manipulative securities transactions or misappropriating corporate resources to their own benefit. The possibility that separating equity holding from control would lead to poor business performance seemed largely academic. Indeed, large, publicly traded companies have dominated the U.S. economy longer and to a greater extent

[1]Smith (1922, p. 233).

than they have any other modern economy. Yet in the six decades since Berle and Means wrote, the U.S. economy has delivered the highest level of incomes and wealth that the world has ever seen.

Observing this performance, academic theorists developed several theories to explain how the system could function so well, despite the problems supposedly associated with separating equity ownership from control. They argued that this separation produces efficiencies that outweigh its costs, and that the efficiencies arise from at least three sources. First, carving up equity claims into smaller units affordable by many small investors makes it possible to amass much larger amounts of capital than could be assembled if investing in corporations were limited to very wealthy individuals who could afford to take large positions. Historian Dow Votaw noted that this ability was especially important in the eighteenth and nineteenth centuries, when the corporate form flourished in the United States— well ahead of the time it became important in Europe. "It was necessary to raise capital through the small contributions of many investors," Votaw wrote, because, unlike in Europe, there were few large family fortunes in the United States.[2]

Second, separating equity holding from control greatly expands the pool of people who can manage corporations, because managers need not be extremely wealthy. This permits the development of a class of professional managers.[3] It also permits some participants in the corporation to specialize in managing, while others specialize in risk bearing.[4] Third, if equity interests are divided into small packages and held by many investors, capital providers can diversify their risks by holding smaller stakes in many different companies. Moreover, the availability of sophisticated and active securities markets

[2]Votaw (1965, p. 22).

[3]Votaw (1965, p. 31) gives this as one explanation for the popularity of the corporate form. See also Chandler (1977, pp. 8–9).

[4]Fama (1980).

for trading these shares makes these investments much more liquid than they would otherwise be, further reducing the risks associated with investing in corporate equities. It is a basic tenet of finance theory that shareholders must be compensated more highly—that is, receive a higher rate of return—as the riskiness of their investment increases. Thus liquid security markets and portfolio investing, which can reduce or even eliminate a large part of the risk that investors must bear, have helped to reduce the cost of capital because shareholders are willing to settle for a lower average rate of return.[5]

The Problem of "Agency" Costs

None of these arguments in favor of separating equity holding from control negates the basic validity of Berle and Means's point, however, because these benefits of efficiency come at a cost. Managers are supposed to be the "agents" of a corporation's "owners."[6] But managers must be monitored, and institutional arrangements must provide some checks and balances to make sure they do not abuse their power. The costs resulting from managers misusing their position, as well as the costs of monitoring and disciplining them to try to prevent abuse, have been called "agency costs." For many participants in the corporate governance debate, controlling management

---

[5]Brealey and Myers (1991, pp. 136–49) provide an accessible discussion of why diversification reduces risk.

[6]I have already discussed the ambiguity of the words "owners" and "ownership" as they apply to large, publicly traded corporations and alluded to the problems with mindlessly identifying shareholders as the owners. For purposes of discussion in the next three chapters, however, I adopt the conventional view that the shareholders are the owners and that the managers and directors are, therefore, agents of the shareholders. In the final chapters, I discuss whether shareholders should be viewed as the owners and managers as the agents for the shareholders.

abuses while minimizing agency costs is and has been the central problem to be solved. "The search [for effective corporate governance arrangements] is directed toward ways of limiting or governing power that may be used against the interests of others while keeping as much as possible of the ability to act in [the manager's] own or his organization's interest," Edward S. Mason wrote in 1960, for example.[7]

As chapter 2 illustrated, many of the developments in securities and corporate law since the 1930s have been aimed at preventing managers from engaging in fraud or deceit, from siphoning off resources to their own benefit, or from entering into financial transactions that advantage themselves at the expense of the company or some subset of its shareholders. The law has very clearly prohibited self-dealing transactions that harm the company. Although checks and balances and legally enforceable fiduciary duties have been imposed, the law until very recently has generally given managers and directors increasing freedom to make strategic planning and day-to-day management decisions for their firms. In many areas courts have told shareholders, in effect, that they may not interfere with the "business judgment" of managers.

For the first few decades after World War II, the managerial class grew, both in numbers and in "professionalization." The latter, Mason explained, "means, among other things, selection and promotion on the basis of merit rather than family connections or social status, the development of a 'scientific' attitude towards the problems of the organization, and an expectation of reward in terms of

---

[7]Mason (1960, p. 7). More recently, Gilson and Roe (1993, p. 874) assert simply that "analysis of American corporate governance has always sought to solve the problem of separation of ownership and control." The framing of the problem as a "principal-agent" one is attributed to Ross (1973), and Jensen and Meckling (1976) are credited with the first use of this concept to characterize the problem of governing the relationship between shareholders and managers.

relatively stable salary and professional prestige rather than in fluctuating profits."[8] Management came to be regarded as a generic skill that
could be learned, taught, and readily transferred from one line of business
to the next, as long as managers had the right information available to
them. Internal accounting and reporting systems were standardized and
made much more sophisticated, and management "by the numbers"
became popular. These tendencies were carried to their logical conclusion
during the conglomerate merger movement of the 1960s, when huge
corporate empires were built by assembling dozens of businesses under
the same corporate umbrella, to be directed by a central office of executives and their number-crunching support staff.[9]

At the time, financial markets were convinced the approach would
work. Shareholders of the companies that led the way in conglomerate
building were rewarded with large increases in their stock prices, at
least until the merger movement peaked in 1968. David J. Ravenscraft
and F. M. Scherer show that an investment of $1,000 each in thirteen
large conglomerates made in June 1965 would have grown in total
value to more than $63,000 by June 1968. By contrast, an investment of
$13,000 in a portfolio of 425 large industrial companies made at the
same time would have grown in value to only $17,382. All of that
surplus value, and more, was lost by 1974, however, when conglomerates went out of favor on Wall Street.[10]

Empire Building and the Market for Corporate Control

The merger boom of the 1960s and subsequent decline of stock
prices in the 1970s led many academics and finance theorists to

---

[8]Mason (1960), p. 12).

[9]Chandler (1990, p. 622) has argued that the executives who built the great
conglomerates were also motivated by a belief that few growth opportunities remained in the industries in which their companies originally operated.

[10]Ravenscraft and Scherer (1987, p. 40).

change their thinking about the nature of the problem most likely to arise from separating equity ownership from control. Their fears shifted from a concern that nonowner managers would be lazy or negligent or would defraud the owners to a concern that managers would use their positions to build empires—building ever larger companies even at the expense of profitability. Economists and organizational theorists such as Robin Marris and Oliver Williamson noted that compensation and prestige were highly correlated with the size of the companies the executives managed, which, they argued, gave management an incentive to try to maximize size or growth rates of their firms rather than profitability.[11]

Marris, Williamson, Henry Manne, and other theorists argued, however, that empire-building tendencies were held in check by an essential feature of the U.S. economy, one that the simple Berle-Means argument did not take into account. This mechanism, the market for corporate control, works by threatening managers with takeover to keep them from abusing their power or misusing corporate resources.[12] If managers were to abuse their positions or fail to perform well for any reason, the stock price of their firms would fall, attracting buyers who would acquire the firm and correct the abuses.

---

[11]Marris (1964, chs. 2 and 3) and Williamson (1964, ch. 3). Williamson argued that managers would be motivated by a preference for certain expenses that enhanced their sense of power and prestige. Marris and Williamson were interested in these problems primarily because of their implications for pricing and production decisions of firms; they wanted to know whether models based on profit maximization would generate the right predictions about the effects of tariffs, supply and demand shifts, or other changes in the operating environment. Most theorists who looked at this question assumed that management would optimize something, even it it was not profits. Only a few were seriously concerned that the separation of ownership from control would lead managers not to optimize anything. An example is the work of Leibenstein (1976), who argued that, for a variety of reasons, bureaucratic organizations tend to settle for suboptimal solutions.

[12]Marris (1964), Williamson (1964), and Manne (1965).

Performance would then be reoptimized, and the buyers would earn a profit for making the improvements.

How can takeovers be both a correction for management abuses and evidence of empire-building behavior by management? It is worth taking a moment here to clarify this point. Many economists and finance theorists believe that companies that acquire other companies are, more often than not, building empires simply to satisfy the egos of their executives. And, indeed, plenty of evidence has been developed showing that acquisitions rarely add new value for the shareholders of the acquiring company.[13] But many of these same economists and finance theorists also believe that an important mechanism for discouraging managers from engaging in value-reducing takeovers and other forms of poor management is the threat that their own company will become a takeover target. According to this argument, the mere threat of takeover should discourage this sort of empire building.

This whole line of reasoning was largely academic until the advent and widespread use of the hostile takeover in the 1980s. Before the mid-1970s, financial institutions in the United States seldom provided backing to "raiders" who attempted to take over companies that did not wish to be taken over. But this tradition quickly broke down after Morgan Stanley backed an unfriendly tender by

[13]See Jensen and Ruback (1983) for a summary of early evidence on the benefits of takeovers for shareholders of both target firms and acquiring firms. The studies they summarize conclude that bidding firms in successful tender offers have an average positive stock return (corrected for market returns) of about 4 percent, while bidding firms in successful mergers have an average return (corrected for market returns) of zero. Unsuccessful bidders have negative average returns. Scanlon, Trifts, and Pettway (1989) found that, for transactions in the 1980s, the returns to bidders were, on average, negative. See also Ravenscraft and Scherer (1987) for evidence that many acquisitions are subsequently sold off because they fail to perform well after the acquisition.

International Nickel Company against ESB Inc. in 1974.[14] Just as Marris and Manne had predicted, some of the earliest raiders justified their tender offers or proxy fights on the grounds that the target companies were poorly managed and that they (the raiders) could do a better job. In defending his bid to acquire Gulf Oil Co. in the early 1980s, for example, T. Boone Pickens told *Fortune*, "I am fighting as an investor to create value for Gulf shareholders, and I am shocked at the hostile reaction from Gulf. I can't figure out what they're afraid of."[15]

Even the most ardent proponents of takeovers as a means to keep bad management in check do not have a very good explanation for how takeovers correct the empire-building tendencies of management. Why should the new management be any more disciplined than the old one?

One answer comes from finance theorists, who argue that the high level of debt imposed on the target firm after the takeover helps keep management on a tight leash. Takeover activity of the 1980s was accompanied by a dramatic increase in financial innovation, especially in the use of new kinds of debt instruments. Banks were willing to provide previously unheard-of levels of debt financing; managers of mutual funds and pension funds were happy to sell out their shares in tender offers to secure premiums that were often 40 to 50 percent above previous stock prices; pension funds, insurance companies, and savings and loans were willing not only to sell out, but also to buy the junk bonds issued to provide long-term financing for the deals—in effect, trading their equity for high-risk debt.[16]

---

[14]Wigmore (1995) provides a detailed account of the transformation of attitudes toward hostile takeovers on Wall Street during the late 1970s and early 1980s.

[15]Peter Nulty, "Boone Pickens, Company Hunter," *Fortune*, December 16, 1983, p. 54.

[16]Volumes too numerous to summarize here have been written about this episode of U.S. history. Some of my own contributions include an edited volume of essays (Blair, 1993); a collection of summary data (Blair and Uppal, 1993); and a *Brookings Review* article (Blair, 1991).

The use of highly leveraged transactions to accomplish takeovers seemed to clinch the argument that takeovers were the financial market's mechanism for correcting bad management. As a result of leveraged buyouts, the target firms typically were closely held by investor groups that sometimes included top management. Thus equity ownership was no longer separated from control in these companies. In other words, the casual evidence appeared to suggest that, when the threat of takeover failed to prevent bad management, actual takeovers, accompanied by a recapitalization that substituted large amounts of debt for equity, would remedy the problem.

Not surprisingly, corporate executives, whose competency was being challenged and whose jobs were threatened, resisted this interpretation of hostile takeovers and leveraged buyouts. They fought back by blaming takeovers and the threat of takeovers for the widespread layoffs and plant closings that occurred in many industries in the 1980s. Fred Hartley, then chairman and CEO of Unocal, for example, told a Senate committee in 1985 that, if outsiders were to take over, Unocal might "go down the tube and there would be 22,000 people out of work."[17]

Similarly, Philip R. O'Connell, then senior vice president and secretary of Champion International Corp., argued in a *New York Times* op-ed piece that the widespread threat of takeover "breeds a climate of fear, with hardly any companies safe from attack. Looking over their shoulders, managers focus on short-term results and defense mechanisms that often place additional high burdens of long-term debt on their companies. High leveraging not only makes companies more vulnerable to recession and high interest rates, but also undercuts product development, innovation and international competitiveness."[18]

---

[17]Epstein (1986, p. 36).

[18]Philip R. O'Connell, "A Timely Halt to the Raiders' Shell Game," *New York Times*, December 22, 1985, p. 2-2.

The charges and countercharges surrounding the takeover movement of the 1980s blew open corporate governance questions that had been dormant for decades. Are takeovers constructive mechanisms of governance that impose discipline on management, or are they acts of megalomania on the part of the acquiring company management? Even worse, are they tools in the hands of speculators and thieves? Is the financial market a powerful mechanism for guiding capital to its best uses, or is it a casino whose influence on the boardroom can only be pernicious? More fundamentally, do shareholders have too much influence, or not enough? Who, after all, really "owns" big public corporations? And whose interests should they serve?

These questions prompted dozens of scholarly studies into the effects of takeovers. Finance scholars did many of the early studies, which purported to show that takeovers resulted in efficiency gains. The evidence cited in these studies was that stock prices of target firms rose on the announcement of a tender offer or other move toward a takeover and declined in response to events that seemed to reduce the possibility that the deal would be consummated. The increases in stock prices of target firms were generally not offset by declines in stock prices of acquiring firms.[19]

Subsequent studies looked for evidence that would shed light on the source of the gains to shareholders and, in particular, whether those gains might come at the expense of bondholders, employees, taxpayers, or even suppliers, customers, or the communities where the target firms operated. That evidence can be summarized as follows:

- No consistent pattern of operating changes has been observed for ordinary (nonhostile) mergers or acquisitions. In other

---

[19]Several of these early studies, as well as a good summary of their findings, were published in a special issue of the *Journal of Financial Economics* in April 1983.

words, ordinary transactions in the market for corporate control do not appear, on the whole, to be either a particularly good or a particularly bad feature of the corporate governance system.[20]

- For hostile takeovers, the gains to shareholders of target firms have been explained partly by the subsequent sell-off of assets, frequently to acquirers in related lines of business.[21] But it has not been determined whether the higher value of these assets to the ultimate buyer results from an improvement in the way the assets are managed or from the acquiring company's power to raise prices because it now has a larger share of the market. Some evidence suggests that the gains may occur because the new managers of the target firms often renege on "implicit contracts" or understandings the firms had with their workers to pay higher-than-average wages or provide exceptional benefits or job security, or because the new managers often drained assets out of overfunded pension funds. In other words, some of the value transferred to the shareholders of the target company in takeovers may have come from laying off workers, reducing their wages and benefits, or both.[22]
- For leveraged buyouts the gains have partly been explained by the decreased tax liabilities of the target firms.[23] Highly lever-

---

[20]Ravenscraft and Scherer (1987) used evidence based on accounting data of the operating effects of acquisitions that had occurred during the 1960s merger wave to show that the deals of that era did not, on balance, improve the performance of target companies. For more recent mergers Lichtenberg and Siegel (1987, p. 659) found that changes of control led to improved productivity. Hall (1990) found no evidence that changes in control (unaccompanied by significant increases in leverage) were followed by reductions in investment in R&D.

[21]Bhagat, Shleifer, and Vishny (1990, p. 2).

[22]For theory and anecdotal evidence, see Shleifer and Summers (1988). For more systematic empirical evidence, see Neumark and Sharpe (forthcoming). See Pontiff, Shleifer, and Weisbach (1990) for evidence that some of the gains from takeovers came from raiding employee pension funds.

[23]Kaplan (1989) and Long and Ravenscraft (1993, p. 205.

aged companies pay less in taxes because more of their operating income goes to making payments on their debts, which are deductible, and less goes to paying dividends to stockholders, which are not deductible.

- Leveraged buyouts also appear to have produced improvements in operating earnings (at least for transactions that took place in the early part of the 1980s), but reductions in capital spending, and reductions in spending on research and development. Buyouts that took place after 1986, as a group, did not lead to significant increases in cash flows, however. Moreover, buyers paid higher prices and used more debt relative to cash flows than they did in earlier transactions.[24]

So far, none of the studies has accounted for all of the gains to shareholders of target companies. Those who believe that the central problem of corporate governance is how to get managers to do what shareholders want and who also believe that takeovers provide an enforcement mechanism for shareholders take the unexplained residual gain as evidence of improvements in operating efficiency. Indeed, all of the evidence cited above (except that on gains from reduced tax liability) is interpreted as showing that takeovers are good for corporate performance because they correct managerial empire-building behavior and increase value for shareholders. This is true even of the evidence that takeover gains came from reducing wages, employment, or investment. The cutbacks were necessary, takeover defenders argue, because the companies were overreaching and committing themselves to spending they could not afford.

---

[24]Long and Ravenscraft (1993), Kaplan and Stein (1993), and Hall (1990). Hall found that the impact on R&D was associated with the increase in leverage, not with the change in control.

Lessons of the Finance Model

In the rest of this book, the phrase "finance model" refers to the theoretical underpinnings for the cluster of arguments that have been used to defend takeovers and that are now used to advocate enhanced rights for shareholders in corporate governance. According to finance theory, the price set in the financial markets for a company's common shares fully and efficiently reflects all the available information about the company and is thus the best measure of the net value of the firm. This tenet, sometimes called the "efficient markets model," is fundamental to finance theory. The theory implies that anything that causes the stock price of a company to rise, such as a planned takeover of that company, must be creating value (unless it can be shown explicitly that the value came from some other source, such as a decline in the value of the acquiring company's stock).

True believers in this finance model interpret the events of the last twenty or so years roughly as follows: corporate performance (as measured by stock prices) declined in the 1970s because executives had been making unrelated acquisitions and otherwise building empires rather than paying close attention to the bottom line. The financial markets, through hostile takeovers, the threat of hostile takeovers, leveraged buyouts, and other leverage-driven restructurings, were correcting that problem as quickly as they could during the 1980s. "Takeover activities were addressing an important set of problems in corporate America, and doing it before the companies faced serious trouble in the product markets," Michael Jensen argues. "They were, in effect, providing an early warning system that motivated healthy adjustments to the excess capacity that began to proliferate in the worldwide economy."[25]

[25]Jensen (1993, p. 839).

Toward the end of the decade, however, state legislatures passed a series of laws making takeovers more difficult, and state and federal courts upheld these and other company-specific defenses such as poison pills. By 1990, according to one count, more than seven hundred companies had adopted poison pills.[26] The powerful financial machine that made the market for corporate control an effective constraint on managers finally collapsed when the SEC and the office of the Manhattan U.S. Attorney brought indictments in 1989 against Michael Milken and Drexel, Burnham Lambert for various securities law violations. Milken and the investment company had devised many of the financial innovations that helped fuel the takeover frenzy. By March 1990 Drexel Burnham had filed for bankruptcy, and the takeover era of the 1980s was brought to an end.

Of course, the situation was more complicated than this explanation suggests, and there are several other theories about what triggered the takeover movement of the 1980s and its rather abrupt end in 1990. By itself, for example, the finance model does not explain why the long-dormant problems supposedly associated with separating equity ownership from control suddenly came to a head in the 1970s and 1980s. In my own work, I have argued that a dramatic increase in real (inflation-adjusted) interest rates in the early 1980s drove up the opportunity cost to investors for investing in corporate equities while simultaneously reducing the number of attractive investment opportunities available to corporations. When real interest rates are low, it is usually in shareholders' interest for companies to retain cash flow and invest it as fast as they can. But when real interest rates are high, as they were in the 1980s, reinvesting cash flow is less likely to be optimal for shareholders, who could put that cash into safer securities and still earn a very high rate of return. In response to high real

---

[26]Investor Responsibility Research Center (199_) and Roe (1993d).

interest rates, then, the financial markets set in motion a whole array of pressures in the 1980s—including threatened and actual takeovers—to compel firms to pay out more cash flow to shareholders rather than retaining it for reinvestment.[27]

I thus accept the argument that financial markets were trying to correct a tendency for firms to overinvest or build empires, but I view that tendency not as proof of bad management, but as a consequence of the changed macroeconomic environment. I also agree that the changes in state takeover laws and the prosecution of Drexel Burnham Lambert contributed to ending the takeover craze, but many other factors were also at work.

Despite other theories and outright objections to the reasoning offered by proponents of the finance model, the free-market, finance-driven perspective on takeovers dominated the academic debate and much of the policy arena through the late 1980s. For those who continue to view the world in these terms, if anything is ailing corporate America in the mid-1990s, it is that shareholders in general are still too passive, that executives are not being held accountable to shareholders, and that the chief mechanism that had existed to make them accountable—the threat of takeover—has been dismantled or at least crippled.[28] Thus, the corporate governance problem to be solved is one of restoring an active market for corporate control or, failing that, creating other institutions that can more effectively hold executives accountable to shareholders.

---

[27]Blair and Litan (1990) and Blair and Schary (1993).

[28]Not all of those who advocated an active takeover market in the 1980s hold this extreme view. Some accept the critique that many of the deals of the 1980s were disruptive and resulted in precarious levels of debt. They are ready to concede that a free-wheeling market for corporate control might not be the best mechanism for reining in managers. For example, Pound (1992b, p. 20) concedes that "the all-or-nothing aspect of the takeover remedy is often the wrong approach to solve corporate problems."

To this end, finance model advocates and other defenders of shareholders' rights have put forth a variety of reform proposals (detailed in appendix 3-1). These proposals would restrict management's ability to issue new classes of stock, discriminate against particular stockholders in making any distributions, or take actions that would reduce shareholder power without permitting shareholders to vote on the change. Other proposals would enhance shareholder voice by making it easier or cheaper for shareholders to communicate with each other or with management, protect voting confidentiality, allow shareholders to critique management in the proxy filings, and permit shareholders to call meetings or nominate directors. Another group of proposals would require directors to present all bona fide takeover offers to shareholders and would prohibit certain takeover defenses such as poison pills. And still other proposals would commit companies more firmly to using internal measurement systems that focus on shareholder returns, reform corporate boards so they represent shareholders more effectively, and tie compensation of executives much more tightly to stock price performance.

One controversial but recurring proposal is to move the power to incorporate firms from the state level to the federal level. Consumer groups and other reformers first raised this proposal in the 1960s and 1970s, arguing that a federal corporation law would be less subject than the various state laws to manipulation by corporate executives.[29] More recently, some shareholder rights groups have taken up the argument. For decades legal scholars have charged that corporate executives seek out the most lenient states in which to incorporate, and states, in turn, offer lenient laws to compete for corporate law

---

[29]"State chartering is a costly anachronism," wrote Nader, Green, and Seligman (1976, p. 70). "To control national and multinational corporations requires national authority."

business. Some finance model advocates and other shareholder rights proponents argue that a federal-level law could help to reduce this tendency toward excessive leniency in the existing system.[30] Others caution that a federal law is the wrong remedy, however. Legal scholar Roberta Romano, for example, believes that such a law would not serve shareholder interests because service to corporations would have much less priority on a national agenda than it does on the agenda of a small state, such as Delaware, that counts on the revenues from the incorporation business.[31]

Another recurring but controversial proposal concerns whether companies should be required to adhere to a one-share, one-vote rule for their common shares. Multiple classes of voting stock with different voting rights are commonly used in start-up companies that are issuing publicly traded stock for the first time, where the founding entrepreneur wants the advantages of access to public markets for financing but does not want to give up control.[32] They are also used for similar purposes by publishing companies. At the Washington Post Co., for example, Class A shares, held almost entirely by the Graham family, elect nine directors to the board, while Class B shares, held mostly by outsiders, elect five directors to the board. The rationale for this practice in publishing companies is to protect the firm from undue pressure by shareholders to compromise editorial integrity in search of higher profits.

Throughout the 1960s and 1970s, the New York Stock Exchange (NYSE) prohibited listing of nonvoting shares of common stock, a practice that had the effect of setting a one-share, one-vote standard for most large companies. Until recently, companies that trade over

---

[30]Monks and Minow (1991).

[31]Romano (1993, p. 149).

[32]Different classes of common stock are issued to give some shareholders more voting control per share than other shareholders have. Although some state corporation laws require one vote per share, many states, including Delaware, do not.

the counter were not so restricted, and the American Stock Exchange (Amex) rules were also not so restrictive. The issue became important in the 1980s, when some companies issued stocks with extraordinary voting rights to "white knights" or other parties aligned with management to help fend off unwanted takeovers. As a result, the practice of issuing multiple classes of shares with different voting rights came to be regarded as a takeover defense.

During the 1980s the NYSE became concerned about competition from other securities exchanges and relaxed its rules. The SEC, which has veto power over exchange rules, blocked the proposed change and in 1987 promulgated a rule banning multiple classes of stock. The Business Roundtable, which represents the interests of executives of large corporations, challenged this rule, and a federal appeals court overturned it in 1990. At the urging of the SEC, the NYSE, as well as the Amex and the Nasdaq Stock Market, which governs trading in over-the-counter stocks, all adopted a uniform one-share, one-vote standard as of the first quarter of 1995. This standard still permits multiple classes of stock, including nonvoting stock, to be listed under special circumstances, however.[33] Thus the controversy still rages, and some shareholder advocates would still like the one-share, one-vote rule made into a legal requirement.

One proposal would solve both the one-share, one-vote question and the problem of companies reincorporating in other states in search of a legal environment that would help to protect management from shareholder pressure. That is to expand the list of actions that require shareholder votes. For example, Michael Jacobs, an investment consultant and former Treasury Department official, has proposed adoption of laws that would allow shareholders to initiate a reincorporation action and would require reincorporation upon a

---

[33]Lang (1995).

majority vote of the shareholders.[34] Others have argued that share-holders be allowed to vote on issuing any stock that violates the one-share, one-vote rule.

A final category of reform proposals that have come out of the finance model camp concerns bankruptcy. Leading proponents of leveraged buyouts in the 1980s argued that the threat of bankruptcy was not great enough nor actual bankruptcy costly or disruptive enough to make high levels of debt a prohibitively expensive mechanism for reducing agency costs. But as the 1980s unfolded and several major companies entered long and protracted bankruptcy proceedings, that argument seemed less convincing.[35] In response, some finance model proponents now argue that bankruptcy laws should be restructured to minimize conflicts of interest among creditors and between creditors and shareholders; to encourage low-cost private workouts, in which the firm and its creditors renegotiate their contracts privately, resolving distress without resorting to the bankruptcy courts; and, if a case does go into the bankruptcy courts, to foster a smooth shift in control and absolute clarity about the priorities of the various claims against the corporation. Advocates of reform argue that current law does none of these things very well.

Mark Roe has argued that bankruptcy proceedings would be much less disruptive if the underlying value of a firm in financial distress could be determined quickly and security holders paid off according to strict rules determining priority of claims. Under current law, the

[34]Jacobs (1991, pp. 228–29). Under current corporation law in most states, shareholder resolutions are advisory only. Hence, even if a majority of shareholders were to vote for a proposal that the company reincorporate into a state with more stringent laws, management would not be compelled to heed the proposal. Jacobs does not explicitly say that his proposal should be passed at the federal level, rather than at the state level. But a federal law appears to be necessary if his proposal is to be effective.

[35]Wruck (1991), for example, has analyzed the bankruptcy process at Revco.

various claimants enter into a lengthy and cumbersome negotiating process, which the court oversees. The uncertainty surrounding the company's future during this process makes it difficult for the company to continue operating, and often the resulting settlement violates the priority rules that were supposed to apply to various securities. Equity holders often receive some payment, for example, even when more senior claimants have not been fully compensated. Thus, in practice, some of the risk of the enterprise borne in principle by shareholders is shifted onto creditors.

As an alternative, Roe has proposed that an auction be held as soon as possible after a company seeks bankruptcy protection to determine the value of the company as a going business. The entire company or a certain percentage position in the company could be sold to a new group of shareholders, whose claims would take priority over all existing claimants. New common stock, whose value would be based on the implied valuation for the whole firm, could then be issued and the stock allocated to existing claimants according to a predetermined and strict set of rules about whose claims have priority. If the firm were insolvent, for example, existing shareholders would probably end up with nothing under this sort of arrangement, and existing creditors would end up with the new common shares. The company would thereby be given a new, more sustainable capital structure quickly and without the haggling and uncertainty that usually engulfs bankruptcy proceedings.[36]

My own view on these various reform proposals is mixed. Shareholders should have the right to vote on more issues, they should

---

[36]Roe (1983, p. 559). Aghion, Hart, and Moore (1992, pp. 532–36) suggest a similar procedure in which all debts are immediately cancelled and converted to equity when a bankruptcy petition is filed. A judge would determine the conversion ratios on the basis of the relative seniority of the different classes of claims. The judge would also immediately solicit bids from competing management groups for the whole company, and the new shareholders would vote on which bid to accept.

have better access to the proxy process, and voting should be confidential. Shareholders need to have effective mechanisms in place for challenging management when they believe management is doing a poor job. Directors and managers should be paid (at least partly) in stock, so that their assets are at risk in the same way that other shareholders' assets are. But there is no reason to compel companies to have only one vote per share of common stock. Such a restriction could inhibit some interesting and and potentially productivity-enhancing financial innovations. Nonetheless, existing shareholders should be allowed to vote on any action to issue new stock that would substantially water down the voting rights or financial claim of existing shareholders.

I have strong reservations about proposals that would give large shareholders significantly greater access to directors and managers or encourage them to communicate with each other about voting matters without at least requiring that all other investors be notified of the actions being taken by the large shareholders. One of the strengths of the U.S. system of securities laws is the great protection it provides to small investors, which encourages more equity ownership by them. This strength should not be undermined.

My other reservations about the reform agenda laid out in appendix 3-1 derive from a more general critique of the finance model. In most large corporations shareholders are not the only parties who have substantial ownership-like stakes in the firm; other participants have often made firm-specific investments that are at risk in the same way that equity capital is at risk. These participants often share in the residual gains and in the residual risks. If control rights tilt too strongly toward shareholders at the expense of these other stakeholders, the corporate governance system in the United States would tend to discourage investments by those other participants. These are complex arguments, which are developed in chapters 7 and 8.

APPENDIX 3-1

Reform Proposals Designed to Protect Shareholder Interests and Enhance Shareholder Power and Influence

LAWS AND REGULATIONS

Corporation Law

1. Corporations with at least 500 shareholders should be required to adhere to a one-share, one-vote standard. That is, each share of common stock, regardless of its class, should be entitled to vote in proportion to its relative share in the total common stock equity of the corporation. The right to vote should be inviolate and must not be abridged by any circumstance or any action of any person. (Council of Institutional Investors, 1989, p. 1)*

2. Each share of common stock, regardless of its class, should be treated equally in proportion to its relative share in the total common stock equity of the corporation, with respect to any dividend, distribution, redemption, or tender or exchange offer. (CII, 1989, p. 1)

3. A vote of the majority of shareholders should be required to approve corporate financial decisions that would materially affect the financial position of the company and its shareholders, including the adoption of greenmail, poison pills, or other actions triggered by an outsider's acquiring a significant share of the voting power of the corporation; golden parachutes; disposition of certain assets; and the incurrence of excessive debt. (CII, 1989, pp. 1–2)

*The list of people, organizations, or commissions credited with each reform proposal is not intended to be comprehensive. In many instances, the same or a similar proposal has been advocated by others as well as those named.

Appendix 3-1 (continued)

Appendix 3-1 (continued)

4. A vote of the majority of shareholders should be required to approve any action that would limit shareholders' rights to elect and remove directors, to determine the timing or length of the directors' terms of office, to consider and vote on other matters relevant to their interests as shareholders, and to call special meetings or take action by written consent, or to affect the procedure for fixing the record date for such an action. (CII, 1989, p. 2)

5. Shareholders should be allowed to decide by a majority vote to reincorporate in another state. (Jacobs, 1991, p. 228)

6. Corporate elections should be decided by the number of votes cast—unvoted shares should never be presumed to be votes in favor of management. (Jacobs, 1991, p. 229)

7. Corporate constituency laws should be repealed because they simply legalize management entrenchment. (Minow and Monks, 1991, pp. 117–21; Twentieth Century Fund, 1992, pp. 81–82; and Jacobs, 1991, p. 76)

Shareholder Voice

1. Corporations should pay for shareholder communications. Management views are already distributed at company expense. (Jacobs, 1991, p. 87)

2. Shareholders who are unhappy with director candidates or who want to register their dissatisfaction with a company that is significantly underperforming should withhold their vote on the entire management slate of directors. They should then send a follow-up letter to targeted management detailing their reasons. (Grundfest, 1992; Wharton, 1991, p. 139; and Minow, 1992, p. 22)

3. Shareholders who meet certain requirements concerning, for example, the size of the block of stock they control or the amount of time they have held the stock, should be given special access to the governance process. Proposals include:

   a. Shareholders with some minimum share of the voting stock of a corporation should be able to publish critiques of corporate perfor-

Appendix 3-1 (continued)

mance in the company proxy. (United Shareholders Association, 1990; and Regan, 1992, pp. 20–25)

   b. They should be able to nominate directors for inclusion on the company's proxy ballots. (Jacobs, 1991, p. 228)

   c. They should be able to call special meetings. (Minow and Bingham, 1993, p. 15)

4. Directors should meet with large shareholders outside of the annual meeting, perhaps through a "shareholder relations committee." (Koppes, 1992, p. 84; Lipton and Lorsch, 1992, pp. 74–76)

5. The entire board should be elected annually—staggered boards should not be permitted. (Minow and Bingham, 1993, p. 14)

6. All companies should adopt confidential voting policies that apply to matters subject to elections, including proxy contests; votes should be tabulated by inspectors of election who are independent of the corporation. (Minow and Bingham, 1993, p. 13; and United Shareholders Association, 1990, pp. 11–20)

7. Companies should permit cumulative voting, so that minority shareholders are assured of representation. (Minow and Bingham, 1993, p. 14)

8. Shareholder lists should be easily available to all shareholders upon request. (United Shareholders Association, 1990, pp. 25–27)

Market for Corporate Control

1. To end coercive two-tier tender offers, any tender offer for control should be required to be an offer at the same price for all the stock. (Epstein, 1986, p. 45)

2. The board of directors should have to present all bona fide takeover offers to shareholders before activating any defense mechanisms. (Epstein, 1986, p. 45)

Appendix 3-1 (continued)

3. Leveraged buyouts should not be discouraged or restricted by law. (Jensen, 1989)

4. Companies should adopt bylaws prohibiting greenmail and blank-check preferred stock. They should also opt out of any voluntary antitakeover laws or stakeholder provisions. (Minow and Bingham, 1993, p. 15)

Bankruptcy

1. Bankruptcy rules should be eased to encourage private workouts of debt through exchange offers. (Jensen, 1991, pp. 72–73)

2. When a firm seeks bankruptcy protection, an auction should quickly be held to determine market value of the firm, and all claimants should then be immediately paid off, in strict order of priority, with cash or new securities that reflect the actual value of the company. (Roe, 1983, p. 530; and Jensen, 1991, p. 73)

3. Chapter 11 should be repealed. When a corporation cannot pay its bills, control should pass from shareholders up to the next class of claimholders, normally the preferred shareholders. Each class of claimholders can choose to pay the bills or pass control up to the next level, until control reaches the most senior creditors. Senior creditors would have the option to liquidate for their exclusive benefit. (Bradley and Rosenzweig, 1992)

INSTITUTIONAL ARRANGEMENTS

Boards of Directors

1. Boards should designate an independent director or a special committee to be assigned special rights and responsibilities for communicating with shareholders at company expense. In exchange, boards should then be given more protection from personal liability. Michigan law already does something like this. (Minow, 1992, p. 22; and Lorsch and MacIver, 1991, p. 70)

Appendix 3-1 (continued)

2. Large shareholders should have direct representation on boards. (Twentieth Century Fund, 1992, pp. 19–20; Lorsch and MacIver, 1991, p. 70; and Jacobs, 1991, p. 204)

3. The board of directors should not include representatives of particular shareholder groups or other stakeholders. It should be a unitary board representing all shareholders and dedicated to keeping shareholder value at the maximum. (Hanson, 1991, pp. 141–43)

4. Directors should be paid in stock. Directors should be required to hold a meaningful amount of the corporation's stock, defined relative to the director's net worth. For example, a director's holdings should amount to at least 5 percent, and perhaps as much as 25 percent of his or her net worth. (Monks, 1993, p. 6; Minow and Bingham 1993, p. 11; and Koppes, 1992, p. 84)

5. Nominating committees of corporate boards should solicit suggestions from large shareholders and should consider all shareholder suggestions. (Koppes, 1992, p. 84)

Management Compensation Systems

1. Accounting and compensation systems should be based on creating value for shareholders. (Rappaport, 1986, pp. 99–104, 1990, p. 104)

2. Compensation systems should tie pay significantly to marginal changes in performance and peg pay to long-term objectives. One recommended split: base salary would represent an average of 25 percent of pay; the expected value of the annual bonus would be another 25 percent; and the expected value of long-term compensation would represent 50 percent (on average) of total compensation. Long-term incentives should be simple but should entail significant downside risk. For example, long-term compensation should be tied to stock price performance over five years. (Jacobs, 1991, pp. 241–44; O'Cleireacain, 1992, p. 91)

3. Director compensation should also be tied to performance. Directors should be paid only in stock, for example. The Financial Accounting Standards Board should change the accounting rules that discourage stock-based compensation, and encourage use of stock op-

Appendix 3-1 (continued)

tions. (Monks and Minow, 1991, p. 177; Jacobs, 1991, pp. 241–44; and O'Cleireacain, 1992, pp. 92–93)

4. If stock options are used, their strike price should increase annually by the interest rate on long-term government securities. Then the manager is rewarded only for beating the return on safe securities. (Jacobs, 1991, p. 208)

5. Executive directors and managers should have significant stakes in their companies, thus reinforcing their commitment to shareholder value. (Hanson, 1991, pp. 141–43)

6. Nonshareholder constituencies deserve to be protected from inordinate risk, but not through corporate constituency laws. Explicit, a priori contracts, such as "tin parachutes" (generous severance packages that apply to all workers if a company is taken over), allow directors to focus on shareholder issues without fear of doing unfair harm to other constituencies. (Gavis, 1990, p. 1483)

4

ARE FINANCIAL MARKETS TOO

SHORT-SIGHTED?

A COMPETING THEORY about what might be wrong with corporate governance arrangements in the United States is that the system encourages corporate managers to focus myopically on short-term performance, often sacrificing long-term performance and "competitiveness" in the process. Proponents of this "myopia" argument include many corporate executives who are convinced that pressures from the financial markets often drive them to engage in perverse behavior that reduces long-term value. Although myopia proponents generally agree in principle with finance model proponents that the appropriate goal for managers should be to maximize long-term value for shareholders, they believe that financial markets often push managers in a different direction in practice. In this chapter I examine the various theories that have been put forward to explain

122

why financial market pressures would be so perverse; I also examine the evidence that has been cited supporting or opposing those theories.

The most simplistic explanation for the myopia argument is that corporate executives do not trust outside investors to make good judgments about "their" businesses. Corporate executives have a long history of mistrusting the financial markets as well as the bankers, brokers, traders, and financial institutions that companies depend on for capital. Professor Mark Roe of Columbia University has argued persuasively in several papers that securities laws and laws regulating financial institutions in this country were devised in part to keep the financial sector from gaining too much power in the governance of public corporations.[1] Many of these laws were written after the stock market crash of 1929, during the subsequent Great Depression. To some extent, these laws were a direct response to widespread belief that the speculative behavior engaged in by financial institutions trading on the stock markets was to blame for the business troubles of the time.[2]

Reflecting that widespread distrust, the economist John Maynard Keynes likened trading on the stock markets to a game in which players try to select winners of a beauty contest not by choosing the contestant they think is most beautiful, but by guessing which contestant the other players would judge to be the most beautiful. More accurately, he said, it is a game in which players try to choose which contestant the other players believe would be chosen by all

---

[1]See, for example, Roe (1991b). Grundfest (1990, p. 89) has made similar arguments: "America seems not to trust her capitalists."

[2]Roe (1993d, p. 329) cites Carosso (1970) for the evidence that financial institutions were blamed for the economic problems of the 1930s. In private correspondence with the author, Roe said that financial fragmentation predated the Depression and the New Deal and that the financial reforms of that era further entrenched the fragmented system instead of moving it toward big government and big finance.

the other players. "We have reached the third degree where we devote our intelligences to anticipating what average opinion expects the average opinion to be," he said. "And there are some, I believe, who practise the fourth, fifth, and higher degrees."[3]

During the highly prosperous three or four decades after the Depression, distrust of the financial markets diminished and arguments about their deleterious influence largely disappeared from major public policy debates about corporate behavior. But the arguments have resurfaced in recent years, reflecting in part widespread underlying skepticism among many corporate executives, their lawyers and advisors, and some economists and policymakers about the way financial markets actually work. One group studying this question recently characterized financial markets as prone to "high-volume, speculative trading and short-lived bubbles and crashes," noting that these "are seen by many as the essence of 'short-termism.' "[4]

Two Harvard Business School scholars, Robert Hayes and William Abernathy, were among the first to argue that a systematic problem in the way U.S. companies are governed or managed was weakening the U.S. competitive position. In a 1980 article in the *Harvard Business Review*, they argued that American management suffered from "competitive myopia." They blamed this myopia on several features of what they called the "new management orthodoxy," including a tendency for managers to rely too heavily on "short-term financial measurements like return on investment for

[3]Keynes (1936, p. 156).

[4]Twentieth Century Fund (1992, p. 7). In another study, Dertouzos, Lester, and Solow (1989, p. 62) noted that the evidence that financial market pressures encourage short-term thinking and that "firms respond to [these pressures] by maximizing their short-term profit in the belief that the market would penalize them for taking the long view . . . comes from business executives describing their own perceptions and behavior."

evaluating performance."[5] In the early 1980s President Reagan commissioned a study on the causes of the decline in U.S. competitiveness. The commission used the notion of "competitiveness" problems to refer to a whole panoply of supposed maladies, including a slow rate of productivity growth, low rates of investment, and loss of market share by U.S. companies in several key industries. That study concluded that U.S. companies were handicapped by a low supply of capital available for investment. The supply of new capital for investors is the net savings of U.S. citizens plus what they can borrow from foreign investors. With demand for capital high and the supply low, the commission argued, U.S. firms faced a much higher "cost of capital" than did their competitors.[6] The high cost of capital of that period provided one possible explanation for why financial markets might be a source of "short-termism" pressures on corporate executives.

High Cost of Capital as a Cause of Myopia

The cost of capital is what businesses must pay investors to compensate them for tying up their funds and incurring the risks associated with the investment. The amount businesses must pay is determined by the minimum return that investors demand.[7] If the interest rates that investors can earn on alternative investments are relatively high, then they will want an even higher return for investing their money in corporate securities. Investors can increase their rate of return either by receiving more money over the same period

---

[5]Hayes and Abernathy (1980, p. 70).

[6]President's Commission on Industrial Competitiveness (1985, pp. 25–27).

[7]The cost of capital can be computed on a pre- or after-tax basis. The difference is important because taxes are one factor influencing the investment climate, but the issue is not material to the present discussion.

of time or by receiving the same money over a shorter period of time. A high cost of capital thus shortens the time horizons for investment. Under this high-cost-of-capital hypothesis, companies that neglect investments with very long lead times before they produce a profit (such as new product development, or market development) are not necessarily poorly managed, nor are their executives necessarily short-sighted or without a vision of the future. They may only be doing what financial market signals are telling them to do—rejecting opportunities whose returns are too slow in coming to satisfy investors demanding high or rapid returns. One advantage, politically, of this explanation for market myopia and related competitiveness problems is that it diffused blame away from individual firms or executives.

The cost of capital is one of those economic concepts that is perfectly clear in theory but very difficult to measure in practice. Finance texts teach that it should be measured as a weighted average of what the corporation would have to pay to raise money in each of several different ways, such as borrowing from a bank, floating bonds, or issuing new stock. Interest rates on securities of comparable risk are thus important components of the cost of capital, as is the expected return to the company's equity. The latter is the hardest to measure. Several common approaches involve using the ratio of the company's earnings per share to the price of its stock, the inverse of the more familiar price/earnings, or P/E, ratio. A stock price that is high relative to earnings suggests that investors are happy to settle for a relatively low rate of return, and vice versa.[8]

---

[8]The return to investors on a share of stock is a combination of the earnings attributable to that share and the expected increase in the price of the share. Because economists and finance theorists do not agree on a method for including expected price increases in the calculation of the cost of capital, I am, for present purposes, ignoring that portion of the equation. The neglect of this factor is important, however, because most of the empirical disagreements about whether the cost of capital has

In the early 1980s the principal evidence for the charge that U.S. companies faced a higher cost of capital than their competitors overseas was that stocks of U.S. companies typically carried much lower P/E ratios than similar Japanese or German companies. These lower P/E ratios were interpreted to mean that U.S. financial markets were demanding a higher rate of return from U.S. companies.[9]

Although one component of the cost of capital fell as U.S. stock prices rose more rapidly than corporate earnings in the 1980s (which pushed the P/E ratio up), the other key components of the cost of capital rose dramatically. The real (inflation-adjusted) rates of interest on debt securities increased both in absolute terms and relative to real interest rates in other countries. So the weighted average cost of capital rose markedly in the 1980s relative to its levels throughout the postwar period, and the gap between the level in the United States and the level in other countries stayed wide.[10]

A high cost of capital deters some investments because fewer investments can provide a high enough return at low enough risk to be worthwhile, given the cost in lost opportunity to invest elsewhere at an assured high rate. But finance model advocates view that as an appropriate market signal that those forgone investments are not worth as much as competing investments. Moreover, if a high cost of capital causes myopic investment behavior, the implied underly-

---

been correctly measured or whether measurements taken at two different countries are comparable come down to disagreements about how to measure the cost of equity capital.

[9]Hatsopoulos (1983) was one of the first to argue that the cost of capital was a primary culprit. The method Hatsopoulos used to calculate the cost of capital relied heavily on a measure similar to an aggregate price-earnings ratio. Subsequent articles, using different methodologies, reached similar conclusions, however.

[10]Blair and Schary (1993) document the change over time in the cost of capital in the United States. McCauley and Zimmer (1989, pp. 10, 15–16) document the higher cost of capital in the United States relative to Japan and Germany in the 1980s. In both of these papers, real interest rates strongly influence the measures of the cost of capital.

ing problem is macroeconomic, such as a savings rate that is too low or a tax rate that is too high. It does not suggest that the governance structure or capital markets need to be reformed.

At any rate, by the early 1990s this cost-of-capital argument seemed less important as an explanation for myopic corporate behavior and continued competitiveness difficulties for several reasons. Real interest rates came back down in the United States in the late 1980s and early 1990s. Meanwhile, the decline in prices on the Tokyo Stock Exchange and the rise in interest rates in Germany and other European countries had narrowed the gap in the cost of capital by anyone's measure.[11]

Other Causes of Myopia

Nonetheless, the "market myopia" argument has persisted. Some advocates of this position argue that the problem arises because stock prices provide a very poor guide to the true underlying value of a corporation. Their critique is based on three related points, which can be summarized as follows: First, stock prices are extremely erratic. In the long run, they may be an unbiased indicator of true value of future earnings, but they vary so much from day to day and week to week that at any single point, they provide almost no interpretable information about the true worth of a company. A joke common among economists is that the stock market has correctly predicted ten of the last five recessions. The point is that stock prices sometimes rise or fall quite markedly without a significant change in underlying fundamental factors. A dramatic example is the 25 percent drop in the value of stocks on the New York Stock

[11]Frankel (1991); Mattione (1992).

Exchange that occurred between October 14 and October 26, 1987.[12] Not only was nothing happening in the real economy that could explain a drop of that magnitude, but the decline in stock prices did not affect the real economy very much, and the market recovered much of its lost ground during the next year. This experience has led some observers to claim that stock prices are irrelevant.

Robert J. Shiller and others have long noted that stock prices are "excessively" volatile because they often move much more than would be warranted by actual ex post changes in the stream of dividends. In other words, they seem to overpredict movements in dividends.[13] Shiller has developed a "group psychology" model of financial market behavior, which he says explains stock price movements better than the efficient markets model and also accounts for this excess volatility.[14]

Second, stock prices are driven by the trading activities of portfolio managers who are rewarded for their performance in the short term (often quarterly). This point explains some of the volatility of stock prices as a natural outcome of the activities of portfolio traders. In a perfectly efficient market, stock prices would be expected to move by small amounts on the announcement of news that genuinely affects a company's future prospects. Even small changes matter to portfolio managers who are judged on quarterly returns, and so they expend a lot of energy trying to anticipate such announcements or to react quickly when announcements are made. But because all traders not only behave the same way, but know everyone trades the same way, they also know that the price movement is likely to be

---

[12]Greenwald and Stein (1988) report eight instances from 1945 through 1987 when the Dow Jones Industrial Average dropped by more than 20 percent. In only two of these instances did output decline in the succeeding twelve months.

[13]Shiller (1989).

[14]Shiller (1989, 1992).

large relative to the true impact of the news. That knowledge means that traders have to react even more quickly to participate in any short-term gains or prevent any short-term losses. This situation is reminiscent of Keynes' notion of the stock market as a game of guessing what everyone else will guess that everyone else will think. These trading practices are said to result in rapid turnover of stock and excessive volatility and supposedly cause portfolio managers to value quarterly earnings and other short-term results too highly.[15]

The third point focuses on the information that portfolio managers use. Because they must track the performance of dozens, sometimes hundreds, of companies, individual portfolio managers do not have time or resources to learn in detail about the businesses of each company they invest in (let alone of companies they might invest in). They thus tend to make judgments on the basis of summary measures of performance, which may be very misleading. In particular, they do a poor job of valuing investment spending, especially "soft" investments such as research and development, training, and market development. These kinds of investments may enhance returns in subtle ways that are difficult to attribute directly to the investment. "Lack of communication prevents investors from understanding management's long-term goals and objectives," Michael Jacobs argues. "Because most U.S. investors are detached from the businesses they fund, they rely on outward manifestation of what is really going on within a company; namely quarterly earnings."[16]

In sum, proponents of this version of the market myopia argument do not trust the signal given by the stock markets about the true value of companies. They claim that executives in other coun-

---

[15]Froot, Perold, and Stein (1992) reach similar conclusions, arguing that shareholder trading practices might affect corporate investment time horizons in two ways—"excess volatility" (similar to my first point) and an "information gap" (similar to my second and third points).

[16]Jacobs (1991, p. 10).

tries are generally less preoccupied with stock prices, and they argue that the wave of hostile takeovers and leveraged buyouts (which finance model advocates regarded as a correction for poor management) put extra pressure on managers. According to this market myopia theory, corporate managers see that the price of their companies' stock is regularly driven down by factors that they cannot control, yet these price declines make them vulnerable to being ousted in a takeover. To protect themselves, corporate executives may be driven to take actions that sacrifice the long-term best interests of the corporation but that send stockholders a short-term message that seems to be positive.

Rebuttal by the Finance Theorists

Perhaps not surprisingly, the myopia critique sounds plausible to many corporate executives and is consistent with the findings of surveys that ask corporate executives to describe their own experience.[17] But it is not consistent with the empirical evidence on the actual behavior of stock prices.[18] The question whether the stock market undervalues long-term returns relative to short-term returns cannot be tested directly, because what matters at any single point is not what the actual performance of the company will turn out to be during the next ten or so years, but what investors think the actual performance will be. The only way to determine what investors think is to see what price they are willing to pay for the stock. So economists have tested the question indirectly by asking whether the stock market marks down companies that invest heavily in

---

[17]See, for example, Business Week/Harris Executive Poll, Bruce Nussbaum, "The Changing Role of the CEO," *Business Week*, October 23, 1987, p. 28.

[18]Marsh (1992) provides a good summary of the evidence on "short-termism."

research and development or other activities whose payoff, if any, is likely to be many years out. Several studies have shown that the stock market does not systematically undervalue such investments.[19]

Advocates of the finance model concede that portfolio managers are evaluated on and rewarded for quarterly results and are therefore focused on the short-term performance of the portfolios they manage. But that does not mean that stock prices reflect only short-term expectations, they argue. "Faced with the demand for better short-term performance, the fund manager . . . cannot sell the future short," finance economist Paul Marsh contends. "The only way he or she can outperform is to identify undervalued shares and buy them, and/or overvalued shares, and sell them. . . . Indeed, the only way they can succeed is through careful analysis of a company's short- and longer-term prospects."[20] According to Marsh, it is exactly this behavior by stock traders and investors that causes the stock prices to reflect quickly all available information. If the finance model is correct, then regardless of whether stock traders and portfolio managers are under pressure to show short-term results, the prices of the stocks in their portfolios should still provide a valid (in fact, the best available) indicator of the long-term value of company plans and strategies and therefore be the best basis for evaluating management performance.

---

[19]For example, see McConnell and Muscarella (1985); Chaney, Devinney, and Winer (1989); Chan, Martin, and Kensinger (1990); and Woolridge (1988). Some studies have found evidence that the financial markets may actually overvalue companies with good growth prospects. See Reinganum (1981); Basu (1983); and Hall and Hall (1993). On the other side, however, Miles (1993) finds evidence that investors in the U.K. stock market in the 1980s systematically undervalued cash flows accruing over long periods of time relative to cash flows accruing over shorter periods, even after adjusting for risk.

[20]Marsh (1992, p. 449).

Finance model advocates have not, so far, come up with a fully satisfying response to the charge that stock prices are not very useful because the amount of real information about the value of a company in a single observation of its stock price is so low relative to the amount of "noise" (random factors that have nothing to do with fundamental values). Nonetheless, many finance model advocates do not accept this uncertainty as a reason to reject stock prices as the best measure of corporate performance.

Although hundreds of attempts have been made to find ways to use accounting information, historic information about stock price movements, and other publicly available information to predict future stock price movements, none has proved consistently successful; the current stock price remains the best predictor of future stock prices, they maintain. It is also virtually the only information about corporate performance that is forward-looking and that management cannot directly manipulate through accounting tricks. Finance theorists also argue that, although short-run price volatility has significantly increased in recent years, price volatility from one month to the next and over longer periods has not increased. Moreover, they argue that price volatility by itself should not lead to shorter time horizons for corporate investments.[21]

Finally, proponents of the finance model do not disagree that the typical portfolio manager does not have the time or resources to investigate and understand the business of every company she invests in. But they respond that, where money is to be made from better information, some investors have the incentive to investigate the business of each company. Stock market prices therefore still

[21]Froot, Perold, and Stein (1992).

quickly reflect the best information available, not just the information used by the typical portfolio manager.[22]

Reform Proposals from the Market Myopia Camp

These differences in beliefs about the underlying causes of corporate malaise mean that proponents of the market myopia theory often part company with advocates of the finance model about the right corporate governance remedies. While finance model advocates want to enhance shareholder oversight and influence on corporate decisionmaking, believers in market myopia would like corporate governance arrangements to shield managers from shareholder pressure, particularly pressure to focus on short-term stock price performance. (Appendix 4-1 lists reforms proposed by market myopia theorists.)

One such reform would eliminate quarterly reports so that managers would no longer be so fixated on quarterly performance. "Doing so might not change attitudes all by itself, but it would symbolize what needs to be done," argues Lester C. Thurow, a professor of economics at the Massachusetts Institute of Technology. "The quarterly profit statement is supposed to improve the information available to investors. It may do this for short-run stock speculators (although even this is open to doubt, given the volatility of the short-run numbers), but from a social point of view there is no payoff to this availability. Not knowing current profits might force

---

[22]Economists and finance theorists distinguish three levels of market efficiency. In the "weak form" of efficiency, current prices reflect all the information contained in the record of past prices; in the "semi-strong form" of efficiency, prices reflect not only all past prices, but all published information; in the "strong form" of efficiency, stock prices fully incorporate nonpublic and public information. In the weak- and semi-strong form situations, attentive investors or insiders might be able to make money by studying a company's prospects or trading on inside information. See Brealey and Myers (1991, pp. 295–96) for a helpful discussion.

short-term investors to understand the firm's technologies and its market position."[23]

Another proposed reform would impose a "transactions tax"— perhaps a few tenths of a percent of the value of any stock bought or sold. This tax would increase the costs of short-term trading and thus supposedly encourage portfolio managers and other investors to "invest for the long term."[24] Believers in the market myopia theory have also argued that companies should have responsibilities under the law to a larger group of constituents than just shareholders.

Finance model advocates reject such proposals altogether. They say that liquidity reduces risk, which should reduce the cost of capital, and that frequent trading improves the information content of stock prices, which should make stock prices more useful as indicators of performance.

Both sides agree that corporate governance would be improved if more and better information were made available to investors so that stock prices would do a better job of measuring the true worth of the equity in public companies. Publication of too many details about the company's plans or performance, however, could damage its competitive position, or create antitrust problems for the company. Moreover, corporate executives often oppose such proposals because additional information would be costly to collect and report in a consistent manner that can be easily interpreted.[25]

[23]Thurow (1988, p. 70).

[24]James Tobin, a Nobel prize-winning economist, has endorsed the so-called "sand-in-the-wheels" approach to reducing the pace of trading activity. See Tobin (1992, p. 23).

[25]The Conference Board and the Business Roundtable, two organizations that represent executives of large corporations, both protested a project by the American Institute of Certified Public Accountants calling for expanded reporting requirements. See Lee Burton, "Companies Pressure Accounting Panel to Modify Demands for More Data," *Wall Street Journal*, August 16, 1994, p. A2. Partly as a result, the AICPA backed down and issued a less stringent reform proposal. See AICPA (1994).

Appendix 4-1 also lists proposed enhancements of the information that market myopia advocates argue management should collect and use internally to plan and evaluate firm performance. In any case, both finance model advocates and market myopia advocates agree that companies should focus on creating value for shareholders. They just disagree about the best way to achieve that goal.

A Subtler, More Complex Market Myopia Story

Proponents of the simple market myopia argument have failed to make a convincing theoretical or empirical case for their position, but some scholars have developed somewhat more subtle versions of the argument that may prove to be more substantial. The central element of these versions posits that the ease with which stocks of large, widely held companies can be traded may not be an unqualified benefit, as finance model advocates generally maintain. In fact, these scholars suggest that the liquidity of the financial markets in the United States may entail more cost than benefit in some circumstances.[26] These costs arise because investors with small holdings or who hold stocks for very short periods and face low transactions costs for getting out of a position have very little incentive to learn about the businesses they invest in or to monitor the operational and business performance of the companies' executives. From the narrow point of view of any one investor, liquidity is good because it gives the investor options and thus reduces that investor's risk. This in turn reduces the return that companies should have to pay such an investor to induce him or her to invest.

---

[26]Coffee (1991) has argued the reverse—that the benefits of control come at a high cost because they probably require sacrificing liquidity. He therefore concludes that investors who want liquidity may rationally avoid exercising more control.

But, this argument continues, liquidity for individual investors may not be good for the economy as a whole because investors, in general, are less likely to be knowledgeable about or committed to specific investments. These uncommitted investors fail to pay close attention to what the company is doing; fail to give management the close supervision, counsel, and advice that one would expect of "owners"; and bail out much too quickly when problems arise. Investors who can exit freely may not be willing to support managers who need time, and perhaps additional resources, to solve a problem. They will probably be inclined instead simply to abandon a troubled business or strategy.

The private Council on Competitiveness and the Harvard Business School jointly sponsored an extensive series of studies of these issues in the late 1980s and early 1990s. In his summary report of the eighteen individual studies by twenty-five scholars, Michael Porter rejects the arguments that the market is myopic because the cost of capital is higher for U.S. companies than for foreign companies or because stock prices overvalue quarterly earnings and undervalue long-term investment. Instead, he offers a more complex and textured argument that, nonetheless, lays the blame for competitiveness problems and low rates of investment in the United States on "the entire system of allocating investment capital within and across companies."[27]

Porter argues that the U.S. system is a "fluid capital" system, characterized by institutional investors who are transient as owners. The stakes they hold in many companies are fragmented, and, as investors, they focus on the profits they can make from each transaction rather than from the relationship as a whole. In deciding whether to buy or sell a particular stock, they must rely on vastly simplified summary information available to all outsiders and ori-

[27]Porter (1992).

ented toward predicting near-term stock price movements. The "value proxies" these investors use "can lead to underinvestment in some industries or forms of investment, while allowing overinvestment in others." For example, Porter cites a survey by James M. Poterba and Lawrence H. Summers, which suggests that, before proceeding with investments, many U.S. executives require a higher rate of return than really makes sense given the other alternatives available, at least according to the appropriate measures of the cost of capital.[28] In other words, these executives act as if investors were demanding a price for the use of their capital that is higher than the raw data suggest it should be.

Similarly, other scholars have argued that investors and corporate executives often fail to include the "option value" of making certain investments or to account for the cost of not making certain investments. Today's investment may prevent an existing business from declining or lead to a new and unexpected opportunity tomorrow. That possibility adds value to today's investment, but corporate executives typically neglect or ignore this value when they use standard capital budgeting techniques.[29] This conservative approach to valuing investments is a reasonable reaction in a world where information is limited and no outside investor is willing to invest the time to understand the full competitive context in which the firm is operating.

Porter argues that, in contrast, Japan and Germany have "dedicated capital" systems with permanent owners who seek long-term appreciation of their investments and who are more interested in their relationship with the company over time than with individual transactions. According to Porter, "the principal Japanese and Ger-

---

[28]Poterba and Summers (1991, p. 10).
[29]Myers (1984a, pp. 134) makes this point. Baldwin and Clark (1992) make related arguments.

man owners engage in ongoing, cumulative information gathering on the company's businesses and prospects. These owners command the respect of management; have access to inside information; and particularly in Germany, exert considerable influence on management behavior."[30] Porter believes that the ongoing nature of the relationships between corporations and their investors in Germany and Japan helps encourage the use of qualitative information as well as the standard financial measures of value and performance. This, in turn, results in better business decisions than does simple reliance on stock market prices, he argues.[31]

Porter advocates a long list of public policy and corporate-level changes aimed at moving the U.S. system of capital allocation toward the dedicated capital model. For example, he would provide tax incentives to encourage longer holding periods, remove tax barriers and other restrictions that limit share ownership by institutions, improve the quality and quantity of information flows between corporate insiders and investors, and link the fortunes of various stakeholders in companies more tightly together (for example, by encouraging employee ownership), and then give these other stakeholders more influence over corporate management (see appendixes 4-1 and 5-1).

Thus, many proponents of the market myopia position are, like some finance model advocates, coming to believe that corporate performance would be improved if large institutional investors, such as pension funds, mutual funds, and other dedicated investors, played a more active (and intrusive) role in selecting and monitoring

---

[30]Porter (1992, pp. 8–9).

[31]The German and Japanese systems have their drawbacks, however. Neither of these systems seems to be as good as the U.S. system at allocating capital to new technologies or risky start-up ventures. Porter (1992, pp. 45–48, 64–65) acknowledges this and suggests that the U.S. system may err by overinvesting in these types of ventures.

corporate directors and in monitoring and evaluating corporate strategies and the performance and pay of top executives. In the early 1990s parties to the corporate governance debates appeared to be converging on the idea that "relationship" investing could solve many corporate governance problems in the United States.[32]

But the two camps were still far apart on the means for achieving these goals. Finance model advocates primarily want to emphasize the rights of shareholders to control corporations and remove legal and institutional barriers that make it difficult for institutional investors to be activists, while market myopia advocates want to emphasize the responsibilities associated with this right. They want to tie the right to play a more active role in corporations to a condition that the financial institutions provide more "patient" capital by taking large positions and committing themselves to holding these positions for a long time.[33] If they did this, they could be a stabilizing influence that would help protect companies and their managements from the vicissitudes of the market as well as provide better monitoring and oversight.

Finance model advocates scored a significant policy victory in the fall of 1992 when the Subcouncil on Corporate Governance and Financial Markets of the congressionally mandated Competitiveness Policy Council rejected Porter's conclusions and policy recommendations outright. In its summary statement following a two-year investigation into the relationship between corporate

---

[32]See, for example, Judith H. Dobrzynski, "Relationship Investing," *Business Week*, March 15, 1993, pp. 68–75; and Myron Magnet and John Labate, "What Activist Investors Want," *Fortune*, March 8, 1993, p. 59.

[33]Some participants in the debate, whose views otherwise more closely resemble those of the finance model, have argued that active monitoring and oversight are indeed responsibilities that go along with ownership of corporate equities. They view these responsibilities as arising from long-term ownership, rather than viewing long-term ownership as a duty arising from exercising the oversight role. See, for example, Monks and Minow (1991, p. 18).

governance and competitiveness, this body essentially espoused the finance model. The final report noted that "many Subcouncil members were not persuaded that we have a pervasive underinvestment or capital allocation problem and did not, in general, find Porter's policy prescriptions persuasive."[34] The subcouncil's reform proposals exhorted boards of directors to establish better procedures and structures, asked institutional investors to do a better job of monitoring, and suggested a few ways to facilitate shareholder communication.

In a footnote attached to its conclusions, the subcouncil further rejected the idea that " 'transient' or fragmented shareholder ownership" creates any time horizon problems for investment. "Owners come from all investment schools and behave with more or less impact on the corporate governance process," the study said. "Our system has many large, long-term owners, some active and some passive. Even passive investors with small blocks of shares, if they are vocal, can have an impact on the corporate governance process. The key is whether investors—regardless of their make-up or time horizons—have the means to monitor and communicate, as well as the will to act to effect changes either in the direction of corporate investment or in the corporate governance/strategic planning process or both."[35]

I am inclined to accept the subcouncil's critique of the simple market myopia arguments. The arguments that financial markets

---

[34]Competitiveness Policy Council, Subcouncil on Corporate Governance and Financial Markets (1992, p. 5).

[35]Competitiveness Policy Council, Subcouncil on Corporate Governance and Financial Markets (1992, p. 3). The subcouncil blamed any competitiveness problem that U.S. companies might have on the "unstable and volatile macroeconomic environment," including "taxes, inflation, interest rates, exchange rates, and legislative and regulatory policies." The subcouncil, however, went on to recommend an enhanced role for institutional investors and relationship investing as a way to improve corporate governance.

are systematically biased against long-term investments are unpersuasive, and the evidence is at odds with this claim. Much more compelling are the more subtle arguments made by Porter and others about the information failures in a fluid financial market with high turnover rates and passive investors and about the advantages of having "dedicated" owners, who can process and use more complex kinds of information in evaluating investment strategies.[36] Moreover, in dismissing the Porter arguments so lightly, the subcouncil fell into the intellectual trap of assuming that shareholders are the only "owners" who matter. Other participants in the wealth-creating process in most corporations also make firm-specific investments, and these investments are at risk in the same way that equity capital is at risk. An effective corporate governance system, one that encourages total wealth creation, must foster and protect these other investments too. But both the finance and market myopia models ignore those other investments. Although Porter's analysis does not explicitly take these other investments into account, his proposals for encouraging dedicated capital and involving other stakeholders more directly in corporate governance at least move in the direction of addressing these issues.

---

[36]In the interest of full disclosure, I should note that I am currently working with Porter and several dozen others on a newly formulated Subcouncil on Capital Allocation of the Competitiveness Policy Council. The subcouncil is jointly headed by Porter and Robert Denham, chairman of Salomon Inc., and is considering several specific policy proposals to try to encourage more involvement in corporate governance by institutional investors and other stakeholders, especially employees, and more and better disclosure.

APPENDIX 4-1

Reform Proposals Designed to Shield Management and Boards From Excessive Influence by Financial Markets

---

LAWS AND REGULATIONS

Corporation Law

1. Directors should be responsible by law, in all states, to constituencies beyond just shareholders. (Lorsch and MacIver, 1989, p. 49)*

Shareholder Voice

1. Special board committees for dealing with shareholders or special shareholder committees should be avoided because there is no guarantee that they represent all shareholders. Shareholders should trust the board they elected or elect a different one. (Cadbury Commission, 1992, p. 48; Millstein 1992, p. 51)

Securities Market Regulation

1. Abolish quarterly profit reports; the SEC should limit earnings reports to one a year. (Thurow, 1988, p. 70; Lorsch and McIver, 1989, p. 70)

2. Transactions taxes should be imposed to limit stock turnover rates. (Tobin, 1992, p. 23)

INSTITUTIONAL ARRANGEMENTS

Boards of Directors

1. Directors should be elected for five-year terms. (Lipton and Rosenblum, 1991, pp. 224–25)

---

*The list of people, organizations, or commissions credited with each reform proposal is not intended to be comprehensive. In many instances, the same or a similar proposal has been advocated by others as well as those named.

Appendix 4-1 (continued)

144

Appendix 4-1 (continued)

2. To preserve their independence, directors should not participate in share option schemes and should be pensionable. (Cadbury Commission, 1992, p. 23)

Internal Controls

1. Alternative measures of performance should be developed, such as profitability, market position, productivity, product leadership, employee attitude, public responsibility, personnel development, and the balance between short- and long-term goals. (Lipton and Lorsch, 1992)

2. Corporations should use a broader definition of assets, including customer relations, brand names, technological resources, and relative position within the market. Financial control systems should focus on asset quality and productivity in addition to quantity and should consider relative rather than absolute measures. (Porter, 1992, p. 95)

3. Corporate investment budgeting methods should be overhauled to take into account the fact that the value of individual investments can usefully be measured only in the context of an entire investment program. All forms of investment, including worker training and other investments in human capital, should be considered in a unified way. (Porter, 1992, p. 96)

4. Codify long-term shareholder value rather than current stock price as the appropriate corporate goal. (Porter, 1992, pp. 86–87)

5. Corporations should design stock option plans so that large bonuses are distributed among all workers. The option plan should be designed to encourage employees to hold their stock over the long term. For example, tax incentives for stock options and stock purchase plans should be limited to those plans with restrictions on selling. (Porter, 1992, p. 86)

5

CAN INSTITUTIONAL

INVESTORS FIX THE

GOVERNANCE SYSTEM?

THE IDEA THAT THE GOVERNANCE PROBLEMS of U.S. companies could be greatly mitigated if only large financial institutions would begin to act like "real owners" surfaced in the late 1980s in the heat of the academic and policy debate surrounding takeovers and their impact on the "competitiveness" of U.S. firms. Both sides in that debate compared the financial systems and institutions for corporate governance in the United States with those in Germany and Japan, whose corporate sectors had shown remarkable strength, profitability, growth, and ability to capture market share from U.S. companies during the previous decade.

Proponents of the market myopia theory noted that there are almost no hostile takeovers in Germany or Japan to plague corporate managers and attributed the competitive strength of companies in

145

those countries to their relative freedom from the tyranny of the stock market. Advocates of the finance model countered that companies in both Japan and Germany (but especially in Japan) are typically very highly leveraged and that banks and other financial institutions own major positions in—and exercise substantial control over—the largest corporations in both countries. The takeover mechanism is not needed to correct bad management in Japan and Germany, they argued, because investors exercise continuous oversight and control so that management never has a chance to steer the companies too far away from the path that investors want them to take.

Both arguments were originally based on sketchy and anecdotal evidence, and both vastly oversimplify the way that U.S. corporate governance differs from that in either Japan or Germany. But the possibility that other countries might have developed a regulatory or financial market structure or set of institutional arrangements that spurs investment or creates wealth more effectively than does the U.S. system was a novel idea in academic, legal, and policy circles. Until the late 1980s most students of corporate governance had assumed that the most "highly evolved" system was the U.S. system, with its fragmented financial institutions, widely traded securities, and deep, highly sophisticated, liquid, and transparent securities markets, with strict rules on what information must be made public and who can trade on what information. (The systems in Great Britain, Canada, and Australia, whose financial and governance structures are similar to those in the United States, would also fall into this category.)

By contrast, most other industrial countries have much thinner financial markets that operate on less public information, and have fewer, but very large and very powerful financial institutions. It was assumed that these more "primitive" systems would evolve to look more like the Anglo-American model. In fact, as OECD (Organization for Economic Cooperation and Development) countries work toward integrating their financial markets, European and Asian countries have been adopting rules, such as limits on insider trading and stiffer capital requirements for banks, that push their systems toward the Anglo-American model.

Nonetheless, the idea that large, powerful financial institutions in other countries might perform a critical governance function that is missing or weak in the U.S. system has opened a whole new line of thinking about financial and regulatory structures and governance systems both in the United States and in other industrial countries.[1] This research is aimed at determining how each system balances the competing goals of corporate governance.

The literature on foreign systems and how they operate is still in its infancy and is not discussed in detail here. This chapter reviews the various types of financial institutions in this country and the role that they currently play in corporate governance. It then looks at how that role has been changing in recent years and reviews the arguments for why certain kinds of financial institutions should be given an expanded and more powerful role, along with a long list of reform proposals that would facilitate this new role. The available empirical evidence on the impact institutional investor activism has had, or could have, on corporate performance is summarized. Finally, the chapter discusses some arguments against enhancing the role of financial institutions in corporate governance in this country and some problems that will ultimately limit the effectiveness of institutional investors in solving the central ills of corporate governance.

Who Are These Big Players?

Financial institutions—including banks and savings institutions, insurance companies, mutual funds, pension funds, investment

---

[1]See, for example, Jacobs (1991); "The American Corporation and the Institutional Investor" (1988); Gilson and Roe (1993); Gerlach (1992); Kester (1992b); Edwards and Eisenbies (1991); Aoki (1988); and Fukao (1995).

companies, and private trusts and endowments—hold more than 40
percent of the total financial claims against U.S. individuals, corporations, and governments. Financial institutions hold more than 80
percent of corporate bonds and almost half of corporate equity
claims. Among the largest and bluest-chip of companies, institutional investors often account for an even larger share—as much as
60 to 70 percent—of corporate equities (see table 2-1 in chapter 2,
which shows how corporate equity holdings are divided among the
major types of institutional investors).[2]

At first blush, then, financial institutions would seem likely to
have a major influence on the governance of corporations. But for
several reasons, that is generally not the case. The claims against
any one corporation are typically divided among dozens, sometimes
hundreds, of financial institutions, each with only one or a few
specialized types of claims. For example, one bank might provide the
construction loan that finances an expansion of the headquarters office,
while another bank heads a consortium to finance the opening of an
assembly plant in Mexico, and still another bank manages a group of
trusts that hold the company's preferred shares. Moreover, the claims
held by each institution may be small relative to the total capitalization
of the company. Meanwhile, each financial institution has its own
agenda, which usually does not include managing or even closely
monitoring the corporations whose securities they hold, and each type
of financial institution faces a different set of regulatory constraints
governing how involved it can get in corporate affairs.

---

[2]Federal Reserve Board numbers show that, as of mid-1994, financial institutions
held 46 percent of corporate equities and 80 percent of corporate bonds. See Board of
Governors of the Federal Reserve System (1994). Brancato (1991) shows that institutional holdings averaged 46 percent of the twenty-five largest U.S. companies but
were much higher for some companies. For example, institutional investors held 69
percent of Eli Lilly & Co., 62 percent of Minnesota Mining and Manufacturing, 59
percent of Philip Morris Cos Inc., and 58 percent of Pepsico Inc.

Banks

As of 1994 banks and other depository institutions (such as thrifts and credit unions) collectively held about $5.3 trillion in financial assets, or 12.4 percent of all financial assets in the United States.[3] A long history of regulation has kept banks from owning controlling blocks of the equity shares in industrial or commercial corporations. The National Bank Act of 1863 gave national banks only limited powers, and these did not include owning stocks. Since passage of the Glass-Steagall Act in 1933, which compelled the separation of commercial banking activities from investment banking activities, neither commercial banks nor bank affiliates have been allowed to deal in corporate equities or to own them for their own account.[4] Today, the regulations on banks are easing, and some large banks have been permitted to acquire securities dealers or engage in brokering activities. Banks can avoid Glass-Steagall limitations somewhat by creating holding companies, which are permitted to buy up to 5 percent of the voting stock of a nonbank company, but they must be passive investors in this stock.[5] In practice, banks rarely hold equities up to the legal limit and are seldom significant holders of corporate equities.

Bank trust departments are permitted to manage private trust funds, but even here the rules are designed to prevent banks from

[3]Data on holdings for banks and other financial institutions discussed in this chapter are from Board of Governors of the Federal Reserve System (1994).

[4]Banks are sometimes permitted to own stocks of corporations for their own account if they acquire the stocks as part of a loan workout agreement. Generally, they would be required to dispose of these stocks within a few years, however. See James (1994).

[5]See Roe (1991b) for a summary of the restrictions on banks and other financial institutions that limit their investments in corporate equities and their activism in corporate governance. The sections on insurance companies, mutual funds, and pension funds also owe a debt to Roe.

having much influence on the corporations in which they invest. Bank-managed trust funds may not put more than 10 percent of their assets into the stock of any one company. And, if banks are to retain the right to trade the stock freely, they must maintain a "Chinese Wall" to separate their investing activities from their lending activities. If, for example, executives in the corporate loan department of a bank were to tip off the trust fund managers that a client corporation was having trouble meeting its loan repayment schedule, then the trust fund manager could not trade on that information without running the risk of violating the prohibitions against trading on inside information.[6]

For many years, banks were major suppliers of short-term (working capital) loans to large corporations, but since the mid-1970s, the "commercial paper" markets have become deep enough and sophisticated enough that most large companies can obtain working capital by issuing short-term notes ("commercial paper") and selling them in public securities markets.[7] Banks continue to provide extensive services to corporations and are important lenders primarily to small and medium-sized companies that do not have access to the commercial paper markets.[8] But even in those companies where they may be major lenders, banks face the problem of "equitable subordination," which restricts how much they can use their lending clout to try to influence corporate management. If a company defaults on its loans and files for bankruptcy protection, for example, any party that is deemed to have had a significant amount of influence over that company's business decisions (including a bank

---

[6]McVea (1993).

[7]Since the late 1970s, a special type of mutual fund, the "money market fund," has emerged as a major investor in commercial paper.

[8]Ralph T. King, Jr., and Steven Lipin, "New Profit Center: Corporate Banking, Given Up for Dead, Is Reinventing Itself," *Wall Street Journal*, January 13, 1994, p. A1.

whose executives had advised the company's directors about a major acquisition or other investments) might find that the debt claims it holds against the company are "subordinated" to other claims in the bankruptcy settlement. If it could be shown that the bank manipulated the corporation to its own benefit, the bank could also be liable for damages to the other creditors.[9] The combination of legal limits on equity holdings and the potential subordination of debt claims has effectively precluded banks from playing an active role in corporate governance in this country.

Banks play a much more prominent role in the governance of both Japanese and European companies. In Japan banks may hold up to 5 percent of a given company's shares, but their influence vastly exceeds the direct influence implied by a 5 percent voting stake. Large Japanese companies typically have a multitiered relationship with their "main banks," which typically also hold significant positions in other affiliated companies within the same *keiretsu*, or industrial trading group. *Keiretsu* member companies, in turn, hold each other's equity. Collectively, Japanese banks and other financial institutions (such as insurance companies) hold about 40 percent of the equity in Japanese corporations, and other corporations hold another 30 percent.[10] These cross-holdings mean that, for most companies, more than half of their stock is in the hands of other commercial and financial companies within their own group. If a *keiretsu* member company encounters financial difficulty, the main bank often arranges for special financing packages to enable the company to restructure its financial obligations and sends senior executives to serve on the board of the troubled company until the problems are resolved.[11]

[9]Lee (1990, pp. 91–107).
[10]Porter (1992, p. 42, table 2).
[11]Aoki (1993b).

Germany and France place no limits on bank shareholdings in other corporations, except those imposed by the size of the bank's capital. In Germany most companies have a strong relationship with one large bank (the *hausbank*), whose executives usually sit on the supervisory board of the company. The European Community is tightening these rules somewhat. Under the second EC banking directive, banks will not be permitted to invest more than 15 percent of their capital in a single nonfinancial company.[12]

Insurance Companies

Insurance companies collectively hold about $2.5 trillion in assets, 5.8 percent of all financial assets in the United States.* Insurance companies are regulated at the state level, and state laws all limit the extent to which they can invest in corporate equities. Although the limits vary somewhat from state to state, life insurance companies typically may put only about 20 percent of their assets into corporate equities, and often only a fraction of that (2 percent of total assets in New York state, for example) may be invested in a single company.[13] Property and casualty companies are not allowed to control noninsurance companies.[14]

Insurance companies often invest in the debt securities of major corporations, but holders of debt securities have few control rights in corporations unless the company defaults or files for bankruptcy protection. If that happens, the holder of the debt securities would not want to be found to have exercised too much influence over the

---

[12]See Fukao (1995) for a comparison of rules governing equity ownership by banks in five countries.

[13]For most of this century, New York-regulated life insurers were barred from owning any stock. See Roe (1993a, p. 651).

[14]Roe (1991b, pp. 22–23).

*Board of Governors of Federal Reserve System (1994, Tables L.121 and L.122).

company, or, as in the case of banks, its claims against the company could be moved to the end of the line. Thus insurance companies, like banks, have been almost completely passive investors in corporations.

Mutual Funds and Investment Companies

Although many mutual funds invest a large proportion of their portfolios in common stock, they face severe restrictions on how they can use their investments to influence corporate managements. The Investment Company Act of 1940 restricts the ability of mutual funds or other investment companies to take concentrated equity positions in the firms in which they invest if they advertise themselves as diversified investment companies. Meanwhile, the tax code imposes significant tax penalties on investment companies that are not diversified by forbidding them to pass income through to their shareholders for tax purposes.[15] Thus the income earned by a company in which an undiversified mutual fund invests could be taxed three times, once as income to the company, a second time as income to the mutual fund, and a third time as income to the shareholder in the mutual fund. This potential for triple taxation gives mutual funds a strong incentive to structure themselves so that they meet the diversification rules.

A diversified mutual fund is permitted to invest up to one quarter of its portfolio in a concentrated way, but if it owns 5 percent or more of the equity of a company, the portfolio company is considered an "affiliate" of the mutual fund. This inhibits the mutual fund from involving itself in the affairs of the company for several reasons. First, mutual funds may not engage in certain kinds of transactions with affiliates without prior approval from the Securities and Exchange Commission. Second, all other investment companies or

[15]Roe (1991b).

individuals who own at least 5 percent of the equity of the portfolio company are also considered affiliates of the mutual fund. A mutual fund cannot collaborate with other affiliates to choose or elect a director or assert its influence in other ways, nor can it engage in certain kinds of transactions with such affiliates, without prior SEC approval. The rule was intended to prevent officers, directors, or other people connected with the mutual fund from engaging in self-dealing transactions at the expense of the fund. One effect of this rule, however, is to discourage groups of mutual funds from trying to exercise joint control over a company. For example, if ten different otherwise unaffiliated mutual funds each owned a little more than 5 percent of a given company, the group of funds would collectively hold a controlling position. But the group could not exercise that control without approval from the SEC.[16]

Mutual funds and other investment companies are also limited by the Hart-Scott-Rodino Act of 1976, which requires any company actively investing in any other company to notify the Justice Department and the Federal Trade Commission.[17] Investment companies are exempted from this filing requirement if their purpose is "investment only," but to meet this test, they must be completely passive investors.

For the most part, these rules have kept mutual funds from actively monitoring and trying to influence the corporations in which they invest, although some funds are now testing the limits of these restrictions and seeking ways around them. In 1986, for example, Fidelity Investments asked shareholders of its Magellan Fund to approve a charter change eliminating the prohibition against invest-

[16]Roe (1991a).

[17]Both the investing company and the target company must also meet certain size tests.

ing in companies for the sake of exercising control.[18] Fidelity general counsel Robert Pozen has also said that Fidelity would not automatically support management when voting on various corporate issues.[19] A few investment banks have also set up so-called "patient capital" funds with the goal of taking large equity positions in limited numbers of underperforming companies and providing management advice and expertise or pressuring directors, if necessary, to help turn these companies around. These funds—which include the 1818 Fund, established by Brown Brothers Harriman, and the Allied Investment Partners fund, established by Dillon, Read—are set up as limited partnerships with fewer than a hundred investors, however, so that the restrictions of the Investment Company Act do not apply. Moreover, because they are partnerships rather than corporations, the investors receive "pass through" tax treatment, which allows partnership profits to be passed through to the individual investors without first being treated as taxable income to the fund itself.

Pension Funds

Pension funds are the least regulated of the four categories of financial institutions considered here. The total financial assets held by

[18]Magellan Fund executives explained in the fund's proxy filing that it wanted to be able to engage in activities such as "seeking changes in a portfolio company's directors or management, seeking changes in a company's direction, seeking the sale of a company or a portion of its assets, or participating in a takeover effort or in opposition to a takeover," but that it did not "intend to become involved in directing or administering the day-to-day operations of any portfolio company." Magellan executives said that its management believed that Magellan was already entitled to do the things it was seeking permission for but that it wanted to clarify the matter to head off potential lawsuits or other litigation. See "Fidelity Magellan Fund Notice of Special Meeting of Shareholders," December 8, 1986, pp. 1, 17.

[19]Susan Pulliam, "Big Investors, Even Money Managers, Join Activist Ranks for Better Bottom Lines," Wall Street Journal, February 5, 1993, p. C1.

pension funds are not as great as those held by any of the other three categories, but pension funds hold more corporate equities than the other categories; indeed, these funds hold more than 25 percent of all corporate equities. But like the other three groups, their holdings are spread out among thousands of funds. Although a few large pension funds have been active in corporate affairs in recent years, most funds are small and have not gotten involved in governance issues.

There are three major subcategories of pension funds, and each faces a somewhat different set of incentives and constraints with regard to engaging in corporate governance activities.

Private (employer-sponsored) defined-benefit plans. Defined-benefit pension plans represent the largest category of private pension plans.[20] In a defined-benefit plan, the employer commits to paying retirees a certain level of benefits and is supposed to set funds aside in a trust fund as the benefits are earned (usually as wages are paid) to pay these benefits. These funds are regulated and supervised by the Department of Labor under the terms of the Employee Retirement Income Security Act of 1974 (ERISA). Under ERISA rules, the payments into the trust fund are supposed to be based on reasonable actuarial estimates of the amount that will be needed at the time the benefits are to be paid. Technically, the employer bears the investment risk associated with the trust fund. If the fund earns a higher rate of return than projected, the employer can reduce its contributions in later years and still meet its commitments to pay promised benefits. But if the trust fund fails to earn a high enough return, the employer is liable for making up the difference.

---

[20]Lakonishok, Shleifer, and Vishny (1992, p. 340) report that more than 80 percent of all pension money was in defined-benefit plans at the end of 1990. More than two-thirds of these assets were in private pension fund accounts; the rest were in public employee plans.

Although the employer bears the risk in principle, employees and retirees are likely to suffer if the pension fund fails. So ERISA rules are designed to prevent self-dealing behavior on the part of employers and to discourage them from taking excessive risks with pension fund assets. The rules forbid such plans to put more than 10 percent of their assets into the sponsoring company and impose strict fiduciary responsibilities on plan trustees that have encouraged pension funds to diversify very broadly.[21] Pension funds also could lose their tax exempt status if they tried to exercise control over an industrial company.

These legal constraints discourage corporate-sponsored pension funds from taking an active role in monitoring corporations, a position that is reinforced by a pension fund culture of passivity regarding corporate governance and, some critics charge, by tacit understandings among executives of sponsoring companies not to use their pension funds to nose around in each other's business.[22] Pension fund managers typically report to the executives of the sponsoring company, who are likely to be displeased if their pension fund pushes for governance reforms, complains about poor performance, or generally makes a pest of itself at some other company. Such

[21]Despite its goal of encouraging prudent pension fund management, ERISA has been criticized for being cumbersome and administratively expensive and for failing to ensure that employers contribute enough to the plans to cover the benefits they promise. ERISA-regulated pension plans are also required to buy insurance through the Pension Benefit Guaranty Corporation (PBGC) that guarantees retirees most of their benefits even if the sponsoring company and its pension fund fail. As a result, employers with responsible, fully funded plans are finding that they have to pay high insurance rates to protect irresponsible employers, and many of the well-funded plans are bailing out of the system by restructuring themselves into defined-contribution plans, which do not have to insure themselves through the PBGC. The funds that remain under PBGC insurance are increasingly the underfunded plans. See Alvin D. Lurie, "Reform Pension Reform," *Wall Street Journal*, December 7, 1993, p. A14.

[22]O'Barr and Conley (1992) use anthropological methodologies to study the cultures in the offices of nine institutional investors, including several pension funds.

activism by one company's pension fund might very well be perceived as an attack on the executives of the other company and could provoke a retaliatory attack on the sponsoring company's executives.[23]

Nonetheless, a few straws in the wind suggest that the trustees of defined-benefit plans are growing more sensitive to corporate governance issues and may become more active. First, the Labor Department has ruled that the fiduciary duties of pension fund trustees require them to exercise the vote of the shares under their control.[24] And trustees are required to vote those shares according to what they regard as the "economic best interest of a plan's participants and beneficiaries, in their capacity as participants and beneficiaries"—that is, in their capacity as investors, not, for example, in their capacity as company employees.[25] This requirement means pension fund trustees may no longer passively vote with management, or fail to vote at all, but must consider the issues carefully, vote their shares, and be prepared with a defensible explanation for their vote.

Pension fund sponsors also have an incentive to see that their pension plans earn the highest return possible for a given risk level. If investor activism can be shown to increase returns without significantly adding to the risks, then fund managers will be encouraged to engage in such activism. A few companies are already testing their wings in this new arena. Campbell's Soup Co., for example, has

---

[23]Roe (1993b, pp. 104–7) argues that control of pension assets by the sponsoring company management is the single most important impediment to activism by these institutions.

[24]See letter from Alan Lebowitz, deputy assistant secretary of Labor, to Helmuth Fandl, chairman of the Retirement Board of Avon Products Inc., February 23, 1988. This so-called "Avon letter" is widely cited as the Labor Department's official position on fiduciary obligations of pension fund managers to vote the shares under their management.

[25]See Department of Labor and Department of Treasury, "Statement on Pension Fund Investments," news release, January 31, 1989.

instituted several shareholder-oriented governance reforms within its own hierarchy and has committed its pension fund managers to an activist approach to monitoring and voting at the companies in which the fund invests.[26] And by early 1994 fifteen corporate pension plans had joined forces with the activist Council of Institutional Investors, which had previously represented primarily public employee and union pension plans (see below).

The Labor Department under the Clinton administration has made increased pension fund activism in corporate governance a high priority.[27] The department is urging employer-sponsored pension funds to draw up procedures for exercising their proxies and is advising them on corporate governance issues and the legal procedures for voting proxies. Labor Secretary Robert Reich has also encouraged pension funds to monitor employment practices in their portfolio companies to help promote greater worker training and involvement in decisionmaking.[28] And several key officials in the administration are interested in broadening the voting criteria plan trustees must consider in voting the shares of portfolio companies to include the total well-being of the plan participants and beneficiaries (as employees and community members, for example, and not just as investors).[29]

One special category of pension plans are multiemployer plans covering union workers. Almost always of the defined-benefit type, these plans are sometimes called "Taft-Hartley" plans, after the Taft-Hartley Act of 1947. This law revised the National Labor Rela-

[26]Susan Pulliam, "Campbell Soup Fund to Take Activist Role," *Wall Street Journal*, July 15, 1993, p. C1. See also Campbell Soup Board of Directors (1994).

[27]See "Secretary Reich Advocates Corporate Activist Role for Pension Plans," U.S. Department of Labor news release, July 28, 1994.

[28]See Kevin G. Salwen and Leslie Scism, "Corporate Pensions Face Proxy Rules," *Wall Street Journal*, December 14, 1993, p. C1.

[29]See Leslie Wayne, "Seeking Investment with Principle," *New York Times*, August 10, 1033, p. D1.

tions Act in a way that forced such plans to be jointly administered by boards consisting of employer and union trustees. Most multi-employer plans have always used conservative investment strategies, with a narrow goal of enhancing value for beneficiaries, but a few multiemployer plans have a long history of investing their assets to "enhance social, political and economic power" of the unions.[30] That such a broad and ill-defined agenda carried the potential for serious abuse and misappropriation of pension assets became painfully apparent with the discovery that corruption plagued the management of the Teamsters Union pension funds from the 1950s through the mid-1970s. Repeated investigations by the Department of Labor, prosecutions, and class action lawsuits by union members against the pension funds of Teamsters' locals and their trustees eventually led to changes in the culture of multiemployer funds, and by 1990 these plans were much more conservatively managed than single-employer plans. Multiemployer plans typically invest in financial securities that are more liquid and stable than equities, and they hold comparatively more cash equivalents and real estate.[31] Union pension funds do hold some equities however, and have stepped up their involvement in corporate governance, submitting a total of seventy shareholder proposals at more than fifty companies in the 1994 proxy season.[32]

Private (employer-sponsored) defined-contribution plans. A variety of provisions in the tax laws encourage employers to set up "defined-contribution" pension plans in which the employer, the employee, or both commit to setting aside a certain amount on a regular basis to provide retirement benefits. These contributions are typically

---

[30]Ghilarducci (1992, pp. 45–46).

[31]Ghilarducci (1992, p. 48).

[32]Adam Bryant, "Subtler than a Picket Line," *New York Times*, April 17, 1994, Sec. 3, p. 7.

handled in one of three ways: they go into professionally adminis-tered trust funds, they go into privately administered funds such as "401(k)" plans, or they are managed by investment companies. TIAA-CREF, for example, administers retirement savings for many of the nation's teachers and college professors. In defined-contribution plans, the employees and retirees bear the investment risk and have some control over how the funds are invested. If the investments earn a high return, the employee gets the benefit, but if they earn a low return, or decline in value, the employee bears the loss. These plans are eligible for many of the same tax benefits that defined-benefit plans are. The employer contribution is tax-deductible to the employer but is not treated as income to the employee until the money is taken out at retirement, and employee contributions, within certain limits, are also made with pretax income. Earnings and capital gains that stay in the fund are not taxable. But these plans escape the most onerous of the ERISA regulations and the requirement that they be insured through the Pension Benefit Guar-anty Corp.

The advantages to employers of using defined-contribution plans have helped make this the fastest-growing category of pension funds.[33] But these funds have not so far been a center of shareholder activism. This is partly because the individual accounts are typically quite small—401(k) accounts are set up separately for each em-ployee, for example—and partly because they are not administered in a coordinated way. Most individuals with assets in 401(k) plans make conservative investments in, for example, high-grade bonds or

---

[33]Clark (1992, p. 67) reports that in 1977, 77 percent of major pension plans, covering 89 percent of all covered workers, were defined-benefit types, with most of the remaining 11 percent covered by defined-contribution plans. By 1983 defined-con-tribution plans represented 29 percent of all plans and covered 17 percent of partici-pants. Anecdotal evidence suggests that the shares have grown considerably since then.

mutual funds. The latter, of course, face the same impediments to shareholder activism that mutual funds face.

TIAA-CREF, which manages $125 billion, is the largest single adminstrator of defined-contribution retirement savings. But TIAA-CREF is really two companies: TIAA (Teachers Insurance and Annuity Association) is an insurance company and is regulated as such, while CREF (College Retirement Equity Fund) is an investment company, regulated like a mutual fund. TIAA-CREF has historically been conservative in its investment approach. It actively manages only about a third of its portfolio and has the remaining two-thirds of its portfolio "indexed." An indexed fund holds securities in the same proportion as they exist in some market index, buying or selling only to adjust its portfolio at the margins so that it continues to represent a fraction of the market tracked by the index. For example, a large indexed fund could buy shares in all of the S&P 500 companies so that it held, say, one-tenth of one percent of every company in the index. If there were no costs of administration, that fund would always perform exactly like the S&P 500 index. Indexed funds are typically extremely passive investors because their investment strategy is based not on trying do a good job of picking companies in which to invest, but on keeping transactions costs as low as possible and riding the movements of the whole market.[34] Thus indexed funds, by definition, do not make money by doing a better job of buying and selling stocks, and they cannot just walk away from stocks that are performing poorly.

TIAA-CREF chairman John H. Biggs has said that even the actively managed part of his fund generally takes long-term positions in the companies in which it invests, usually playing the role of quiet partner rather than vocal activist: "When we take a major

---

[34]Lakonishok, Shleifer, and Vishny (1992) conclude that such a strategy yields better performance, on average, than more active stock-picking strategies.

position in a company—and when we take a position, it's usually 2 percent of the outstanding stock of the company, running up to as high as 10 percent—we are on the phone on a regular basis with that company. We follow them very, very carefully. . . . We'll be regularly probing and questioning the management of the company."[35] Before 1994 the fund rarely sought to influence executive succession or other corporate policies through public statements about a company's management, although Biggs says it was occasionally more aggressive in the background. For example, in 1993 TIAA-CREF called about twenty other large pension funds to encourage them to vote against three Eastman Kodak directors running for reelection. In early 1995 CREF was a major force in pressuring W.R. Grace & Co. to oust its longtime chairman, J. Peter Grace, and restructure its board, and it was one of several institutional investors seeking the resignation of Kmart CEO Joseph E. Antonini.[36] Like other major users of the indexing strategy, TIAA-CREF has realized that, because it cannot always bail out of poorly performing companies, it may have some responsibility to use its ownership clout to try to improve the companies' performance. In this spirit, TIAA-CREF issued a "Policy Statement on Corporate Governance" in September 1993, providing a detailed statement of its views on shareholder rights, proxy voting issues, executive compensation policies, approaches to CEO performance evaluation, strategic planning, social responsibility issues, and organization of boards of direc-

[35]John H. Biggs, Remarks, Forum on Cooperation between Shareholders and Corporations, Investor Responsibility Research Center, Washington, October 27–28, 1993.

[36]Leslie Scism, "Teachers' Pension Plan to Give Firms Tough Exams," Wall Street Journal, October 6, 1993, p. C1; Randall Smith and James P. Miller, "W.R. Grace Under Pressure to Break Up Following the Ouster of the Chairman," Wall Street Journal, March 20, 1995, p. A2; and Stephanie Strom, "Kmart Chief Resigns Post Immediately," New York Times, March 22, 1995, p. D1.

tors and encouraging dialogue between TIAA-CREF and companies.[37]

Public employee pension funds. Public employee pension funds, such as the State of Wisconsin Investment Board, the California Public Employee Retirement System (CalPERS), and the New York City Retirement Systems, are also growing quickly. In 1994 they controlled about $495 billion worth of corporate equities, or 8.4 percent of all outstanding equity; in 1980 they held less than 3 percent.

Although not officially regulated by ERISA, most public employee plans are of the defined-benefit type, meaning that the employer (a state or local government entity) bears the investment risk, and the plans usually adhere to the same fiduciary rules as ERISA-regulated plans. Thus diversification requirements typically limit their ability to take concentrated positions in individual corporations. Before the late 1980s, public employee pension funds tended to be very passive investors.

Nonetheless, several scholars and observers have concluded that public employee funds are "the institutions with the greatest freedom to use their resources to exercise voice" in corporate governance.[38] One of the first studies to look at the role public employee pension funds should be playing was put together by a task force assembled by Governor Mario Cuomo in New York in 1989. That study identified four new obligations that it said should govern the behavior of pension funds. These are a "duty to monitor," a "duty to communicate" with management, a "duty to participate in corpo-

[37]"TIAA-CREF Policy Statement on Corporate Governance," New York, September 30, 1993.

[38]Taylor (1990b, p. 72), who cautions, however, that public employee funds may be the "least equipped to [exercise voice] effectively."

rate governance," including evaluating voting proxies, and a "duty of accountability."[39]

Indeed, some of the most activist institutional investors in recent years have been the public employee funds. For example, several of the largest funds, led by CalPERS CEO Dale Hanson, caused a stir in 1990 when they wrote a letter to the directors of General Motors asking them to explain their procedure for evaluating candidates to succeed Roger Smith as chairman. Some corporate executives and directors regarded the letter as extraordinarily impudent. GM chairman Smith reportedly called the governor of California to complain that CalPERS was out of line.[40]

How the Big Pension Funds Are Flexing Their Muscles

Although CalPERS has been among the most visible of the activist institutions, many others have also begun to flex their muscles. Despite the multitude of legal constraints that have kept most financial intermediaries out of corporate board rooms, public employee pension funds, union pension funds, and a few other financial institutions have begun organizing themselves so that their voice would be heard. In 1985, for example, Jesse Unruh, state treasurer of California, and Roland Machold, director of the New Jersey Division of Investment, organized the Council of Institutional Investors, which has lobbied for legislation and SEC rulings to strengthen the hand of shareholders—including institutional investors—in corporate governance. Shortly after that, former ERISA executive and shareholder activist Robert Monks, and his associate Nell Minow

---

[39]Our Money's Worth: The Report of the Governor's Task Force on Pension Fund Investment, New York State Industrial Cooperation Council, New York, 1989.
[40]Taylor (1990b).

formed the Institutional Investors Service, which provides institutional investors with information on upcoming governance matters at individual corporations and encourages them to vote their shares for reforms that would strengthen shareholder voice.

Initially, these groups put most of their energy into trying to prevent managers from instituting antitakeover measures in their firms. These activists attacked greenmail, poison pills, golden parachutes, "crown jewel" sales, manipulation of voting rights, debt-based recapitalizations, and other devices that corporate managers use to ward off unwanted takeovers. Institutional shareholders mounted campaigns against poison pills at more than fifty corporations in 1987, for example.[41] They also advocated federal laws to protect the rights of shareholders, fought state antitakeover laws, and waged media campaigns in behalf of their position. Institutional investors testified in hearings against Pennsylvania's antitakeover law, for example; the law was passed anyway in 1990 but provided that companies could decide not to avail themselves of the protections it offered. CalPERS and others then sent letters to Pennsylvania companies in which they held stock asking them to opt out of parts of the law that the institutional investors most vigorously opposed. More than 60 percent of all *Fortune* 500 companies with headquarters there did so under threats by institutional investors to sell out their positions.[42] The activist institutions had plenty of allies in this effort among academic theorists and finance market specialists, who were convinced that takeovers had been reforming the corporate sector and that management efforts to impede takeovers were designed only to protect management from that discipline.

---

[41]George Anders, "Institutional Holders Irked by 'Poison Pills,'" *Wall Street Journal*, March 10, 1987, p. 6.

[42]Monks and Minow (1995, pp. 40, 151).

Largely because of that early protakeover stance, most corporate executives were initially wary of activist pension fund managers. But the executives' desire for "patient" capital has made them look at pension funds in a new light. Pension funds, it turns out, have several characteristics that distinguish them from the Wall Street money managers so despised by corporate executives for their asset churning, their herd instincts, and their focus on quarterly earnings. First, pension funds have predictable inflows and outflows, so liquidity is less important to them than it is to other kinds of financial institutions. Moreover, the actuarial factors that drive pension fund investment strategies permit them to buy and hold for a long time. Traditionally, many pension fund trustees have turned over a large part of their assets to money managers who actively buy and sell stocks in an effort to increase returns. But the evidence is mounting that such strategies cannot consistently beat the market averages by enough to justify all the transactions charges.[43] As a result, several large pension funds have adopted strategies such as indexing that greatly reduce their asset churning and increase their average holding periods. Pension funds covering New York state employees, for example, have nearly 80 percent of their portfolios indexed.[44] The annual turnover rate of stocks in the CalPERS portfolio is only about 10 percent (which implies an average holding period of ten years), versus about 50 percent for mutual funds.[45]

Second, the largest pension funds have become so large that their portfolios, of necessity, tend to mirror the whole economy. They cannot easily buy and sell large stakes in individual companies

[43]Lakonishok, Shleifer, and Vishny (1992). Jacobs (1993) has also assembled a large amount of anecdotal evidence to this same effect.

[44]Edward V. Regan, former state controller of New York, now president of the Jerome Levy Economics Institute, private correspondence with the author, Spring 1994.

[45]Hanson (1992).

because their holdings are big enough to move the market. More important, they are much less likely to be interested in engaging in "zero-sum" or "net negative" financial transactions. Pension fund portfolios are so diversified that they are likely to have positions on both sides of most transactions and would therefore oppose transactions that do not create more value on one side than they destroy on the other. Major pension funds provide the highest growth and return for their beneficiaries when the whole economy is growing fastest, and there is very little they can do at the margins to alter that.[46]

These characteristics have led several policy analysts, legal scholars, and others to conclude that corporate management might be better off cultivating financial institutions, particularly pension funds, as active investors, rather than resisting them. "Properly informed, institutional investors . . . may be the long-term owners that managements say they need," lawyer Ira Millstein has suggested.[47]

Institutional investors lost many of their early efforts to crack open the doors to corporate boardrooms. Hundreds of companies succeeded in putting antitakeover measures into place despite the opposition from institutional investors, and nearly every state passed some kind of antitakeover law. But, by the late 1980s, separately and through their new organizations, the institutional investors—especially the public employee and union pension funds—had begun to find their voice. This group is potentially a new political and economic power base, separate from management, separate from

[46]Sarah Teslik, executive director of the Council of Institutional Investors, put it well in a recent newsletter to her members: "Moving in and out of investments in more-or-less efficient markets only puts you ahead if you do it better than others—enough better to cover significant costs plus a bit more. This is . . . virtually impossible if you have to place $50 billion, and keep it invested for years. . . . Fiduciaries of large pension funds ought . . . to be asking if there are other things they can do that will affect all of their investments." Teslik (1993, p. 4).

[47]Millstein (1992, p. 43).

Wall Street, separate from the raiders, separate from the investment bankers. In fact, pension fund managers are unlike any group that has ever before played a role in the governance of U.S. corporations. Many of them came out of the labor movement or are career public servants or politicians.[48] Potentially, they could ally with management, Wall Street, or even labor, but for now they are their own new power center.

In the last few years, pension funds and a few other activist institutional investors (such as CREF and Fidelity Investments) have been trying new ways to exercise this influence. They have used publicity campaigns as bully pulpits to chastize companies that were not performing well, executives who were too highly paid given their performance, and companies that were otherwise not taking the funds' interests into account adequately or giving them the respect they wanted. In the late 1980s CalPERS, still at the lead, began publishing an annual list of poorly performing companies that it intended to target with governance reform proposals. In 1993 the Council of Institutional Investors also published a list of underperforming companies. The clear implication was that its members might consider acting collectively to address the problems at these companies. The institutions have also lobbied for changes in the proxy rules to make it easier for them to communicate among themselves. And they have pressured boards of directors into meeting with them outside of regular annual meetings.

---

[48]Industrialist Charles Wohlstetter (1993, p. 78) snidely suggests that "if the pension fund bureaucrats possessed the skills necessary for running great corporations, they would not be satisfied with government salaries, no matter how high, but would bless the corporate world with their extraordinary insights. . . . We have a group of people with increasing control of the Fortune 500 who have no proven skills in management, no experience at selecting directors, no believable judgment in how much should be spent for research or marketing—in fact, no experience except that which they have accumulated controlling other people's money."

More important, they have been winning. In 1991 the SEC made it easier for shareholders to get certain kinds of shareholder resolutions (including those relating to executive compensation) on the ballot. And in 1992, the SEC instituted two new rule changes that clearly shift power away from corporate management and toward activist shareholders. The first eased the proxy solicitation rules so that shareholders could more easily communicate with each other without triggering the filing and preclearance requirements for a proxy solicitation. The second expanded the reporting requirements so that directors would have to explain and justify executive compensation packages in more detail in a company's proxy statements to shareholders.

Institutional investors have also prodded directors—through both behind-the-scenes negotiations and public exhortations—into acting more decisively to remove poorly performing managers. CalPERS and other institutional investors were vocal in their criticisms of former GM CEO Robert C. Stempel in 1992, for example, and, by some reports, were influential in getting GM's independent directors to press for Stempel's resignation.[49] The success of the institutions at embarrassing GM directors sent shock waves through boardrooms all over the country, galvanizing directors into greater attentiveness and activism in many companies, as well as into greater responsiveness to the desires of pension fund executives.[50]

Since the early 1990s executives at several public pension funds have also sought, and been granted, quiet meetings with directors of companies they have targeted as underperformers. In 1990, for example,

---

[49]Joseph B. White and Paul Ingrassia, "Eminence Grise: Behind the Revolt at GM, Lawyer Ira Millstein Helped Call the Shots," *Wall Street Journal*, April 13, 1992, p. A1. In private conversations with the author, several GM independent directors denied that the public criticism directed at them by the big institutional investors influenced their decision to fire Stempel.

[50]Alison Leigh Cowan, "The High-Energy Board Room," *New York Times*, October 28, 1992, p. D1.

CalPERS voted its shares against the Lockheed board when raider Harold Simmons was trying to take over the company. Although Simmons lost, Lockheed's directors were shaken by CalPERS' opposition, and since 1991 Lockheed's chairman has met regularly with the company's institutional shareholders, instead of communicating with them only through Wall Street analysts as the company had previously done.[51] During a two-month period in late 1994 and early 1995, Time Warner chairman Gerald Levin held private meetings with at least five different large-block shareholders to bolster support for his strategic plans for the company.[52] Shareholders have also found alternatives to submitting shareholder proposals. TIAA-CREF, for example, reported in 1994 that it had submitted eighteen proposals during that proxy season but had successfully negotiated away fourteen of them before shareholders were given a chance to vote on them.[53]

Some companies have begun seeking out institutional investors to get their advice on such issues as how many independent directors should sit on their boards and who they should be.[54] In early 1993, for example, Champion International initiated discussions with its institutional shareholders, including CalPERS and the New York City Employees Retirement System, reportedly inviting them to suggest potential directors. The company was trying to head off a potentially embarrassing confrontation with shareholders at its annual meeting that spring.[55] Institutional investors have also suc-

[51]Richard W. Stevenson, "Large Foot in the Boardroom Door," *New York Times*, June 6, 1991, p. D1.

[52]Geraldine Fabrikant, "Battling for Hearts and Minds at Time Warner," *New York Times*, February 26, 1995, p. F9.

[53]Investor Responsibility Research Center, *Corporate Governance Bulletin*, March–April 1994.

[54]Christi Harlan, "Ten Companies Are Targeted for Action," *Wall Street Journal*, October 6, 1993, p. B1.

[55]Susan Pulliam, "Paper Company Initiates Meetings with Big Holders," *Wall Street Journal*, February 18, 1993, p. A5.

ceeded in passing anti-poison-pill resolutions at a few companies,[56] and in one thirteen-month period, from November 1992 through December 1993, they helped force turnover in top management at American Express, Borden, GM, IBM, Kodak, and Westinghouse.

The Promise of "Relationship Investing"

The effort to define a new and constructive role for institutional investors has generated a new phrase for the lexicon of corporate governance: "relationship investing." There is no agreement on a precise definition of relationship investing, but advocates most often describe it as a situation in which the investing institution is responsibly engaged in overseeing the management of the company, rather than remaining detached or passive, and is committed to the company for the "long term." Michael Jacobs uses the phrase "effective ownership" to describe this role, while Ira Millstein speaks of "knowledgeable and diligent ownership," and others often use phrases such as "real owner."[57] "Major institutions have exactly the right set of characteristics for playing the role of concerned, informed, but low-key monitor," asserts Harvard professor John Pound, one of the leading proponents of this approach to corporate governance.[58]

Advocates argue that involvement by institutional investors who hold a significant position in a company mitigates several of the problems that make it difficult for small, individual shareholders to

[56]The State of Wisconsin Investment Board led the successful drive to rescind a poison pill at Champion International, for example. See Brett Duvall Fromson, "The Big Owners Roar," *Fortune*, July 30, 1990, p. 74.

[57]Jacobs (1993); Millstein (1992, p. 53).

[58]Pound (1993, p. 7).

be "relationship investors." The first of these is the "collective action," or "free rider," problem. To be an effective monitor, an investor must expend resources. But more effective monitoring will benefit all investors, even if they have contributed nothing to cover the costs. Small individual investors therefore have an incentive to wait for someone else to do the job, hoping to get a free ride on someone else's efforts, and, as a result, the job may never get done. These free rider problems are easier to solve when the number of parties is smaller. As the number of investors required to control a company declines to, say, twenty or thirty large institutions, rather than thousands of individual investors, the possibility of coordinated action and cooperation increases.

Second, large institutional investors with many holdings may be more willing to absorb the costs of evaluating certain governance reforms because those costs can be spread across more investments. For example, an institution may be willing to support research investigating whether certain kinds of poison pill provisions help or hurt investors. Do they enable management to resist value-enhancing takeovers, or do they just help management get a higher price for the company once it becomes a takeover target? Once an institutional investor has expended the resources to research this issue and reach a decision at one company, it can apply its findings to dozens, or even hundreds, of other companies in its portfolio.[59]

Proponents of a more activist role in governance for pension funds and mutual funds also argue that these financial intermediaries are less likely to have commercial conflicts of interest that will bias their judgment about a company's choice of strategies or the performance of its executives. Unlike banks or insurance companies, for example, mutual funds and public employee pension funds are un-

[59]Black (1992a).

likely to be trying to win a contract or protect a relationship with a portfolio company that is also a client or customer.[60]

Several proponents of institutional activism also argue that enhancing the influence of institutional investors would benefit society because the interests of large institutional investors such as pension funds tend to coincide with the interests of society at large. Law professor Bernard Black argues, for example that an individual oil company may not find it profitable to invest in preventing oil spills, but a diversified fund that owns many oil companies would fully bear the costs of industry regulation and therefore would be more willing to support investments in preventing oil spills by all the companies in which it invests.[61] Robert Monks and Nell Minow add that pension funds "can be concerned with vocational education, pollution and retraining, whereas an owner with a perspective limited to a particular company or industry would consider these to be unacceptable expenses because of competitiveness problems."[62]

But many advocates of relationship investing caution that the benefits can come only if the investing institution is compelled to stay with the companies in which it invests. That can happen if the size of its stake keeps it locked in or if trading rules or other regulations discourage or prohibit it from selling. "Institutions should not expect to gain greater influence over management, without giving up some of their current trading flexibility," Michael Porter argues.[63] Lester Thurow is even more adamant on this point:

---

[60]Mutual funds may not be completely free of such pressures, because money managers elsewhere in their organization may be trying to win a contract to manage the assets in a company's pension funds. And public employee pension funds may be subject to political pressures that raise other concerns.

[61]Black (1992a).

[62]Monks and Minow (1995, p. 132). To date, however, institutional investors have rarely gotten involved in the kind of management minutia suggested by these arguments.

[63]Porter (1992, p. 74).

"We should also ensure that these institutions—or any shareholder with a dominant position in a company—cannot easily extricate themselves from that role. . . . The United States needs an economy in which finance cannot succeed unless industry succeeds. . . . [We should] put real capitalists back in charge of the American corporation and then box them in so that they have no choice but to improve the nation's productivity and competitiveness."[64]

These arguments reflect Albert O. Hirschman's analysis of the mechanisms available to members of a free society for responding to problems in their important social and governing institutions. In most instances, he said, the choice is between "exit" and "voice." In the case of problems with corporations, that means either selling one's shares or using the rights associated with holding shares to voice one's concerns and try to make changes.[65]

Appendix 5-1 highlights several reform proposals offered by proponents of relationship investing. These proposals address various features of the regulatory environment or of the culture of investment management that are believed to impede institutional activism in corporate governance. Some of them also tinker with the tax laws or with other rules to discourage investors from simply selling poorly performing stocks or to condition enhanced voice on adoption of impediments to exit.

Evidence on the Impact of Relationship Investing

So far, little systematic and direct evidence has been assembled about the effect on U.S. corporate performance of active institutional investors who hold their positions for extended periods of

---

[64]Thurow (1988, pp. 70–71).
[65]Hirschman (1970).

time without engaging in a takeover. This is an area ripe for further research. The evidence that has been brought to bear on the debate is generally either indirect or merely anecdotal. The success stories of extraordinary financiers, past and present, are often cited as examples of what committed, involved investor-owners can accomplish.[66] Other anecdotal evidence cites the performance of firms in Germany and Japan, where monitoring by institutional investors is believed by some scholars to be much more intense.

For the most part, advocates of greater activism by institutional investors rely heavily on indirect evidence to support their views. Professor Black argues that certain systematic tendencies in the behavior of corporations and their boards of directors reduce value and that, at least in theory, institutional influence could help to modify those behaviors. These shortfalls in performance show up in several ways, Black argues. Numerous studies, for example, show that bidders frequently overpay when they make an acqustion and that corporate executives of target companies often resist takeover offers that the stock market believes will be wealth enhancing.[67]

Institutional oversight can add substantial value, Black argues, "if the institutions or their representatives on boards of directors can discriminate" between good acquisitions and bad. Other indirect evidence shows that corporate governance arrangements affect the stock prices of companies. Black summarizes this body of evidence

---

[66]See, for example, Lowenstein (1991) and De Long (1991).

[67]Black (1992b) summarizes the empirical evidence for each of his propositions, but some of that evidence is contradictory. For example, Black cites studies showing that stock price reactions to unrelated acquisitions during the 1980s were negative and lower than returns to related acquisitions; he also cites evidence that stock prices often jump when a confirmed conglomerateur retires; and he cites studies showing that the positive stock price returns from the announcement of conglomerate acquisitions in the 1960s appear to reflect mistakes. Black does not say why the stock market reactions in the 1980s should be any more trustworthy than those of the 1960s, which turned out to be wrong.

too, concluding that "rules requiring a supermajority vote to approve a merger, authorizing blank check preferred stock, adopting a staggered board, or eliminating cumulative voting negatively affect stock prices."[68]

Lilli Gordon and John Pound summarize and critique many of these same studies, arguing, however, that the findings are more complex and difficult to interpret than one might at first think. Some studies show that governance changes making takeovers more difficult have no effect on stock prices, while others show a positive effect.[69] Moreover, they argue, anticipating how a governance change might affect stock prices is not straightforward. A governance change that served to entrench management would be expected to cause stock prices to fall, but if it also signals that management has internal information that it might be a takeover target, stock prices would be expected to rise.

Gordon and Pound analyze their own data on governance changes that inhibit takeovers in more than six hundred corporations and find that firms with no governance restrictions have higher-than-average valuations over the long run, but lower-than-average levels of internally generated resources. Conversely, firms that adopt a large number of new corporate governance protections have, on average, higher levels of internally generated resources and lower market valuation ratios than their industry peers. Gordon and Pound conclude that takeover protection mechanisms are most likely to be adopted by firms that have been relatively successful in the past (so they have high levels of internally generated resources) and that the main effect of such protections is to dampen external market pressures, giving the firms more maneuvering room in case they make investment mistakes in the future. One might also conclude that

[68]Black (1992b, p. 910)
[69]Gordon and Pound (1993). See also Gordon and Pound (1992).

firms that may need to go back to the equity markets to raise funds because their own internally generated resources are low cannot afford this luxury.[70]

In a separate study, Gordon and Pound assembled their own data on a small sample of firms in which a large block of stock was sold to an active, friendly investor who took a seat on the board. They show that, in this small sample, returns for the remaining common stockholders were only average, roughly mirroring the performance of the S&P 500, and that, except for companies in which Warren Buffet was the active investor, they may even have done worse than companies without active investors.[71] The authors provide no explanation for what it is that the successful friendly investors do that accounts for their better performance.

A study by Stephen L. Nesbitt, however, offers some weak evidence that efforts by institutional investors to monitor corporate managers more intensely can produce high returns. Nesbitt studied the performance of forty-two companies that were the target of CalPERS-led governance reform campaigns between 1987 and 1992. The average return for the targeted firms was 29 percent higher than the return on the S&P 500 in the five years after CalPERS initiated its actions with respect to those firms.[72] Nesbitt's findings break out in a very interesting way, however. The firms targeted by CalPERS in 1987, 1988, and 1989 did not perform as well, on average, as the S&P 500 over the subsequent five years. In most of these firms, CalPERS targeted pure governance issues, such as the adoption of

---

[70]This last point is my own interpretation. Gordon and Pound cast the issue slightly differently, arguing that the financial markets believe that the probability that a firm will make an investment error is higher when the firm has high levels of internally generated cash and that this is why such firms also have low valuation ratios.

[71]Gordon and Pound (1992, pp. 32–33).

[72]Nesbitt (1994). The reported returns have been adjusted for differences in risk. Unadjusted for risk, the targeted returns had a 41 percent better return.

poison pills or confidential voting rules. Sometime in 1990, CalPERS shifted strategies and began targeting firms for poor performance. The twenty-four firms targeted in 1990, 1991, and 1992 had subsequent returns that were 99 percent better than the return on the S&P 500 through the end of 1993.[73]

Nesbitt's findings are interesting, but they by no means prove that CalPERS' actions were responsible for the improved returns. CalPERS may simply be good at identifying troubled firms that directors and managements are already scrambling to fix. Moreover, CalPERS' actions amounted, in essence, to publicity campaigns, pointing out the underperformance of the targeted companies. It is unclear whether returns could be similarly improved at the hundreds of other underperforming companies, many of which are smaller and much less likely to attract media interest than, say, American Express, Chrysler, Salomon Brothers, Sears, Time Warner, or W. R. Grace, which were on CalPERS' hit list in 1990 or 1991.

The most systematic evidence to date of the effect of relationship investing was developed by Michael Fleming of the Federal Reserve Bank of New York. He examined data on investors who acquired a large equity stake in firms between 1985 and 1989 but who did not subsequently acquire the firms. He found that such investors did little to enhance the performance of the firms. He shows positive and significant market-adjusted returns to the stock of the target company during the first two months after the announcement of the investor's new position in the company but significant declines in the returns during the subsequent two years. Much of Fleming's sample consists of hostile large block acquisitions by corporate raiders and arbitrageurs such as Victor Posner and Ivan Boesky. Fleming's study also does not control for the presence of sharehold-

[73]Nesbitt (1994, p. 9). Again, the reported relative returns are adjusted for differences in risk.

ers who may have held large blocks of stock throughout the period studied.[74]

The Pitfalls of Relationship Investing

The idea that "relationship investing" by large institutional investors might solve some of the most intractable corporate governance dilemmas led to a rush of euphoria in the late 1980s and early 1990s. Finance model advocates thought they had found a less controversial and less disruptive alternative to corporate takeovers that would still discipline corporate management. Some corporate executives thought they had found a way to insist on more responsible behavior by their shareholders. The media seized on the idea as a brilliant new rescue plan for the corporate sector.[75] Shareholder groups, led by a few activist pension funds, won a larger voice at several major corporations. And academics, policymakers, and legal scholars produced dozens of studies calling for adjustments in certain financial market regulations, adoption of new tax incentives, and clarification of fiduciary duties, so that relationship investing would be free to take off.

By 1994, however, the initial euphoria had turned to studied caution. Several new investment funds and limited partnerships established as relationship-style funds in 1990 and 1991 were still trying to assemble large enough blocks of assets by early 1994 to

---

[74]Fleming (1993).

[75]*Business Week* said relationship investing "could be a tonic for the nation's economy," for example. Judith H. Dobrzynski, "Relationship Investing," *Business Week*, March 15, 1993, p. 75. And *Fortune* said that institutional investors "are the market's most discerning participants" and that they "offer what most managers profess to want." Michael Seely, "In Praise of Institutional Investors," *Fortune*, April 5, 1985, p. 167.

make them credible as major investors in targeted firms. The Lens Fund, headed by Robert Monks, by the spring of 1994 had failed to raise any outside funds toward its $1 billion goal; likewise, Allied Investment Partners had raised only a quarter of the $1 billion it sought. Lazard Freres & Co.'s Corporate Partners, which began in 1988 with $1.65 billion, had run into controversy with its investments in Phar-Mor, Inc. and had shown poor returns on "protective investments" it had made (designed to ward off takeovers) in companies such as Polaroid.[76]

These funds were designed to provide investment vehicles for pension fund managers interested in relationship investing. But their slow start seemed to result from confusion and uncertainty about exactly what relationship investing would mean in practice, as well as what strategies would work. Corporate Partners has had mixed returns with its cooperative approach, for example, while Monks has apparently put off the large institutional investors by his adversarial approach. Some studies suggest that the adversarial approach has produced impressive returns—Nesbitt's study of CalPERS' activism is a case in point—but the samples are small, and separating the effect of a unique contribution by the investor from the effect attributable to media hype is difficult. At any rate, some important potential investors such as CalPERS have been unwilling to make the large commitments to these investment funds that their sponsors had sought.

By late January 1994, scarcely a year after executives at American Express, IBM, and Westinghouse had been forced to resign under pressure from unhappy shareholders and boards of directors, an article in the *New York Times* asked whether shareholder activists had

---

[76]See Susan Pulliam, "CalPERS Won't Invest in Activist's Fund," *Wall Street Journal*, June 22, 1993, p. C1; and Kleiman, Nathan, and Shulman (1994). The Lens Fund continues, but primarily as a vehicle for Monks' personal fortune.

"lost their edge." The article noted several ways in which institutional shareholders had succeeded in gaining power, as well as ways in which managements and boards were accommodating the demands and expectations of the activist shareholders. "What will shareholders do now that a degree of peace has broken out and they have management's attention?" the article asked.[77]

The caution is warranted, because it is not at all clear that most institutional investors have anything of value to contribute to the governance of most companies. Although relationship investing of some type may be a viable strategy for a few major institutional investors and is likely to work for some specialized funds, most well-managed financial institutions are not likely, for several reasons, to try to emulate J. P. Morgan, even if the law permitted them to do so. And there are important reasons why it might not be such good public policy if they did.

Few Incentives

Even when it is done extremely well, as Warren Buffet and a handful of others have done, investing with the intent to hold the stock for the long term and to monitor and engage target company management in ongoing dialogue imposes costs. The investing institution must develop considerable expertise in the industry and in the specifics of the company in which it invests, both before and after it commits its funds. If the investing fund intends to diversify, these costs must be incurred for every company in the portfolio. As noted above, some advocates of institutional activism argue that pension funds and other financial institutions can easily develop policy posi-

[77]Leslie Wayne, "Have Shareholder Activists Lost Their Edge?" *New York Times,* January 30, 1994, p. D7.

tions regarding certain governance issues and apply them broadly to many companies. But in most cases the kinds of policy issues that lend themselves to this sort of wholesale assessment are unrelated to the most important value-creating activities of the company. As one critic put it, "How do shareholders vote on whether a company is introducing important new products fast enough, or on whether low morale among middle managers is hurting the implementation of brilliant strategic plans? The answer is, they don't."[78] Even an institution large enough to hold as much as 5 or 10 percent of the stock of companies in which it invests may still not be able to reap a large enough reward to justify the effort necessary to investigate and evaluate idiosyncratic matters affecting each company.

Michael Jacobs, Nell Minow, and other proponents of relationship investing argue that pension funds and other institutional investors should not try to micromanage the companies in which they invest, but should instead place their money with specialized funds who will undertake the monitoring service and develop the necessary expertise.[79] Some of these funds may prove successful at relationship-style investing. But this type of investing is likely to remain a tiny proportion of total equity investments in the United States. "I cannot imagine the United States accepting what in effect is control of its economy by private cartels," writes Peter Drucker, the famed management guru who, in the 1970s, wrote about the rapid development of pension plans as owners of corporate equity. "I also wouldn't know where to find the geniuses to run them. . . . I see no possibility at all of the thousands of pension funds—let alone the 250 very large ones that matter—entrusting their investment deci-

---

[78]Taylor (1990b, p. 78).

[79]Jacobs (1993); Monks and Minow (1995). All three authors are associated with organizations that are trying to provide such services or create such funds—Jacobs with Kurt Salmon Associates in Atlanta; Monks and Minow with the Lens Fund.

sions and their decisions on corporate management to these new financial capitalists."[80]

The high costs of developing sufficient information to monitor companies effectively enough to outperform the indexes was what drove many of the big pension funds to adopt indexing strategies in the 1980s. They found that neither they nor their money managers could develop enough expertise to know when to buy and when to sell. How reasonable is it, then, to expect them to develop enough expertise to know whether a three-year capital spending plan laid out by the CEO of a portfolio company should be adjusted up or down? Hindsight makes it easy to say that IBM overcommitted itself to mainframe computers and tried to be too many things to too many computer users. But even the best-informed investors still seemed satisfied with IBM's strategy right up until early 1991 when IBM's earnings and stock prices collapsed.[81] No evidence suggests that greater activism by the seven hundred or so institutional investors who hold about 31 percent of IBM's stock could have helped that company see its problems coming any sooner or solved the internal management problems any faster even if they had.

Should an institutional investor decide that it wants to take on the task of monitoring from a more knowledgeable vantage point, it could develop or acquire special expertise in certain areas and then

---

[80]Drucker (1991b, pp. 168–69). See also Drucker (1991a).

[81]IBM's earnings per share peaked in 1987 at $175.9 and then began slipping, but the company moved to shift its strategy and by 1988 had reversed the slide and appeared to be returning to health. Revenues per share and earnings per share peaked again in 1990, and the company's stock price peaked again in early 1991 at $139.75. The collapse of earnings at IBM in early 1991—and the corresponding collapse in the stock price—caught even the most seasoned financial analysts completely off-guard. See *Value Line Investment Survey*, Pt. 3: *Ratings and Reports*, 50 (January 27, 1995), p. 1094 for historical information on stock price, earnings per share, and revenue per share. See also Jeffrey M. Laderman, "Red-Faced over Big Blue: Why the Analysts Blew It," *Business Week*, April 8, 1991, pp. 77–78.

engage management in a dialogue about the special problems and opportunities facing the company. But if it does so, it may be compelled to accept limitations on its ability to sell the company's stock. For many institutions, the sacrifice of liquidity will simply not be worthwhile because it would undercut the advantage the investor would gain from expending the resources to develop the special knowledge. Columbia University law professor John C. Coffee, Jr., notes, for example, that very few bank holding companies come close to the level of share ownership permitted by law, which he says suggests that something other than the legal constraint on ownership is holding them back.[82]

Advocates of institutional activism argue that the presence of one or a few large institutions in a company would mitigate the free-rider problem. But the opposite could easily happen. As soon as one investor assumes the role of monitor, other investors might have less incentive than ever to expend the resources necessary to monitor the company. One solution is for the monitoring investor to cut a special deal with the company so that only that investor can reap most of the benefits of its monitoring. Warren Buffet's Berkshire Hathaway, for example, often invests in companies through special issues of preferred stock. Buffet invested $700 million in Salomon Brothers in 1987 by buying a special issue of preferred stock with a yield of 9 percent, convertible into common stock at Buffet's option. He thereby locked in a respectable return even if Salomon's performance stayed at the same level or declined, but he also ensured that he would enjoy the full fruits of any improvement in performance. In the first eighteen months after Buffet bought in, holders of Salomon's common stock suffered losses of 12.6 percent, while Buffet's convertible preferred shares continued to provide the promised 9 percent annual return.[83]

[82]Coffee (1991, p. 1320).
[83]Kleiman, Nathan, and Shulman (1994).

Such sweetheart arrangements set up a potential conflict of interest between the monitoring investor and the other investors. It is
exactly this type of conflict that the elaborate system of securities
laws in this country was designed to mitigate. These laws make it
difficult for investors to gain control, or even exercise significant
influence, without subjecting themselves to potential liability
claims from other creditors and investors and without accepting
limits on their ability to trade.

Although large public employee pension funds have demonstrated
that they can make waves in corporate boardrooms, relatively few
have done so, and William Taylor argues that relatively few more are
likely to become active in corporate boardrooms. Trustees of public
employee funds share two characteristics that constrain their activism, he says: "First, their personal agendas are more political than
economic. Second, none of them are chosen for their fiduciary role
based on their capacity to function as effective corporate owners."[84]
Robert Monks and Nell Minow point out a third problem: a trustee
or manager of a public pension funds "bears none of the risk of loss
if the value of the investment declines; his own career progress is
only tangentially related to the performance of a particular company;
. . . he appears to be prohibited from involving himself as a director
in the affairs of the company; and it is virtually inconceivable that
even the most outstanding performance will result in personal
profit—pecuniary or otherwise."[85]

Questionable Social Benefits

This last problem—that pension fund managers are unlikely to
have the right incentives to be effective corporate monitors—sug-

---

[84]Taylor (1990b, p. 72).
[85]Monks and Minow (1995, p. 161).

gests why encouraging financial institutions to play that role might be poor public policy. Designating institutional investors as the monitors of the corporate sector does not solve the agency problem inherent in the widely traded corporate form, but exacerbates it by adding yet another layer of oversight between management and the ultimate beneficiaries of the wealth-creating activities of corporations. It is already the job of boards of directors to monitor management and to insist that the company create value for investors. If shareholders are invested in the company through a pension fund, and pension fund managers are expected to look over the shoulders of boards of directors who are supposed to be monitoring management, another layer has been added between management and shareholders. If pension fund managers turn their portfolios over to investment fund managers who are supposed to monitor boards of directors, then still another layer has been created. These extra layers of monitors, each one further removed from the ultimate beneficiary, seem highly unlikely to enhance the effectiveness of the monitoring that gets done. The same questions about incentives and accountability that were first raised by separating management from equity ownership arise for each additional level of monitoring.

Some of those who argue that institutional investors should have a much stronger role in the governance of U.S. corporations are simply misinterpreting the analogies to governance structures in Japan and Germany. Japanese corporate ownership and control is decidedly *not* in the hands of otherwise disinterested financial institutions, but is, as Taylor puts it, "built around reciprocal shareholdings between companies and their banks, suppliers and customers. . . . What most distinguishes these *keiretsu* industrial groups is the vast amount of information sharing and expertise transfer. . . . Another big difference between the U.S. and Japan [is that], since big owners have other business relationships with group companies, they have opportunities for creative problem solving during periods of trouble. . . . Shareholders can sacrifice some value in their equity stake in return for other financial benefits that grow out of their group relationship."[86]

The shareholder rights advocates in this country would scream that such multilayered relationships are poisoned by "conflicts" of interest. Such advocates believe that companies should be run solely for shareholders and that introducing other interests into the board-room threatens this primary interest. To that end, they argue, for example, that corporate directors should be "independent," that is, directors should have no relationship whatsoever to the company on whose board they serve, except that they are themselves sharehold-ers.

I argue in the following chapters that individuals whose only interest in a company is ownership of common stock also have skewed incentives. A firm that wants to maximize its total wealth-creation activity must pay attention to the costs, rewards, and risks imposed on other stakeholders in the firm. A director who represents only shareholders may be in a poor position to understand and weigh the effects of the company's actions on these other stakeholders. By contrast, directors who represent multiple stakeholders and who understand their job to be maximizing the total wealth creation of the firm, are more likely to be sensitive to these other effects.

An example illustrates the point. Institutional investors with diversified portfolios care not about "firm-specific" risk, but only about the "systematic" risk in their total portfolio of investments. The overall return on an institution's portfolio will be higher for a given level of overall risk if all the firms in the portfolio engage in highly risky strategies that have very high payoffs (if they succeed), as long as the probabilities of failure are uncorrelated across firms in the portfolio. The successes will more than make up for the failures, and the institutional investor will be happy to move its capital as

---

[86]Taylor (1990b), p. 81.

quickly as possible from failing companies to succeeding companies. In effect, the institution does not really care about the individual failures.

Advocates of institutional activism hail this ability to absorb risk through diversification as one of the great benefits of financial institutions as investors in corporations. They claim that it reduces the cost of capital to firms and encourages risk-taking. But what this argument fails to take into account is that, other than shareholders, most participants in the portfolio companies cannot fully diversify their risks. When large companies fail, key suppliers or customers are usually also hurt, and employees are often devastated. These other players generally do not have an alternative customer whose demand is increasing, or another set of skills whose value is rising, to compensate for the losses they suffer in their relationship with the failed company Diversified institutional investors have no incentive to consider these other losses in deciding whether to promote risky strategies or discourage costly investment programs in their portfolio companies. Even if institutional investors had the right incentives, they are unlikely to have the information they need to make this calculation.

This last argument is likely to be regarded as especially controversial because most participants in the debates about corporate governance are accustomed to thinking of shareholders as the residual risk bearers and to assuming that all other participants, if they bear risk at all, are fully compensated for the risks they bear. Chapter 7 explores why these assumptions are not necessarily true, and in fact, not likely to be true in most large modern companies.

What Boards of Directors Are Supposed to Do

The discussion to this point has focused on the role of major investors as monitors of corporate performance and has proceeded as if an investor-monitor (a "relationship investor"), if it existed, would meet regularly with management and review detailed information about the operations of the company and its strategic plans. But that is precisely what boards of directors are supposed to do. In fact, the most adamant advocates of institutional activism concede that, if directors were doing their jobs right, additional layers of monitors would not be needed. And the most thoughtful of the shareholder rights advocates concede that, if a company has a good board and strong management, the details of its corporate governance arrangements (from whether it permits cumulative voting, to how it determines CEO pay, to whether it has a major investor-monitor), are not terribly important.[87] Ideally, they say, corporate governance reforms should create structures that will encourage boards to do a better job in the first place. Mechanisms that enable owners to compel changes when and if a company's performance is slipping and the board fails to act should be used only as a last resort.

Acknowledging this central role of boards of directors, reform advocates on all sides have weighed in with suggestions about how board structures and practices, information flows to the board, and incentive systems facing boards should be reformed. Appendix 5-2 presents a long list of such proposals. Board reform is not discussed at length in this book, not because such reforms are unimportant, but because I believe that another issue must be resolved first: Whose interests should boards of directors be serving?

---

[87]Shareholder rights advocates often cite Motorola as an example of a company with several less-than-ideal governance arrangements. The company has charter provisions allowing it to issue "blank check" preferred stock, for example, and has a poison pill. But the company's track record for responding to shareholder concerns, and for performance generally, has been stellar in the early 1990s (providing shareholders a five-year average annual return of 36.3 percent through spring 1994.) As a result, the Institutional Shareholder Services has consistently recommended that its clients vote with management. See Institutional Shareholder Services, Inc., "Proxy Analysis Report on Motorola Inc.," Bethesda, Md., March 15, 1994.

The importance of resolving this question becomes clear in the first of the board reform proposals listed in appendix 5-2, which calls for all publicly traded companies to have a majority of "outside" directors. Scholars, reform advocates, corporate lawyers, and even many corporate executives have gradually come to agree that giving boards of directors some independence from management is essential to good governance. If "insiders," that is, executives of the company who report to the CEO, make up more than half of a given board, clearly that board cannot be considered independent. But, beyond that, what criteria help ensure that the board of directors represents the constituencies it is supposed to represent and does not merely serve as a rubber stamp for the CEO?

Two competing theories have emerged. One holds that directors should be completely independent of all interests except those of shareholders. A director who reports to the CEO, who comes from a firm that has a business relationship with the company, or who represents any special interest group such as employees should not be considered independent. The strongest advocates of board independence also generally argue that directors should be required to hold a significant amount of stock in the company.[88] This emphasis on board "independence" is thus a mask for the true agenda of shareholder advocates, which is shareholder dominance.

An alternative theory about whose interests boards should represent is implicit in the recommendation by Michael Porter that boards of directors should include representation from all significant stakeholders, including major customers, suppliers, financial advisors, employees, and even the surrounding community.[89] Porter's proposal is extremely controversial as applied to large, publicly traded companies, but it is a model widely used in many smaller,

---

[88]See Monks and Minow (1995, p. 224), for example.
[89]Porter (1992, p. 86).

high-tech start-up companies. Clearly, the definition of "independent" depends on the definer's beliefs about whose interests corporations should serve—an issue taken up in the remaining chapters.

APPENDIX 5-1

Reform Proposals Designed to Encourage Institutional Investor Activism (But Limit Their Liquidity)

LAWS AND REGULATIONS

Corporation Law

1. Corporate stock should have no voting rights until it has been held for at least two years, and then voting rights should increase with the length of time shares are held, for example, one-third vote per share in year three, two-thirds vote per share in year four, and full voting power in year five and beyond. (Thurow, 1988, p. 70)*

Shareholder Voice

1. Shareholder groups who hold at least 0.5 percent of shares of a company for at least five years should be allowed to submit a 300-word statement on management effectiveness for inclusion in the proxy. (Regan, 1992)

2. Any shareholder group owning at least 5 percent of a company's shares should be given free access to the company-paid proxy statement to nominate directors. (Jacobs, 1991, p. 228)

3. Corporate democracy should be tied to relationship investing; pursued for its own sake, corporate democracy leads to adversarial relationships. (Twentieth Century Fund, 1992, p. 19)

4. Institutional investors should become more active owners. Institutional investors should have regular contact with managers at the senior executive level and should fully understand management's strategies. (Cadbury Commission, 1992, pp. 51–52)

*The list of people, organizations, or commissions credited with each reform proposal is not intended to be comprehensive. In many cases, the same or a similar proposal has been advocated by others as well as those named.

Appendix 5-1 (continued)

Appendix 5-1 (continued)

5. Institutional investors should stay out of the day-to-day management of a company. If shareholders are dissatisfied with the way directors or managers are performing, they should replace them. (Working Group on Corporate Governance, 1991, p. 143; Koppes, 1992, p. 82)

6. Institutional investors should be subject to scrutiny, however. Public and private pension funds should be required to disclose publicly their proxy voting and investment decisions on certain corporate matters such as takeovers, proxy contests, restructuring, and shareholder-rights plans. (Millstein, 1991, pp. 166–67, 1992, p. 62; and Monks and Minow, 1991, chap. 6)

Tax Laws

1. The tax system should be used to create an incentive for long-term equity investment. Moreover, such incentives must be extended to untaxed investors such as pension funds. (Porter, 1992, pp. 81–82)

2. Taxes on intercorporate dividends should be eliminated to encourage intercorporate supplier-customer cross-shareholding. (Roe, 1993c, p. 1988)

Securities Market Regulation

1. A "safe harbor" should be provided under Section 16(b) of the Securities and Exchange Act (prohibiting trading by insiders) to promote large stakeholding and corporate monitoring. (Coffee, 1991, p. 1346)

2. Regulations affecting banks, insurance companies, mutual funds, and investment companies should be revised to eliminate or reduce the restrictions on concentrated share ownership. Financial institutions should be able to buy up to 10 percent of a company (some advocates say 15 percent), for example. Investment companies or other financial institutions that take large long-term positions in companies and become active monitors should not be subject to Hart-Scott-Rodino Act liabilities nor to the unrelated business income tax. The Department of Labor should remove a barrier to pension fund activism by clarifying that pension funds that invest in at least fifty stocks, not generally from the same small set of industries, are diver-

Appendix 5-1 (continued)

sified enough to satisfy fiduciary obligations. (Porter, 1992, p. 77; Jacobs, 1991, p. 224; Black 1992a, pp. 822–23; and Roe, 1993b, pp. 97–99)

3. Portfolio diversification, including indexing, should be restricted to a level consistent with the institution's ability to monitor. (Coffee, 1991, p. 1355)

4. The Labor Department and the Internal Revenue Service should clarify that cross-investments through pension plans (corporate pension plans holding blocks of each others' sponsors' stocks) can be prudent and will not be subject to unrelated business taxation. (Black, 1992a, p. 846)

5. The Employee Retirement Income Security Act (ERISA), which governs pensions, should be revised to encourage, even require in some instances, activism by these pension funds as shareholders. Diversification requirements under ERISA should be relaxed. The Labor Department, which oversees ERISA, should make it clear to corporate pension fund managers that simply hiring traditional money managers does not necessarily fulfill fiduciary duties. (Coffee, 1991, p. 1365; Monks and Minow, 1991, p. 254; and Jacobs, 1991, pp. 49–50)

6. Anyone who holds a dominant position in any company—say, 20 percent or more—should be forced to give the public one day's notice of the intent to sell shares. (Thurow, 1988, p. 70)

INSTITUTIONAL ARRANGEMENTS

Boards of Directors

1. Restrictions on board membership by institutional investors should be loosened. (Porter, 1992, p. 86)

2. Institutional investors should be encouraged to sit on the boards of directors of companies in which they invest, to actively hire and fire managers, and to participate in developing the strategies that will make their investments useful. (Thurow, 1988, p. 69)

Appendix 5-1 (continued)

Internal Controls

1. Long-term shareholders should be provided with "inside information" but prevented from trading on it. (Porter, 1992, p. 85)

2. Incentive compensation should be linked to competitive position. (Porter, 1992, p. 94)

Financial Structure

1. Today's laws draw too sharp a distinction between loans and equity. Institutions that provide major long-term loans to companies should take an active role in their strategic direction. To bring this about, long-term loans should have voting rights or be coupled with issues of stock with voting rights. (Thurow, 1988, pp. 69–70)

Ownership Structure

1. Restrictions on joint ownership of debt and equity should be eliminated. (Porter, 1992, pp. 82–83)

Institutional Behavior

1. Institutional investors should more carefully select companies based on fundamental earning power and should increase the size of their stakes. (Porter, 1992, p. 89)

2. Pension funds and other institutional investors should support the creation of investment funds that actively monitor instead of trying to do the monitoring themselves. (Jacobs, 1991, pp. 220–21; Porter, 1992, p. 70)

3. Some institutional investors need to wean themselves away from overwhelmingly reflexive indexing and move toward more direct investment in fewer companies or at least toward obtaining sufficient knowledge about some of the companies represented in an institution's indexed portfolio to enable intelligent appraisals of their boards and managements. (Millstein, 1992, p. 48)

APPENDIX 5-2

Reform Proposals Designed to Improve Performance of Boards of Directors and to Improve Information Flows and Incentives

BOARDS OF DIRECTORS

1. All publicly traded companies should have a majority of outside directors.

   a. GM model: Outside directors should be "independent" directors; that is, they should have no business or other relationship with the firm, other than as a director and shareholder. (GM Board memo; National Association of Corporate Directors, 1992, p. 21; Koppes, 1992, p. 84; and many others)

   b. Porter model: Boards of directors should include representation by significant customers, suppliers, financial advisors, employees, and community representatives. (Porter, 1992, p. 86)

2. The chairman of the board should be an outside director, and not the CEO. (Lorsch and MacIver, 1989, p. 70; Cadbury Commission, 1992, pp. 21–22; Stern, 1993, p. 9; and Koppes, 1992, p. 84)

3. Boards should include a certain number of "professional" outside directors. These could be drawn from a pool of candidates identified by institutional investors. (Gilson and Kraakman, 1993, p. 82)

4. Each board should formally recognize a chief outside director, or, as one advocate calls it, "deputy chairman of the board." (Lipton and Lorsch, 1992, pp. 70–71; and Cadbury, 1993, p. 8)

5. Boards should be smaller. They should have no more than ten members, and outside directors should outnumber inside directors by at least two to one. (Lipton and Lorsch, 1992, pp. 67–68)

6. CEOs should serve on no more than one other corporate board in addition to their own. (Minow and Bingham, 1993, p. 12)

Appendix 5-2 (continued)

197

Appendix 5-2 (continued)

7. Outside directors should meet alone (without the CEO or other inside directors) regularly—at least once a year; some proponents say as often as four times a year. (Working Group on Corporate Governance, 1991, p. 142; Minow and Bingham, 1993, p. 13; and Koppes, 1992, p. 84)

8. Directors should be required to make a specific commitment of time and should be permitted to sit on no more than three boards at once. Each day of board meetings should be matched by one to two days of preparation. (Minow and Bingham, 1993, pp. 11–12; Lipton and Lorsch, 1992, pp. 69–70)

9. There should be term limits for outside directors, for example, ten to fifteen years, and a mandatory retirement age. (Lipton and Lorsch, 1992, p. 68)

10. Boards should meet monthly or even bimonthly for a full day, and should have one two- to three-day strategy session each year. (Lipton and Lorsch, 1992, pp. 69–70)

11. Compensation committees should consist of no more than five people and should be staffed by independent directors. CEOs should not sit on each others' compensation committees. Compensation committees should be able to hire their own pay consultants. The board should provide the details of its compensation contract with the CEO to the shareholders. (O'Cleireacain, 1992, p. 90; Minow, 1992, p. 14; Cadbury Commission, 1992, p. 31; Business Roundtable, 1992, p. 2; and Koppes, 1992, p. 84)

12. Boards should have audit committees staffed only by independent directors. This committee should meet with the external auditors at least twice a year, with no executive board members present. (Cadbury Commission, 1992, pp. 28–29; National Association of Corporate Directors, 1992, p. 11; and Koppes, 1992, p. 84)

13. Boards should have nominating committees staffed by outside directors. (Lorsch and MacIver, 1989, p. 173; Cadbury Commission, 1992, p. 27; Koppes, 1992, p. 84)

Appendix 5-2 (continued)

14. Outside directors should screen and recommend candidates for the board based on qualifications established by the board. (Working Group on Corporate Governance, 1991, p. 143; Monks and Minow, 1991, p. 259)

15. Directors should be allowed to contract out for professional advice. (Cadbury Commission, 1992, p. 24; and Koppes, 1992, p. 84)

16. To maintain control and safeguard against illegal practices, boards should formulate a specific list of matters reserved for their collective decision. (Cadbury Commission, 1992, p. 25)

17. Directors should meet with outside shareholders, with officers and employees of the company, and, as necessary, with outside advisors, to ensure they have the information they need to do the job. (Minow and Bingham, 1993, pp. 11–12)

18. Companies should provide an annual informal setting in which up to ten of the larger shareholders can meet directly with the board of directors, with the goals of improving understanding between institutional shareholders and directors and thus avoiding much of the letter writing, meeting requests, board-seat requests, and proxy proposals some institutional investors have been pursuing. (Lipton and Lorsh, 1992, p. 74)

19. Companies should set up a binary board structure. German AGs for example, have two-tiered boards. Another possibility is the institution of a "corporate senate," which has veto power over the actions of the board that involve conflicts of interest. The corporate bylaws would give the senators (as well as all directors) access to all corporate information and oblige each director to report any conflicts of interest to the senate. Senators would be elected on the basis of one vote per shareholder, giving small shareholders the same power as large shareholders. (Turnbull, 1993, pp. 1–3)

20. The courts should formulate a duty of independence as a halfway point between the duty of care and the duty of loyalty. Informed, disinterested directors should be required to approve any corporate transaction in which management or any other director has a stake, other than the corporation's stake. (Palmiter, 1989, p. 1461)

Appendix 5-2 (continued)

ENHANCED INFORMATION AND INTERNAL CONTROLS

1. Boards of directors should establish formal criteria for picking directors and formal performance standards against which they evaluate strategy, judge themselves and the CEO, and measure the long-term performance of the company. (Competitiveness Policy Council, 1992, pp. 12–13)

2. Corporations should establish specific long-term quantitative performance objectives, and these objectives should be disclosed to all corporate investors. Investors and directors should periodically appraise the progress of corporate management toward reaching these goals. (Lipton and Lorsch, 1992, pp. 72–73)

3. Directors should perform an annual evaluation of CEO performance that reviews company operating performance as well as major extraordinary initiatives the CEO has set out to achieve. (Lipton and Lorsch, 1992, p. 73; Working Group on Corporate Governance, 1991, p. 142)

4. A chosen leader of the outside directors should meet with the CEO after the performance review session to relay the main points of that discussion. The CEO should then meet with the outside directors to provide a reaction. (Wharton, 1991, pp. 137–38)

5. Directors should clearly communicate qualifications for board members to shareholders. (Working Group on Corporate Governance, 1991, pp. 142–43; Competitiveness Policy Council, 1992, pp. 12–13)

6. Before new directors are hired, they should be required to write a letter informing the CEO of their time restrictions. Corporate counsel should explicitly spell out to new directors the duties and responsibilities for which they will be accountable. (Lorsch and MacIver, 1989, p. 192)

7. Independent directors should include their own statement in proxy filings (especially after a period in which the company does not meet its performance targets). (Lipton and Lorsch, 1992, p. 75; Minow and Bingham, 1993, p. 14)

Appendix 5-2 (continued)

8. Outside directors should meet regularly with security analysts and selected large institutional investors. (Wharton, 1991, p. 138; and others)

9. Directors should be compensated in part with stock options. (Crystal, 1992, p. 245)

10. Tax incentives for stock options and stock purchase plans should apply only to plans with restrictions on selling, such as options that cannot be activated for at least five years, or that otherwise penalize the early exercise of stock options. (Porter, 1992, p. 87; Baily, Burtless, and Litan, 1993, p. 103)

11. Shareholders should have to approve compensation contracts every three years. (Cadbury Commission, 1992, p. 31)

12. If a company underperforms for three consecutive years, the board should publish a report for shareholders detailing the nature of the problems the company faces. Large shareholders would then be allowed to include statements in the proxy on management performance. (Lipton and Lorsch, 1992, p. 75)

13. Companies should undergo periodic "business audits" by outside experts to provide perspective in evaluating a company's performance. (Drucker, 1991a, pp. 113–14; Lipton and Rosenblum, 1991, pp. 235–36)

14. Management should maintain an appropriate, arms-length relationship with auditors. Firms should disclose all fees paid to the auditors for services other than the audit. (Cadbury Commission, 1992, p. 39)

15. Auditors should have legal protection against defamation and breach of confidentiality suits when reporting suspicion of fraud. Few auditors are in a position strong enough to challenge management. (Cadbury Commission, 1992, p. 40)

16. Companies should be required to disclose information about how compensation of the top executives is related to performance, including the performance factors that compensation is tied to and precisely how compensation would vary with variations in those factors. Companies should also be required to disclose the market value of all perquisites provided for executives. (Crystal, 1992, p. 247)

6

WHOSE INTERESTS SHOULD

CORPORATIONS SERVE?

THE FINANCE AND MARKET MYOPIA VIEWS of the central problem of corporate governance start from an assumption that the appropriate social purpose of corporations is to maximize shareholder return. They differ only over how best to achieve this goal. Finance model advocates believe that shareholder interests are best served by policies and actions that maximize share price in the short run because they accept the central maxim of finance theory: that the price of a share of stock today fully reflects the market's best estimate of the value of all future profits and growth that will accrue to that company. Thus they advocate an unfettered market for corporate control and other reforms that enhance the power of shareholders. Market myopia advocates, however, question whether today's stock price is a reliable enough guide to the future value and returns from the company's investments to be the exclusive focus of managerial attention. They fear that pressures from the financial markets impart a bias in managerial judgments against managing for the long term.

A third point of view is occasionally voiced in the corporate governance debates. This view has two distinct incarnations, but both versions start from the premise that corporations do not exist solely to provide returns to shareholders. Instead, they must serve a larger social purpose. The more familiar version of this idea holds that corporations should be "socially responsible" institutions, managed in the public interest. This idea was popular among consumer advocates, environmentalists, and social activists in the 1960s, 1970s, and early 1980s and was used in the 1980s by some corporate executives as an argument in support of policies that would inhibit takeovers or give companies more defenses against them. The idea never had much theoretical rigor to it, failed to give clear guidance to help managers and directors set priorities and decide among competing socially beneficial uses of corporate resources, and provided no obvious enforcement mechanism to ensure that corporations live up to their social obligations. As a result of these deficiencies, few academics, policymakers, or other proponents of corporate governance reforms still espouse this model.

Nonetheless, the idea that corporations should have some social purpose beyond maximizing returns to shareholders survives, and a new view about what this purpose should be is just beginning to emerge among the leading thinkers about corporate governance issues. It is that corporations exist to create wealth for society.[1] Ac-

---

[1] A few of the leading lawyers and management specialists active in corporate governance reform issues have begun describing corporate goals in these terms. Drucker (1991a, p. 112) argues that institutional owners of German and Japanese companies "do not attempt to maximize shareholder value or the short-term interest of any one of the enterprise's 'stakeholders.' Rather they *maximize the wealth*

cording to this view, the goal of corporate governance mechanisms and the responsibilities of corporate directors are to see that the firm maximizes wealth creation. In some instances this broad goal may be equivalent to maximizing returns to shareholders, but that will not always be the case.

To those who believe that corporations must serve some larger social purpose, governance reform proposals from the finance and market myopia camps might do damage to this larger social purpose if they tilt too strongly toward compelling corporate executives and their boards of directors to focus exclusively on maximizing shareholder returns.

Reconsidering an Old Question

Whether it is in the public interest for widely held corporations to be run exclusively for shareholders is an old question. Although seemingly forgotten by most advocates of the finance model, a major issue that Berle and Means originally raised was whether shareholders in widely held companies should be given the same legal rights and protections as owners of other kinds of property. Their answer was no. Because shareholders could not adequately undertake all the responsibilities that ownership of, say, real property normally implies, Berle and Means wrote, they should not necessarily be given all of the rights normally associated with ownership.

The property owner who invests in a modern corporation so far surrenders his wealth to those in control of the corporation that

---

producing capacity of the enterprise [emphasis in the original]." Similarly, Millstein (1992, p. 42) writes about the role that "knowledgeable and diligent ownership (relationship investing) can play in causing corporations to better *maximize their wealth producing capacity in the global economy* [emphasis added]."

he has exchanged the position of independent owner for one in which he may become merely recipient of the wages of capital.

. . . The owners of passive property, by surrendering control and responsibility over the active property, have surrendered the right that the corporation should be operated in their sole interest,—they have released the community from the obligation to protect them to the full extent implied in the doctrine of strict property rights. At the same time, the controlling groups, by means of the extension of corporate powers, have in their own interest broken the bars of tradition which require that the corporation be operated solely for the benefit of the owners of passive property.[2]

Nonetheless, Berle and Means were careful not to imply that corporate management should be free to run companies in their own interest.

Eliminating the sole interest of the passive owner, however, does not necessarily lay a basis for the alternative claim that the new powers should be used in the interest of the controlling groups. The latter have not presented, in acts or words any acceptable defense of the proposition that these powers should be so used. No tradition supports that proposition. The control groups have, rather, cleared the way for the claims of a group far wider than either the owners or the control. They have placed the community in a position to demand that the modern corporation serve not alone the owners or the control but all society.[3]

Finance model advocates often cite Berle and Means as their most important intellectual ancestors, but, curiously, they have ignored or dismissed as trivial the key question of whose interests corpora-

[2]Berle and Means (1932, pp. 3, 355).
[3]Berle and Means (1932, pp. 355–56).

tions should serve. Moreover, proponents of the finance model have so dominated the debate over corporate governance in recent years that those who might have raised the question have largely been silenced or have been driven to make circuitous arguments that soft-pedal or sidestep the question.[4] By the early 1990s, for example, it had become quite unfashionable for corporate executives to talk about their jobs in any terms other than maximizing shareholder value. Similarly, in his critique of the U.S. system of capital allocation and corporate governance, Michael Porter never explicitly challenges the notion that corporations should be driven by the goal of maximizing value for shareholders. Instead, he refers repeatedly to the "divergence of interests between owners and corporations" and the need to align the goals of investors with those "of the corporation" or to align the goals of management or employees with those "of the corporation."[5]

For these kinds of arguments to make sense, we must think carefully about who and what the corporation is, what goals it should have, and whose interests it should serve. These questions can be asked as legalistic or descriptive ones: What does the law say? Or they can be asked as questions of public policy: What *should* the law say?

---

[4]An exception was an essay by Epstein (1986, p. 3) that at least acknowledged the question. "Out of this bitter debate [the 1980s takeover battles] emerged a sharp divergence of views on the purpose of the corporation in the American system of capitalism. Whereas many shareholders thought of it in terms of its profitability, corporate management tended to define it in terms of service to the community, suggesting that their corporations were 'institutions,' much like museums or hospitals, that served a public interest as well as the private interest of shareholders." Epstein goes on to defend a view that companies should be run for shareholders and that shareholders should be given more control. Thus Epstein's piece supports my fundamental point about the dominance of the finance model.

[5]See, for example, Porter (1992, p. 20).

What the Law Says

From its earliest evolution, corporate law has always been a bit schizophrenic about the right to form corporations.[6] On one hand, the right to incorporate was viewed as a simple extension of property rights and the freedoms of association and contract on the part of property owners. Under this "inherence" theory, the right to incorporate is inherent in the right to own property and write contracts. It follows that corporations should be legal extensions of their "owners" in the sense that they should have all the same rights and responsibilities as the individuals who own their equity.

The earliest corporations were "joint stock companies," which in the seventeenth and eighteenth centuries were set up for limited durations to accomplish specific tasks.[7] They were mechanisms for amassing capital to finance trading expeditions, for example, or to finance the construction of roads or canals. The joint stock companies were typically owned by a relatively small group of wealthy people who exercised close control over them.

But from the beginning, these joint stock companies and their successors, first the "trusts" (which were really holding companies), and, ultimately, modern corporations, required some sort of grant or charter from the state to exist.[8] These charters were granted in part

---

[6]The section that follows draws heavily on an article by William T. Allen, chancellor of the state of Delaware. See Allen (1992). I have credited Allen where I have taken his arguments directly. See also Votaw (1965, chap. 1) for an informative essay on the evolution of the corporate form.

[7]The first joint stock company was formed in 1555, but the form was rarely used before the 1600s. See Votaw (1965, pp. 13–17).

[8]The original trusts were voluntary associations of small companies that each agreed to turn their stock over to a common board of trustees, in exchange for trust certificates of equal value, so that the operations of the companies could be managed in common. Their purpose was to formalize the otherwise unenforceable agreements

because the projects to be undertaken were believed to be in the public interest. Under the "concession" theory, corporations owe their existence to a special concession from the state. This theory considers corporations to be separate entities from the owners of their equity, with a separate right to own and dispose of property, to enter into enforceable contracts, and to engage in business transactions. But their rights and responsibilities are defined and limited by the state and are not equivalent to those of the individuals who own their equity.

For complex historical reasons, the corporate form was used in the nineteenth century much more extensively in the United States than it was in other countries. So corporate law was more fully developed at an earlier date here than elsewhere. The earliest corporations were not granted perpetual life, nor were equity holders granted limited liability, but by the 1820s, most states had passed general incorporation acts that granted both of these features. By the middle of the 1800s, most states permitted the formation of corporations "for any legal purpose" and imposed no limitations on their accumulations of wealth and property. Thus, the right to form corporations became available to all individuals (a fact that supports the inherence view), but corporations themselves had characteristics that were not available to individuals and that only the state could grant (a fact that supports the concession view).

The 'Property Conception' of the Corporation

Before the rise of the large, multiunit, modern business enterprise in the late 1800s, "owners managed and managers owned," as professor

---

among companies to fix prices or control supply. The trust form came under attack by state and federal courts, and, in response, the state of New Jersey passed a generalized incorporation law permitting the formation of holding companies. The Standard Oil Trust and the other well-known "trusts" of the late 1800s and early 1900s were actually holding companies. See Chandler (1977, pp. 318–20).

Alfred D. Chandler, Jr., put it.[9] Although the notion existed that corporations were special entities with some public purpose aspects, there was no real question in the law about who should have control over corporations and in whose interest they should be run. William T. Allen, chancellor of the state of Delaware, notes that a leading corporation law treatise of the mid-1800s regarded corporations as "little more than limited partnerships, every member exercising through his vote an immediate control over the interests of the body."[10] He further notes that the law had not yet established with certainty that the state even had the right to impose taxes on corporations (separately from taxing their shareholders), and that shareholder liability was not limited to the extent that it is today.

The Pujo Committee report of 1913 detailed the loss of control by shareholders as corporations grew and shareholdings became more dispersed, but by 1919, the law still held that corporations were supposed to be run for the benefit of the stockholders.[11] That point was made crystal clear in a famous case before the Michigan Supreme Court, *Dodge v. Ford Motor Co.* The Dodge brothers had sued Ford Motor Co., complaining that Henry Ford suspended dividend payments, choosing instead to retain $58 million in profits to be used to expand the business and lower the price of its products. As shareholders, the Dodge brothers wanted Ford to pay out some of those accumulated profits instead and asserted that, because shareholders owned the enterprise, they could force directors to pay out the profits. The Michigan Supreme Court agreed:

[9]Chandler (1977, p. 9).

[10]Allen (1992, p. 8).

[11]*Report of the Committee Appointed Pursuant to House Resolution 429 and 504 to Investigate the Concentration of Control of Money and Credit*, House Report 1593, 62d Cong. 3d sess. Government Printing Office, 1913, as cited in Herman (1981, p. 7).

A business corporation is organized and carried on primarily for the profit of the stockholders. The powers of the directors are to be employed for that end. The discretion of directors is to be exercised in the choice of means to attain that end, and does not extend to a change in the end itself, to the reduction of profits, or to the nondistribution of profits among stockholders in order to devote them to other purposes.[12]

According to Allen, this decision is "as pure an example as exists" of what he calls the "property conception of the corporation." Allen's property conception, which conforms closely to my finance model, is based on an inherence view of the corporation, a view that in modern times has been associated with the "Chicago School" of law and economics (much of the theoretical basis and analytical techniques used to defend this position was largely developed at the University of Chicago). Central to the property conception is the treatment of the corporation as a "nexus of contracts," through which the various participants arrange to transact with each other.[13] In this conception, assets of the corporation are the property of the shareholders, and managers and boards of directors are viewed as agents of shareholders, with all the difficulties of enforcement associated with agency relationships, but with no legal obligations to any other stakeholders. Under this view, "the rights of creditors, employees, and others are strictly limited to statutory, contractual, and common law rights," Allen says.[14]

The 'Social Entity Conception'

The property conception of the corporation held sway in U.S. corporate law throughout the 1800s and early part of the 1900s. But with

---

[12]204 Mich. 459, 170 N.W. 668 (1919), cited in Allen (1992, p. 10).
[13]Jensen and Meckling (1976, pp. 305–60).
[14]Allen (1992, p. 10).

the separation of ownership from control, the development of so-phisticated securities markets, and the emergence of a class of pro-fessional managers who viewed themselves as "trustees" of great institutions, a competing view began to take hold. "It was apparent to any thoughtful observer that the American corporation had ceased to be a private business device and had become an institu-tion," Berle wrote in the preface to *The Modern Corporation and Private Property*.[15] Similarly, historian Dow Votaw noted that "the buccaneers of the late nineteenth century gave way to the more statesmanlike professional managers of the twentieth. The aggres-sive, profit- and power-seeking individualist was replaced by the arbitrator and diplomat whose motivations included organization survival, professional reputation, and equitable balancing of inter-ests, as well as profit-making. The modern corporation has been aptly described as a 'constellation of interests' rather than the instru-ment of the acquisitive individual."[16]

Allen calls this view the "social entity conception," noting that the purpose of the corporation is seen as "not individual but social." As he puts it:

> Contributors of capital (stockholders and bondholders) must be assured a rate of return sufficient to induce them to contribute their capital to the enterprise. But the corporation has other pur-poses of perhaps equal dignity: the satisfaction of consumer wants, the provision of meaningful employment opportunities and the making of a contribution to the public life of its commu-nities. Resolving the often conflicting claims of these various corporate constituencies calls for judgment, indeed calls for wis-dom, by the board of directors of the corporation. But in this view,

[15]Berle and Means (1932 p. v).
[16]Votaw (1965, p. 28).

no single constituency's interest may significantly exclude others from fair consideration by the board.[17]

This idea, of course, is a direct descendent of the point Berle and Means made in the conclusion to their work in 1932. To be sure, Berle was concerned about the potential for corporate managers to abuse the powers implied in this conception. "Now I submit," he wrote in a later essay, "that you cannot abandon emphasis on 'the view that business corporations exist for the sole purpose of making profits for their stockholders' until such time as you are prepared to offer a clear and reasonably enforceable scheme of responsibilities to someone else."[18]

Until the 1980s the social entity conception of the corporation was never given official legal sanction, although many social activists and several business leaders adopted the idea.[19] As the modern

[17]Allen (1992, p. 15).

[18]Berle (1932). The Berle essay was one of a series of essays in a scholarly debate between Berle and Professor E. Merrick Dodd. Despite his apparent interest in the idea of the corporation as a social institution as expressed in the conclusion to *The Modern Corporation and Private Property*, Berle argued that giving corporate executives too much power "might be unsafe, and in any case it hardly affords the soundest base on which to construct the economic commonwealth which industrialism seems to require." (p. 1372) Dodd, by contrast, argued that the law was moving in the direction of viewing the corporation as "an economic institution which has a social service as well as a profit-making function." See Dodd (1932, p. 1148).

[19]In 1946 Frank Abrams, then chairman of Standard Oil Company of New Jersey, described the role of the modern manager as maintaining "an equitable and working balance among the claims of the various directly interested groups—stockholders, employees, customers, and the public at large." See Rostow (1960). In 1978 directors of Control Data Corp. gave formal recognition to the view of corporations as social entities in its proxy statement to shareholders, urging them to pass several amendments to the company's articles of incorporation that would require the board to consider the effect of any takeover proposal on the company's employees and other "stakeholders." "The Board is mindful and supportive . . . of the growing concept that corporations have a social responsibility to a wide variety of societal segments which have a stake in the continued health of a given corporation," the proxy letter stated. See Control Data Corp. Proxy Statement, May 3, 1978, p. 4.

corporation grew in size and power after World War II, the central concern of legal scholars was not so much whether corporations should or should not be run primarily for shareholders, and certainly not whether the separation of ownership from control would make corporations inefficient or uncompetitive. Rather, the concern was about who should control the vast economic, political, and social power of these large and powerful wealth-generating machines and how that power should be restrained. "It is not enough that the great corporation be a paragon of efficiency and production," Votaw wrote in 1965, expressing a view quite typical of the era.

> The large corporations are the possessors of substantial amounts of this power, and properly so. Without it they could not perform the tasks society demands of them. In a free society, however, we cannot leave the subject there. Power, in either private or public hands, raises difficult questions: How much power? In whose hands? Power for what purposes? To whom are the wielders of power responsible? What assurances are there that the power will be used fairly and justly? and, Is there machinery by which the power and the method of its exercise can be made responsive to the needs of society?[20]

Votaw noted that the political legitimacy of the corporation was challenged during the Depression, when it appeared that this power was not being used responsibly. But then "the corporation . . . performed brilliantly during World War II" and "the performance of the corporate system since the war has also been very good, as a whole, [producing] rising prosperity and standards of living." As a result, he said, "issues of legitimacy moved into the background."[21]

[20]Votaw (1965, p. 87).
[21]Votaw (1965, p. 102).

Questions of legitimacy faded in part because corporations were assuming more and more responsibilities as social institutions. By the late 1960s and early 1970s, corporate responsiveness to a broad group of stakeholders had become accepted business practice (for pragmatic reasons if nothing else).[22] Consumer advocates and religious and political groups that wanted to influence corporate behavior bought token shareholdings so that they could introduce resolutions and vote on important corporate policies. They also staged boycotts and waged publicity campaigns. Although no corporation ever went so far as to, say, elect Ralph Nader to the board of directors, many of them created public affairs offices, added consumer hotlines, gave research grants to universities and other special research institutes, contributed to charity, agreed to divest from South Africa, and engaged much more directly in political dialogue. They also gave their employees paid leave to engage in public service activities and participated in community development programs. Wages were still rising rapidly during this period, and large corporations were increasing the noncash benefits they gave their employees, such as health insurance, pensions, education and training support, and vacation and sick leave. In addition to paying relatively high taxes, they also became significant supporters of public institutions such as theaters, parks, schools, museums, and hospitals. Most companies looked upon such "socially responsible" behavior as a way to improve the general business climate.

The law moved to accommodate the social entity view by protecting companies that engaged in such activities, even when these

---

[22]Accepted, at least, by most business leaders. Economists and legal scholars of the Chicago School railed against such behavior, however. For example, Milton Friedman wrote that "businessmen who talk this way are unwitting puppets of the intellectual forces that have been undermining the basis of a free society these past decades." See Milton Friedman, "The Social Responsibility of Business Is to Increase Its Profits," *New York Times Magazine*, September 13, 1970, p. 33.

activities were clearly not directly related to maximizing profits for shareholders. The courts, for example, generally upheld corporations that had made donations to museums or hospitals or had otherwise expended corporate resources on community-enhancing activities against challenges from shareholders. By the 1970s, in fact, forty-eight states had passed laws "explicitly providing that chartered corporations could give to charities without specific charter provision."[23] A clever legal device was developed to justify these kinds of activities without conceding that directors did not have a primary duty to maximize wealth for shareholders. The courts held that, while it might divert shareholder wealth in the short run, responding to the needs and interests of other stakeholders was good for shareholders "in the long run," because the good health and well-being of the communities in which companies operate was considered important for business. "The law papered over the conflict in our conception of the corporation by invoking a murky distinction between long-term profit maximization and short-term profit maximization," Allen writes. "The long-term/short-term distinction preserves the form of the stockholders-oriented property theory, while permitting, in fact, a considerable degree of behavior consistent with a view that sees public corporations as owing social responsibilities to all affected by its operation."[24]

Breakdown of Accommodation

For nearly half a century, this practical accommodation in the law worked. These activities were seldom challenged by shareholders, but when they were, they were successfully defended as being bene-

---

[23]See Herman (1981, footnote 40, p. 401). Herman cautions that "corporate largess for purposes not readily reconciled with profit-effectiveness is still subject to legal challenge." (p. 256)

[24]Allen (1992, pp. 16–17).

ficial to shareholders in the long run. And, until the 1970s, it appeared that shareholders were benefiting—along with employees and
communities—from the broad social role that most large corporations played. An investment made in the Standard & Poor's composite companies in 1945 would have yielded a compound annual rate
of return of 7.59 percent by 1972, compared to an average annual
yield on high-rated corporate bonds during this same period of about
4.30 percent.[25]

The "in the long run" device for reconciling the goal of maximizing value for shareholders with a more broadly defined goal of social
responsibility for corporations broke down in the 1980s for three
reasons, according to Allen: the rise of global competition; interna-
tionalization of financial markets; and the emergence of the hostile
takeover. To these a fourth should be added: the collapse in stock
market returns in the 1970s, followed by the rise in the cost of
capital in the early part of the 1980s.

The rise of global competition contributed to an irregular but
steady erosion of corporate profitability in the post-War decades,
especially in the manufacturing sector. Meanwhile, the investment
options overseas were expanding, and, by the early 1980s the real
return on bonds and other, safer investments in the United States

---

[25]These calculations are unadjusted for inflation. The difference between the
return earned by bondholders and that earned by stockholders over the period may
simply be an appropriate level of compensation for the additional risk borne by
stockholders. There is no way to measure how much shareholders should be paid for
risk. One can only measure how much more they, in fact, earned on high risk
investments relative to lower risk investments. The point here is only that shareholders shared in the wealth creation by large corporations, as they should have.

The end date for this analysis was not chosen at random. By 1974 the S&P 500
average had fallen by 24 percent, wiping out all of the gains it had seen in the previous
ten years (and reminding investors that investing in stocks did entail some significant
risks). This loss in value was not fully regained until 1980. Many observers believe
this poor performance by the stock market in the 1970s helped set the stage for the
battles for corporate control in the 1980s.

had climbed to new heights. Together, these changed the expectations of the financial markets about the return that corporations should provide, and the resulting discontent among investors opened the way for hostile takeovers and leveraged restructuring.[26]

The emergence of tender offers and hostile takeovers shattered the uneasy "in the long run" legal device for reconciling the property conception and the social entity conception. To shareholders who had been offered an immediate 35 or 40 percent premium to tender their shares, the possibility that the company might perform better as an independent entity "in the long run" seemed irrelevent. Even in terms of evaluating more ordinary business decisions, the extraordinarily high cost of capital that prevailed in the 1980s greatly weakened the defense for expenditures that would show returns only in the long run. At discount rates of 10 to 15 percent, the return on investments of any kind, whether in new plants and equipment or in community relations, must be much higher and come in much faster than it must at discount rates of 5 to 10 percent.[27]

The legal response to the breakdown of the accommodation between shareholder wealth maximization and corporate social responsibility has not been completely worked out. Throughout the 1980s, for example, the American Law Institute worked to develop a new consensus statement on principles of corporate governance. Reflecting the political dominance of the "finance model," or "prop-

---

[26]This hypothesis about the cause of highly leveraged corporate restructuring activity in the 1980s was first presented in Blair and Litan (1990) and is a major thesis of several essays in Blair (1993).

[27]Based on a survey of 228 Fortune 1000 firms conducted in 1990 and 1991, Poterba and Summers (1991) estimate that corporate executives use an average real (inflation-adjusted) "hurdle rate" of 12.2 percent to evaluate investments. More recently, the *Wall Street Journal* reported that corporations were setting very aggressive hurdles on return on investment—some as high as 20 percent—for capital spending planned for 1994. See Fred R. Bleakley, "As Capital Spending Grows, Firms Take a Hard Look at Returns From the Effort," *Wall Street Journal*, February 8, 1994, p. A2.

erty conception" of that decade, early drafts were strident in tone, asserting that corporations should absolutely and unequivocally be treated as the property of shareholders, that the goal of the corporation should be to maximize value for shareholders, and that the well-being of shareholders should take precedence in every corporate decision. The tone was softened considerably in the final document, which states that the objective of corporations should be "the conduct of business activities with a view to enhancing corporate profit and shareholder gain." In so doing, the document said, corporations "may devote a reasonable amount of resources to public welfare, humanitarian, educational, and philanthropic purposes." Nonetheless, this document still insists that shareholder interests should dominate and that directors should consider nonshareholder constituencies only when "competing courses of action have comparable impact on shareholders."[28]

At the state level, the rejection of the strict property conception (at least in the context of takeovers) was much more explicit. At least twenty-seven states have passed laws since 1985 that specifically make it legal for (and in at least one state, require) directors to consider other interests in addition to shareholders when making major business decisions, mainly in deciding whether to accept or fight a tender offer. (Two states, Pennsylvania and Ohio, had such a law before 1985.)[29] Typically, these statutes require directors to consider the "best interests of the corporation" as a whole, and then identify a specific set of stakeholders, including employees, creditors, suppliers, and the community in general in addition to shareholders, whose interests are considered tied to the corporation. "States saw a different side of the rampant takeover activity—the social responsiblity side—and began to question whether attaining

[28]The American Law Institute (1994, pp. 55, 405).
[29]See Wallman (1993) for a list of the states with corporate constituency laws.

takeover benefits for shareholders was as consistent with other important interests as economic and legal orthodoxy presumed," says law professor Alexander C. Gavis.[30]

Steven M. H. Wallman, an SEC commissioner who helped to draft the original "corporate constituency" law passed in Pennsylvania in 1983 and its amendment in 1990, defines the corporation's interest as "enhancing its ability to produce wealth indefinitely . . . [including] both profit from today's activities and expected profit from tomorrow's activities."[31] This wealth-producing language is not in the statutes, but Wallman's subsequent explication of what it means for directors to act "in the interest of the corporation" suggests that these laws, if interpreted and applied as Wallman believes they should be, could provide a legal basis for a new conception of the proper goals of corporate governance.[32] Linking the interests of the various constituencies to the interest of the corporation, he asserts, "resolves much of the tension that would otherwise exist from competing and conflicting constituent demands."[33] Defining the interests of the corporation in terms of maximizing the wealth-producing potential of the enterprise as a whole also provides the beginning of a way to resolve the long-term, short-term conflict, as well as a basis for deciding which corporate constituencies matter under what circumstances.

Many legal scholars, policy analysts, and others have sharply criticized these corporate constituency laws. Their only application is in the takeover context, critics say (because the "business judgement rule" still applies in other contexts). In this context, their

---

[30]Gavis (1990, p. 1461).

[31]Wallman (1991, p. 170).

[32]In private correspondence with the author Septempter 7, 1993, Wallman took pains to distinguish his "wealth-producing notion" of the duty of boards and the role of corporations from the "social responsibility model."

[33]Wallman (1991, p. 170).

effect is to give corporate executives and directors carte blanche to do whatever they want, the critics say, because almost any decision can be justified on the grounds that it benefits or protects some constituency. Thus, finance model advocates and even some market myopia advocates disparage these laws as no more than knee-jerk reactions by state legislatures to try to protect management and workers in their states from the threat of hostile takeovers.

The state of Delaware, where more than half of the Standard & Poor's 500 corporations are incorporated, has not passed such a statute, but the decision of the Delaware Supreme Court in *Paramount Communications v. Time Inc.* in 1989 was widely interpreted as giving similar leeway to management of Delaware-chartered firms. It did so, however, by again invoking the "long-term/short-term" distinction rather than by directly addressing the question of whose interests should take precedence. In that case, the board of directors of Time Inc. thwarted a takeover bid by Paramount Communications by quickly executing a tender offer for Warner Communications. Paramount's initial cash offering price represented about a 40 percent premium over the price at which Time's stock had been trading just before Paramount's offer, and Paramount later raised the bid, with the higher bid representing a 60 percent premium. But for months (indeed, years) before the Paramount bid, Time had been negotiating a stock-for-stock merger with Warner Communications and had announced a merger plan a few months before the Paramount offer was made. The Delaware Supreme Court refused to stop Time from proceeding with the tender offer for Warner, even though, in taking that action, Time's board foreclosed any opportunity for Time shareholders to accept the Paramount offer or even to vote on the merger with Warner. "The fiduciary duty to manage a corporate enterprise includes the selection of a time frame for achievement of corporate goals," the court ruled. "That duty may not be delegated to the stockholders. . . . Directors are not obliged to abandon a deliberately conceived corporate plan for a short-term shareholder profit unless there is clearly no basis to sustain the corporate strategy."[34] Allen, who wrote the chancery court opinion in the case, later wrote that the ruling "might be interpreted as constituting implicit acknowledgement of the social entity conception."[35]

Four years later, in a case again involving Paramount Communications, the Delaware Supreme Court appeared to shift its stance again, this time toward placing more weight on getting the highest value for shareholders, regardless of the effect on management's carefully laid long-range strategic plans. In this case Paramount was negotiating a merger agreement with Viacom when Paramount CEO Martin Davis learned that QVC Network was interested in acquiring Paramount. In response, Paramount put together a deal with Viacom to exchange Paramount shares for a mix of Viacom stock and cash that was estimated to be worth about $70 per Paramount share, and that gave Viacom an option to buy 19.9 percent of the stock of Paramount if the Paramount-Viacom deal were canceled for any of a number of reasons, including an acquisition of Paramount by some other bidder. The options included several unusual features that would be highly disadvantageous to QVC if it proceeded with a tender offer. Nonetheless, QVC did proceed, offering $80 a share for 51 percent of Paramount's stock and filing suit to have the stock option agreement invalidated.

In contrast to its assessment of the facts in the earlier case, the Delaware Supreme Court ruled that Paramount was embarking on a plan to sell control of Paramount and that Paramount's board was therefore obligated to consider all offers in order to get the best price for the company. "The pending sale of control implicated in the

---

[34]See Supreme Court of the State of Delaware, *Paramount Communications, Inc. v. Time Inc.*, 571 A.2d 1140–1155 (Delaware 1990).

[35]Allen (1992, p. 20).

Paramount-Viacom transaction required the Paramount Board to act on an informed basis to secure the best value reasonably available to the stockholders," the court ruled.[36]

Technically, the difference between these two cases hinged on whether the defendant directors (Time's board in the first case, and Paramount's board in the second) had put their companies up for sale when they announced merger plans. But in the first case, the court seemed to give directors considerable leeway to reject takeover bids in order to protect long-range strategic plans, and in the second case, the court seemed to sharply circumscribe the types of long-range plans that would be so protected. Thus it remains unclear whether directors of companies incorporated in Delaware can consider the effect of a takeover decision on stakeholders other than just shareholders.[37]

So far, no stakeholder has tested the limits of the "corporate constituency" laws by attempting to enforce his or her claim to

---

[36]See Supreme Court of Delaware, *Paramount Communications Inc. v. QVC Network Inc.*, 637 A.2d 34 (Del. 1994).

[37]Takeover lawyer Martin Lipton says that the two cases "can be summarized as holding that under Delaware law the objective of the corporation is the *long-term* growth of shareholder value; assuming the board of directors has used due care (followed reasonable procedures) and did not have a conflict of interest, the board may prefer *long-term* goals over *short-term* goals except when the decision is to sell control of the corporation or to liquidate it in which case the board must use reasonable efforts to get the best value obtainable for the shareholders. Under this standard the board has the right to invest for the *long-term* in people, equipment, market share and financial structure even though the financial markets do not recognize (or overly discount) the future value and even though the board's strategy results in elimination of dividends and reduction in market price of the stock. Also under this standard, the board has the right to 'just say no' to a premium takeover bid. However, the board does remain subject to shareholder control and the shareholders have the right at least once a year to replace at least some of the directors who have followed a strategy or taken a position disliked by the shareholders." [Emphasis in original] Private correspondence with the author, April 5, 1994.

consideration in the courts.[38] Unless and until these laws are over-turned, however, they give formal legal sanction to the idea that corporations have social purposes in addition to providing profits for shareholders.

What Should the Law Say?

Although the law has still not resolved the issue unequivocally, the belief that the primary goal of corporate endeavors should be to maximize value for shareholders still dominates the public policy debates and has largely been accepted even by corporate executives who not long before tended to resist that idea.[39] Three theoretical arguments are typically given for why it is in society's interest that corporations should be run for shareholders and why shareholders, in turn, should be given control.

Shareholders as 'Owners'

The first of these arguments holds that shareholders should have the right to control corporate resources and ensure that they are used to their own benefit because they are the "owners." The right to con-

---

[38]"Case law interpreting nonshareholder constituency statutes appears to be non-existent," says Gavis, who suggests that states with these laws have relatively little corporate activity in them. See Gavis (1990, p. 1446). But some of the laws include language intended to rule out, or at least discourage, such enforcement action. See Sommer (1991b, p. 46). Such provisions reinforce the view of some legal scholars and observers who believe that the statutes were intended to protect management, not to give other stakeholders access or standing to make specific claims against corporations.

[39]Lazonick (1992, pp. 467, 469) argues that corporate executives have been co-opted by this finance-oriented view because they have risen to the tops of their organizations in an era that rewarded financial market performance more than innovative activity or growth in market share and because their own compensation is now, more than ever, tied to stock price performance.

trol private property is an essential part of what it means to own something, and ownership rights are a vitally important social norm and important for efficiency reasons.

By now, that argument—that shareholders own the corporation, so therefore they should be able to exercise control over it—should have been put safely to rest. It is simply circular logic. Shareholders own equity, and the question is what control rights ought to accompany that kind of claim against the company. The de facto separation of equity ownership from control, Votaw noted, changed the whole legal concept of property, at least with respect to corporations.

> Property consists of a bundle of rights which the owner of property posesses with regard to some thing—rights to possess, use, dispose of, exclude others, and manage and control. The corporate concept divides this bundle of rights into several pieces. The stockholder gets the right to receive some of the fruits of the use of property, a fractional residual right in corporate property, and a very limited right of control. The rights to possess, use, and control the property go to the managers of the corporation.[40]

When property rights have been broken up in this way, trying to identify one party as the "owner" is neither meaningful nor useful. "To assume that we can know who property owners are, and to assume that once we have identified them their rights follow as a matter of course, is to assume what needs to be decided," Joseph William Singer wrote in an essay on whether steelworkers have any legitimate property rights in the plant where they work.[41]

Building on the idea of property as a bundle of rights, Thomas Donaldson and Lee E. Preston argue that the various property rights that societies grant are generally based on some underlying concept

[40]Votaw (1965, pp. 96–97).
[41]Singer (1988, pp. 637–38).

of justice, especially distributive justice. Notions of distributive justice, in turn, are based on some socially constructed notion of who has what moral interest in the use of the asset—for example, who has contributed what effort or made what sacrifice, who has what need, or who has made what prior agreement about the uses of the asset. In modern corporations, by definition, all stakeholders have some stake or moral interest in the affairs of corporations, Donaldson and Preston observe and conclude that "the normative principles that underly the contemporary pluralistic theory of property rights also provide the foundation for the stakeholder theory as well."[42]

Management Accountability

The second argument for why it is in the public interest to operate corporations for shareholders holds that, as a normative matter, corporate executives should not be allowed to make arbitrary decisions to use other people's property for their own interest or even for what they believe to be in the public interest. Managers must be held accountable to someone. Diffusing this responsibility among many groups of stakeholders means, in practice, that managers are accountable to no one.

Ronald Coase has argued that, if property rights are clearly established and if all parties can contract freely over the use of resources, then those resources will be used efficiently.[43] According to Coase, it makes no difference (from an efficiency standpoint) whether the factory owner has the right to pollute or the townspeople have the right to clean air. If the property rights are clearly established, the various parties can write a contract in which the townspeople pay

[42]Donaldson and Preston (1995).
[43]Coase (1960, pp. 15–16).

the factory owner not to pollute or the factory owner pays the townspeople for the right to pollute. In either case, the process of contracting will determine a socially optimal "price" for polluting, and the factory owner will end up spending the right amount on pollution abatement equipment.[44]

But even if one agreed in principle that clearly established property rights would be socially useful, establishing completely clear "property" rights in complex organizations such as corporations is impossible in practice, in part because the concept of "property" is so complex and multifaceted. The question is which of the many "control" rights should be assigned to shareholders, which given to other stakeholders, and which left to managers.

Nonetheless, if managers do not themselves bear the full costs of their decisions and if they are not held accountable to someone for something, they will be accountable to no one, and they will have few incentives to use resources under their control efficiently.

Versions of this argument were often heard in the debates of the late 1960s and early 1970s about the "social responsibilities" of business. In its simple version, it says that performance is easier to monitor if only one dimension of performance, such as profits (or, in their capitalized form, share value) is measured. In more sophisticated versions, the argument is concerned about private uses of power. As Friedrich A. Hayek puts it, "the tendency to allow and even to impel the corporations to use their resources for specific ends other than those of a long-run maximization of the return on the capital placed under their control . . . tends to confer upon them undesirable and socially dangerous powers."[45]

---

[44]The information requirements are quite severe for this hypothesis to hold, however, and the difficulties in enforcing contracts could easily be insurmountable.
[45]Hayek (1985, p. 100).

The central point here is the need for mechanisms to ensure that management is accountable for its decisions. Managers should be held accountable precisely because they are managing assets that are not their own and because they do not personally bear all of the costs of their decisions. But this argument fails to make the case that the objective of managers should be to maximize share value; it therefore also fails to make the case that the shareholders should necessarily be given greater control rights.

The third public interest argument used to justify assigning control rights to shareholders is that shareholders are the residual claimants.[46] They receive the residual gain and bear the residual risk associated with the corporate enterprise, this argument goes, and they therefore have the best incentive to monitor. To the extent that this is true, maximizing value for shareholders is equivalent to maximizing the social value of corporations, and it follows that it would be socially optimal to give control rights to shareholders to ensure that share value is maximized.

At first glance, this argument would seem to be the same as saying that the shareholders should monitor because it is their money that is being managed. But saying that it is the shareholders' money does not resolve the underlying questions about the meaning of "ownership" in this case. Ronald Gilson and Mark Roe make the distinction clear: "Equity has governance rights because the holder of the residual profits interest has the best incentive to reduce agency costs; the right to control rests with those who stand to gain

[46]This is the cornerstone of the corporate governance arguments made by Easterbrook and Fischel (1991). Shareholders hold voting rights, as opposed to bondholders, management, or employees, they argue, because shareholders are the residual claimants on firm income and are therefore willing to pay most for voting rights. When a firm is in distress, shareholder incentives become skewed and other constituents receive voting rights. "The fact that voting rights flow to whichever group holds the residual claim at any given time strongly supports our analysis of the function of voting rights," they wrote (p. 405). See also Easterbrook and Fischel (1983).

the most from efficient production."[47] Previously, Gilson had held that the "description of shareholders as the 'owners' . . . derives . . . from the need for those holding the residual interest in corporate profits to have the means to displace management which performs poorly. . . . This position is based on matters other than a preconception of the rights associated with 'ownership'; indeed, if the statute did not provide for shareholders, we would have to invent them."[48] This argument is the product of a long and somewhat arcane scholarly effort to explain large enterprises in a way consistent with neoclassical economic theory. In very simplified terms, the theory that has been developed goes as follows: Team production is often much more efficient than individual production. But, because it is sometimes hard to tell who is responsible for what portion of the output produced by teams, individual team members might try to shirk. Team production thus requires that someone serve as monitor to be sure that no one shirks. What keeps the monitor from shirking? The monitor enters into contracts with all of the other input providers to pay each of them according to their opportunity cost (that is, what they could get if they sold their services or materials to the next highest bidder), and the monitor receives all of the extra value created by the enterprise, over and above these costs. In other words, the monitor bears the residual risk and receives the residual gain.[49]

In a small, entrepreneurial firm, this monitor is the owner-manager. But who bears the residual risk and receives the residual gain in large, widely held corporations? Scholars who have worked on these questions of organizational theory have generally assumed

---

[47]Gilson and Roe (1993, p. 887).

[48]Gilson (1981, p. 34).

[49]See Alchian and Demsetz (1972), who wrote the classic article that marked the beginning of the development of this view of corporations.

that it is the shareholders.[50] From that assumption, they have argued that hierarchical decisionmaking and oversight by boards of directors were institutional arrangements developed as substitutes for direct monitoring by shareholders.[51] And, from that argument, they conclude that boards of directors should represent the interests of shareholders above all other competing interests.

In the idealized model of a corporation described by these scholars, institutional and legal arrangements that direct as much of the oversight and control responsibilities as possible to shareholders or to their representatives make impeccable sense. But shareholders were long ago granted limited liability, which, of course, shifted some of the residual risk onto creditors and others. Moreover, the risks that shareholders bear can largely be diversified away by holding the shares as part of a balanced portfolio. Finally, shareholders generally have unrestricted rights to sell their shares, which means that shareholders, perhaps more than any of the other stakeholders in firms, have the option to "exit" if they are dissatisfied with the performance of the firm. Thus, the notion that shareholders bear all of the residual risk seems doubtful on its face.[52]

[50]In nearly all of the finance literature and much of management and economics literature, shareholders are assumed, without question, to play this role. A few organizational theorists and labor economists interested in the problems introduced by firm-specific investments in human capital have come to appreciate that shareholders are generally not the only residual risk-bearers, and that the assumption that they are is not inconsequential. But the implications of this fact for efficient corporate governance have not yet been acknowledged or studied by finance theorists nor have they been formally acknowledged in the law.

[51]Fama and Jensen (1983) made this argument in their now classic article.

[52]Finance specialists have long understood that the value of a company's equity can be increased by shifting some of the risk onto debt holders. Wallman (1991, p. 178) provides an easy-to-understand example. In this case, maximizing value for the shareholders is clearly not equivalent to maximizing social value. But finance model advocates tend to assume away the implications of this insight for corporate governance by asserting that creditors can write contracts that prohibit the managers of the firm from shifting more risk onto them than they initially bargain for.

For it to be be strictly true that shareholders receive all of the residual gain and bear all of the residual risk, the suppliers of all other inputs into the corporate enterprise would have to be compensated by means of "complete" contracts (that is, contracts that specify exactly what is to happen in all circumstances). These contracts would have to compensate other input providers at their social opportunity cost (including compensation for any explicit, predictable risk they were bearing). If such arrangements were, indeed, the norm, it would not make any difference to employees, lenders, materials and equipment suppliers, dealers, communities, or other stakeholders if a corporation suffered losses and had to go out of business. That is because the inputs supplied by these other parties could be readily redeployed at the same price or wages they had commanded in their service to the corporation or because the providers of these inputs were compensated in advance for any losses they might incur at such time.[53]

Curiously, although this assumption about the allocation of risk and rewards in the corporate enterprise would appear patently wrong, it is almost never challenged outright. In fact, among true believers in the finance model, this assumption is dogma. But labor economists have long noted that workers in large corporations, especially in certain industries, earn higher wages and benefits than do

---

[53]Fama and Jensen (1983, pp. 302–3) assert (but do not demonstrate empirically) that "the contract structures of most organizational forms limit the risks undertaken by most agents by specifying either fixed promised payoffs or incentive payoffs tied to specific measures of performance. The residual risk–the risk of the difference between stochastic inflows of resources and promised payments to agents–is borne by those who contract for the rights to the net cash flows. . . . Moreover, the contracts of most agents contain the implicit or explicit provision that, in exchange for the specified payoff, the agent agrees that the resources he provides can be used to satisfy the interests of residual claimants. . . . Having most uncertainty borne by one group of agents, residual claimants, has survival value because it reduces the costs incurred to monitor contracts with other groups of agents. Contracts that direct decisions toward the interests of residual claimants also add to the survival value of organizations."

workers with comparable skills and comparable jobs who are self-employed or who work for small entrepreneurial firms.[54] This differential would suggest that some of the residual gains from team production in large corporations are being shared with workers. Neoclassical economists have argued that apparent labor market differentials can be explained by unmeasured differences in labor quality and working conditions. An alternative view is that firms may, in some circumstances, pay higher wages to improve motivation, morale, and job stability, to make recruiting easier, and to encourage employees to develop special skills that may be valuable only to that employer. In other words, the higher productivity justifies the cost of paying wages above the competitive rate. Either way, the residual gain from team production is being shared with workers. And, as the next chapter shows, sharing the residual gain with workers necessarily implies that these workers are sharing in the residual risk associated with the ability of the enterprise as a whole to continue to generate those gains.[55]

It is easy to see why the assumption that shareholders are the residual claimants is so important to those who maintain that shareholders should have control. If other stakeholders could be shown to share in the residual gains and risks, their interest in being able to exercise some control over corporations would be significantly legitimized.

Despite the empirical weakness of the assumption that shareholders receive all of the residual gain and bear all of the residual risk, the underlying point of the finance model argument is quite important—corporations are more likely to be managed in ways that maximize social value if those who monitor and control firms re-

[54]See, for example, Dunlop (1988, p. 56).

[55]This last point is probably not obvious, but it arises from the fact that the workers have made firm-specific investments in human capital as part of the process of wealth creation in the enterprise.

ceive (at least some of) the residual gain and bear (some of) the residual risk, and, conversely, if those who share in the residual gains and risks are given the access and authority they need to monitor. Put more simply, corporate resources should be used to enhance the goals and serve the purposes of all those who truly have something invested and at risk in the enterprise. Those parties, in turn, should be given enough of the control rights to ensure that corporate resources are used to those ends. If control rights could be allocated in this way, all of the participants would have an incentive to see that the total size of the pie is maximized, and any one stakeholder group would have trouble increasing the value of its stake simply by pushing costs and risks onto other stakeholders.

In short, it is possible to reject the simplistic finance model or property conception of the corporation to the extent that it implies that directors' only duty is to maximize value for shareholders, and still retain the compelling logic that private control of private property leads to the most efficient use of society's resources. In the next chapter I argue that the view of corporations as wealth-creating machines, with a social purpose of maximizing wealth, provides a clear basis for thinking about how control rights to that machine should be allocated. My conclusions differ from those of most finance model advocates, however, because I make a much more general assumption about what the source of value creation is, and who it is that bears the risk and receives the gains in most corporations today.

The primitive model of corporations in which shareholders are seen as earning all the returns and bearing all the risk is a throwback to an earlier time when the typical corporation owned and operated a canal, a railroad, or a big manufacturing plant. Entrepreneurial investors put up the financial capital, which was used to build or buy the railroad, canal, or factory and to make initial payments to hired managers. The managers, in turn, arranged to buy raw materials and energy, hire labor, oversee production or manage the operations, and (in the case of the factory) ship the goods to market. The proceeds from the sale of those goods was used to meet payroll (including the manager's salary), pay taxes, buy more raw materials, keep the machinery in working order and pay off any loans, and all of these inputs were acquired at the going market rate. Anything left over after that was "profit," and it seemed reasonable and appropriate that the profits belonged to the initial investors (shareholders), who were the only parties with significant assets tied up and at risk in the enterprise. These assets consisted of some inventories and receivables, the entrepreneurial know-how of the owner-manager, and, most, the canal, the roadbed and railcars, or the factory.[56]

For enterprises that fit this model, it may be a reasonable approximation of the truth that the capital investments and the entrepreneurial efforts of the investor are the sources of the wealth and that shareholders capture all of that wealth and bear all the associated risk. For firms that look like this, corporate governance arrangements that provide for them to be run for shareholders and that accordingly give as much control to shareholders as possible, serve to encourage wealth creation by fostering and protecting investments in physical capital and entrepreneurial effort.

But in the 1990s, fewer and fewer publicly traded corporations actually look like the factory model. Much of the wealth-generating capacity of most modern firms is based on the skills and knowledge

---

[56]"How can residual-claimant, central-employer-owner demonstrate ability to pay the other hired inputs the promised amount in the event of a loss?" Alchian and Demsetz ask. "He can pay in advance, or he can commit wealth sufficient to cover negative residuals. The latter will take the form of machines, land, buildings, or raw materials committed to the firm." See Alchian and Demsetz (1972, p. 791). Historians Galambos and Pratt (1988, p. 20) note also that most of the technology that was the source of added value in early factories was embodied in the capital—the physical plant and equipment—and that the employer-owner was often an engineer who was largely responsible for technical decisions about plant design or addition of new equipment.

of the employees and the ability of the organization as a whole to put those skills to work for customers and clients. Even for manufacturing firms, physical plant and equipment make up a rapidly declining share of the assets, while a growing share consists of intangibles (some recognized on the books and given an accounting value, some not) such as patent rights, brand reputation, service capabilities, and the ability to innovate and get the next generation product to market in a timely manner.[57]

It is commonplace to hear chief executives of major corporations say "our wealth is in our people."[58] Although such lines are probably not taken seriously nearly as often as they are said, there are important economic reasons why they should be taken seriously. Moreover, the idea that the wealth of a corporation is in its people has important implications for corporate governance arrangements.

[57]A rough measure of this is the share of the market value of assets accounted for by property, plant, and equipment (PP&E). I calculated these numbers using data on all manufacturing and mining firms listed in Compustat for which the relevant information was available. In 1982 PP&E accounted for 62.3 percent of the market value of mining and manufacturing firms; by 1991, PP&E accounted for only 37.9 percent of the market value.

[58]A quick review of interviews with twelve CEOs (on many topics) in recent issues of the *Harvard Business Review* produced the following quotes: "Our employees aren't just agents for the company, they are the company," – Robert F. McDermott, CEO of USAA. "A company is not bricks and mortar or money and finance. It's people;" and "profit is in the hands of employees." – Frederick C. Crawford, CEO of TRW; "If the people on the front line really are the keys to our success, then the manager's job is to help those people that they serve. That goes against the traditional assumptions that the manager is in control," – Robert Haas, CEO of Levi Strauss & Co.

7

TOWARD A NEW VIEW

OF CORPORATE GOALS

AND GOVERNANCE

I BEGAN THIS BOOK BY ARGUING that the role of public policy in the governance of large publicly traded corporations is to provide a legal and institutional environment that supports the development of efficient governance structures—that is, those that foster the most efficient use of resources to create wealth for society as a whole. One of the most important institutional arrangements for encouraging efficient use of resources is private property. If the party who controls the use of an asset also reaps the benefit of using it efficiently—and bears the cost of its misuse—that party has a significant incentive to see that the asset is used well. Hence institutional arrangements that bundle the right to control and benefit from assets together with the responsibility for bearing the risks associated with the use of the assets are likely to lead to efficient use of those assets.

In large, publicly traded corporations, those ownership or property rights have been unbundled and carved up among the many participants in the corporate enterprise. There are, of course, some important efficiency advantages from dividing up these ownership rights. Day-to-day decisionmaking has been turned over to hired managers, who have much better and more detailed information than do shareholders about the operations of the firm. Meanwhile, shareholders are better positioned than managers to bear certain kinds of risks because shareholders can more readily diversify their holdings. But a major governance problem arises as soon as decisions are made and control rights are exercised by parties who do not bear all the risk associated with the use of the assets. Mechanisms need to be devised so that the parties whose assets are at risk can monitor the managers; and contingent control rights need to be established so that, if the assets are grossly mismanaged, the at-risk parties can wrest control from and replace the poorly performing managers.

To date, most participants in the legal and policy debates about corporate governance have assumed that the monitoring group should be the shareholders. In one situation or another, the debate has considered whether shareholders should be given more or less power relative to management or has asked how the incentives facing shareholders or the information available to them might be improved to encourage them to perform their monitoring role more effectively.

Good reasons support this focus on shareholders. In the basic model of the firm discussed at the beginning of chapter 2, the shareholders' claim against the company is treated as a residual one—all other creditors and claimants are supposed to be paid first. Moreover, important contingent control rights are assigned to shareholders. Legal scholars Frank H. Easterbrook and Daniel R. Fischel explain this arrangement as follows:

Voting exists in corporations because someone must have the residual power to act (or delegate) when contracts are not complete. Votes could be held by shareholders, bondholders, managers, or other employees in any combination. . . . One might expect voting rights to be held by a small group with good access to information—the managers. Yet voting rights are universally held by shareholders, to the exclusion of creditors, managers, and other employees. . . .

The reason is that shareholders are the residual claimants to the firm's income. Creditors have fixed claims, and employees generally negotiate compensation schedules in advance of performance. The gains and losses from abnormally good or bad performance are the lot of the shareholders, whose claims stand last in line.

As the residual claimants, shareholders have the appropriate incentives . . . to make discretionary decisions. The firm should invest in new products, plants, and so forth, until the gains and costs are identical at the margin.[1]

Finally, because shareholders are residual claimants, Easterbrook and Fischel argue, shareholders have the moral and legal standing to be treated as "owners" of the corporation and to be given important control rights.

The Easterbrook and Fischel analysis reflects the standard view of corporations used in most introductory economics textbooks and serves as the basis for most discussions about corporate governance (typically without examination or reflection). I do not take issue with the logic of this analysis. Undoubtedly, in some corporations shareholders are the only residual claimants, and in such cases, wealth is created most effectively by maximizing the stream of

---

[1]Easterbrook and Fischel (1991, pp. 67–68). This book is an excellent analysis of the structure of corporation law and its relation to economic efficiency from a Chicago School perspective.

profits earned for shareholders. In such cases, the most efficient use of corporate resources is probably encouraged by giving shareholders control over residual decisionmaking. Instead, I argue that, as an empirical matter, most modern corporations do not look like this model and that, in practice, shareholders are rarely the only residual claimants.

Employees, for example, inevitably bear many of the risks associated with certain kinds of investments, especially investments in "human capital." Hence, when investments in highly specialized human capital are important to the way that a firm creates wealth, employees, as well as shareholders, are likely to be residual claimants and, therefore, residual risk-bearers.

Investments in human capital are most likely to be important in technology-intensive or service-oriented enterprises, where most of the value added comes from innovation, product customization, or specialized services.[2] These kinds of enterprises account for a growing share of economic activity and are vital to the long-term productivity and prosperity of the U.S. economy. In such enterprises employees whose skills are specialized to the company will inevitably bear some of the risk associated with the enterprise, and this fact gives them a "stake" in the company that is at risk in exactly the same way as the stake held by shareholders.[3]

---

[2]Paul M. Cook, founder and CEO of Raytheon Corp., stresses the importance of investments in human capital in his business. His company, he says, restricts its charter "to the world of material science, and within material science, to niches . . . in which we can be pioneers, the first and best in the world. And I mean *the* first. That means we can't just go to universities and find trained people; we have to train them ourselves." See Taylor (1990a, p. 102).

[3]Stanford professors Paul Milgrom and John Roberts draw the same conclusion in their work on organizational economics. "With high levels of firm-specific human capital, the decisions taken by the firm place risks on employees' human assets that are comparable to those borne by investors in physical capital. Protecting the value of this human capital then requires that employees' interests figure into the firm's decisionmaking." Milgrom and Roberts (1992, p. 351).

In firms where highly specialized skills are important, then, employees may be as highly motivated as shareholders to see that the firm's resources are used efficiently. Moreover, the employees of such enterprises exercise de facto control over many important decisions and, because of their inside knowledge of the business and their stake in its success, may be much better situated than distant and anonymous shareholders to act as monitors of management.

All of this implies that, for many kinds of corporations, employees (and sometimes other major stakeholders) have as much claim to being owners of the corporation as do shareholders, and perhaps more so. I am not suggesting that employees or other major stakeholders be given voting rights *instead* of shareholders, nor certainly that traditional shareholders be disenfranchised. But a clear understanding of what ownership means and of who has what investments at risk in most corporations suggests the need for the following.

First, management and boards of directors should understand their jobs to be maximizing the total wealth-creating potential of the enterprises they direct. In doing this, they must consider the effect of important corporate decisions on all of the company's *stakeholders*. For this purpose, stakeholders should be defined as all parties who have contributed inputs to the enterprise and who, as a result, have at risk investments that are highly specialized to the enterprise. These parties inevitably share in the residual risk of the firm. The law and the culture of the boardroom should support this broader view of the role of management and directors. In practice, the interests of various stakeholders can be taken into account in several ways, and some of these will be discussed in the remaining chapters.

Second, depending on the issue and the enterprise at hand, some stakeholders will matter more than others in some decisions. To provide better guidance for managers and directors, more research into the sources of wealth creation is needed, together with a better understanding of the organizational forms and governance structures that enhance wealth creation.

Third, where employees or other stakeholders have significant specialized investments at risk, their rights and obligations as owners should be formalized through compensation schemes, organizational forms, or other arrangements that place significant amounts of the company's equity under the control of the at-risk stakeholders and that assign control responsibilities commensurate with their equity stake to this group. Compensating employees who have investments in specialized human capital at risk with shares in the company can be a mechanism for aligning their interests with those of other shareholders.

Sources of Wealth Creation

In general, a business enterprise can generate wealth in three ways. First, it can provide products and services that are worth more to the customer than the customer pays for them. Customers capture the benefits of this activity in the form of "consumer surplus." Second, it can provide opportunities for workers to be more productive at their jobs than they could be in other available employment. To the extent that they earn higher incomes than they could elsewhere, the employees of such a company capture some of the wealth created by the enterprise.[4] Third, the enterprise can provide a flow of profits to its investors that is greater than those investors could get by invest-

---

[4]A full analysis would include "psychic incomes" of employees—that is, the satisfaction they get from a particularly interesting job or from working with colleagues whose company they enjoy. To the extent that some wealth is created because the employee works at a satisfying job, it should manifest itself partly in total income to the employee that is higher than his money income, or it may show up as lower costs to consumers or as higher returns to investors than they would otherwise earn, because the employee is willing to work for a lower money wage than he would demand at a less satisfying job. All of these ways of creating wealth are hard to measure.

ing in alternative activities.[5] If the wealth captured by consumers, employees, and suppliers of capital (the sum of consumer surplus, labor surplus, and capital surplus) exceeds any external costs (such as air pollution) imposed on the surrounding community or on others who are not direct participants in the enterprise, the enterprise is creating wealth.[6]

According to economic theory, if all of the firm's labor, raw materials, and capital inputs are acquired in perfectly competitive input markets and all the firm's products are sold into perfectly competitive product markets, all of the wealth created by that enterprise would be captured by consumers. The prices of the firm's products would be equal to their long-run average cost of production. No "economic profits" would accrue to the firm or to its input providers, either in the form of higher-than-normal profits for shareholders or higher-than-competitive wages for the firm's workers.

But perfectly competitive markets rarely exist, so participants in a firm may often earn economic profits, or *rents*. Rents are returns that are greater than the minimum required to induce the firm to supply a good. In the long run, a company earns true rents only if the returns are greater than the minimum required to induce the firm to make new investments to supply additional quantities of the good. But in the short run, a firm earns *quasi rents* as long as the return is

[5]An investment that earns only "normal" profits does not create wealth for the investor because the return equals the opportunity cost. Once an investment has been made, its value is determined by the actual returns it earns. If it earns a lower-than-normal return, wealth was destroyed by making the investment. If it earns a higher-than-normal return, wealth was created. Nonetheless, once the investment has been made, it is a "sunk cost." From that point on, using that asset in ways that provide a return higher than other alternative uses maximizes wealth creation.

[6]The enterprise could also provide a flow of benefits to other input providers, such as suppliers or creditors, but in such cases, the analysis could simply be repeated for those providers. Communities that provide the infrastructure in which the firm operates represent a special case that may deserve separate consideration.

higher than the minimum required to induce the firm to continue supplying the good, given that the required investments have already been made.[7] Firms in perfectly competitive markets can never earn true economic rents, but they may earn quasi rents.

Companies sometimes earn rents by colluding or by monopolizing a market to keep the supply of a product artificially low or to keep the price above its competitive level. Although firms have incentives to try to earn rents in this way, these rents do not result from new wealth being created; they are merely a transfer of wealth to firms from customers. In fact, extracting rents by artificially reducing supply and raising prices reduces total social wealth, which is why price collusion is prohibited under the antitrust laws.

Companies can also earn rents by creating and capturing new wealth if they meet one of two conditions. Either they must provide products that are unique or specialized enough that their prices have not been "competed" down to the long-run average cost of production, or they must have a technological or organizational advantage that enables them to produce the products or services with less labor or raw materials than their competitors use or to deliver them to customers in a more convenient way. If companies capture the wealth they create in this way, that wealth should show up as higher profits, higher wages for employees, or some combination of the two.

Management specialists have long understood that an important factor in business success for firms is to find and develop special

---

[7]For example, suppose I can break even by building a house and renting it for $1,000 a month. If I rent it for $1,000 a month, I earn zero economic rents. But if the demand for rental property allows me to rent the house for $1,200 a month, I can earn $200 a month in true economic rents. Now, suppose I have already built the house, that I have no alternative use for it, and that it costs $250 a month in out-of-pocket costs for me just to own the house. If I rent that house for $1,000 a month, I earn zero economic rents but $750 in quasi rents.

niches or sources of competitive advantage and to exploit them so that they can capture some of the rents available in these special niches.[8] The important point here is that, for a firm to earn rents in ways that create new wealth, it must utilize some inputs in ways that produce a higher value than they do in any other use.

To be sure, not all wealth-producing inputs must be organized and managed within a firm, and not all inputs used by firms must generate returns that exceed their opportunity cost. But economists and organizational theorists who have puzzled over why some economic activity is organized within firms and some is organized through a series of market exchanges are increasingly coming to believe that the key is whether there are specialized inputs that are more valuable when used in the context of an on-going, administered relationship among the various parties to the enterprise than when they are used in a series of market transactions.

In principle, for example, an entrepreneur could contract with a factory owner to rent a factory on a day-to-day basis and hire workers on daily spot markets to work in that factory. That does not happen because factories are complex systems, which can be run more efficiently by a regular team of workers familiar with each other and with the factory. Organizing production through a firm permits the use of specialized inputs—the dedicated plant and equipment and the "organizational" capital embodied in the knowledge of the team of people who regularly work in the factory and in the routines they have developed for working together.[9]

---

[8]See, for example, Porter (1980), the classic textbook used in "corporate strategies" classes to teach management students how to identify such competitive opportunities.

[9]Nelson and Winter (1982, p. 134) argue that much of the knowledge that firms have about how to produce goods and services and deliver them to customers is embedded in the "routines" that guide actions and decisionmaking by various employees. This knowledge, they argue, is "tacit knowledge of the organization, not consciously known or articulable by anyone in particular."

Where investments in such specialized inputs can create value, it is advantageous for the participants in the enterprise that uses the inputs (for example, the factory owner, the management, and the team of workers) to maintain long-term relationships with each other in order to extract the full value from the investments each has made. But governing those long-term relationships is complicated. Governance structures must be devised that give all of the participants incentives to work together efficiently and that minimize costs of coordination and dispute resolution. Corporations can be viewed as one kind of solution to this complex governance problem: they are an institutional structure whose role is to administer the contractual relationships among all parties that contribute highly specific inputs. Economist and organizational theorist Oliver Williamson uses the phrase "relationship-specific investments" to describe the kinds of inputs whose use calls for organizing work within a firm.[10] The firm, Williamson says, substitutes a "hierarchical" governance structure for a series of market transactions.

In setting up a corporation or other kind of business firm, Easterbrook and Fischel argue that rules for team production that cover all contingencies generally cannot be written in advance. They, as well as most other writers on corporate governance, usually assume, however, that satisfactory long-term contracts can be written with most participants in the firm, including employees, suppliers, and creditors, so that such participants are paid fixed amounts that are not contingent on how well the enterprise as a whole functions. But, they argue, some participants in the firm must have residual authority to make decisions about matters that have not been decided or explicitly contracted for in advance. And because the returns from the enterprise are uncertain, all participants cannot be guaranteed a

---

[10]Williamson (1979a, 1979b). Williamson also uses the phrase "asset specificity" to capture this idea.

fixed payment. At least one participant, therefore, must contract to receive the residual returns—to get the profits if there are any and to suffer the losses if the enterprise does not do well. In the case of the entrepreneurial firm, a single entrepreneur is assigned both residual control and residual returns and is referred to as the "owner" of the firm.

In the simplest model of the corporation, where shareholders are assumed to have close control over management, the shareholders play this role. Easterbrook and Fischel argue that, even where shareholders are not in a position to have close control over residual decisionmaking, they are always the residual claimants and therefore are always given voting control over management. The following series of examples shows that, in practice, shareholders are not always the only residual claimants. In many important cases, wealth is created by means of a complex interaction between technological and organizational innovation that includes input by skilled employees for which the managers of the firm are not able to contract explicitly in advance. In these cases, the skilled employees must necessarily make investments in specialized skills and take risks for which they cannot be fully compensated by means of complete contracts. They must also, by necessity, share in the residual risk.

The Simplest Example

Suppose an individual designs a special piece of equipment that would enable her to make widgets with less raw material than is used by competitors who make similar widgets.[11] Consider first

---

[11]To keep matters simple, suppose also that this machine generates no pollution so that the gain in productivity does not come at the expense of some higher cost imposed on society.

whether the entrepreneur would create wealth for herself if she were to build the machine and embark on a widget-making enterprise.[12]

The cost to the entrepreneur to build the specialized equipment can be measured quite accurately.[13] So too can the "scrap" value of that equipment once it is built. The hard part is calculating the "value-in-use" of the equipment as a widget-maker. This is done by estimating the present value of the expected stream of operating profits (revenues from the sale of widgets, minus raw materials, energy, maintenance costs, and labor costs) from using the machine to make widgets.[14] These three measures of value may be very different. Moreover, a great deal of uncertainty will surround the estimate of the value-in-use of the widget-maker.

The entrepreneur must make a sequence of decisions. She must decide first whether to proceed with the investment; if she makes the investment, she must then decide, again and again, whether to continue to operate the machine and make widgets, or to abandon the business, shut down the widget machine, and sell it for scrap.

For the first decision, the entrepreneur must make the best estimate she can of the present value of the expected stream of operating

---

[12]The following examples have been developed in a more formal, mathematical way in Blair (1995).

[13]At least, her out-of-pocket costs can be measured; there may be no way to assign a cost figure to her creative efforts, a fact which goes to the heart of the arguments I make later about the contributions of skilled employees in general.

[14]If widgets are sold into perfectly competitive markets, this measure of the value-in-use is equal to the scrap value of the machine plus the present value of all the rents and quasi rents derived from using the widget machine. The value to the entrepreneur may diverge from this if she must pay out part of the operating profits in taxes, or, as we shall see in the subsequent example, in the form of higher wages to employees. Assume for now that the entrepreneur pays "normal" wages and no taxes, and therefore gets all of the rents and quasi rents. The "present value" of a stream of payments is calculated by summing over all of the expected future payments, with each payment "discounted" by a factor that takes into account how many months or years in the future the payment will come, and the interest rate or some other measure of the time value of money.

profits from using the widget-maker (taking into account uncertainty about the future prices of raw materials and other inputs, as well as of widgets), and if that estimated value equals or exceeds the up-front costs of building the machine, then it would be wealth creating and therefore socially beneficial for her to proceed with the investment. Assuming for the moment that the entrepreneur captures and keeps all of the rents and quasi rents herself, then it would also be privately beneficial for her to proceed with the investment. Once the investment has been made, she will find out whether she succeeded in creating wealth for herself. If the value-in-use of the machine turns out to exceed her cost of having built the machine, then she will, indeed, have created and captured new wealth.

If the value-in-use of the machine turns out to be high enough, the entrepreneur will most assuredly want to go forward with the business. How high is high enough? Suppose, for example, that the value-in-use of the machine turns out to be less than it cost her to build the machine. At that point, the only way the entrepreneur can recover any wealth from the machine is either to operate it or to sell it for scrap. And, as long as the value of the stream of operating profits generated by the machine exceeds the value of the machine as scrap, it makes sense for the entrepreneur to operate the machine (or to sell it to someone else who will operate it). In other words, after the machine has been built, its production cost becomes irrelevant to its value. Even if the initial investment failed to create wealth, once the resources have been expended to build the machine, wealth is maximized by continuing to use that machine to produce widgets as long as the present value of the operating profits it produces exceeds its scrap value.[15]

---

[15]This may seem like an obvious point, but it bears repeating because, as we shall see, it often seems to be ignored when it comes to thinking about the value of investments in "human" capital. I will take up that problem in the next example.

Suppose the entrepreneur wants to form a corporation, WidgInc, to own the widget machine and operate the widget business. One reason she might want to do this is that her own personal resources might not be great enough to supply all the start-up capital herself. She may also want the advantages of limited liability and perpetual existence for her enterprise. How should she finance that corporation? Finance scholars have long debated the question of whether there is an "optimal" debt-to-equity ratio, but one thing seems clear empirically: debt is used more often when the business has tangible assets to serve as collateral, while equity is more likely to be used when the assets of the business are intangible.[16] Suppose, for the sake of argument, that the entrepreneur issues debt equivalent to the scrap value of the widget machine (so that the debt is completely collateralized) and issues enough equity to finance the remaining cost of building the widget machine and putting it into production.[17] The entrepreneur then buys raw material and labor at the going market prices for these inputs.

If the equity is initially sold to a small group of family and friends of the entrepreneur, the resulting corporation would closely resemble the basic model of the corporation presented in chapter 2. The value of the equity in WidgInc would be equal to the present value of the expected stream of rents and quasi rents from the machine (minus the outstanding debt, plus the scrap value of the machine, which are exactly equal so they cancel each other out). This value would rise and fall with fluctuations in the demand for widgets and the price of inputs. But shareholders would bear all of the risk

---

[16]Long and Malitz (1985).

[17]She could issue less debt, but that would not affect the argument I am making. She could also issue more debt, but if so, the creditors would presumably require a higher rate of return because they would then bear some of the business risk associated with the enterprise. That would complicate my story somewhat, but not change my essential results.

associated with these fluctuations in business conditions. To maximize the value of the equity of this company, the entrepreneur should operate the machine as long as the value of the stream of operating profits exceeds the scrap value of the machine (that is, as long as there are some positive rents or quasi rents), but she should shut the machine down whenever the value of the stream of operating profits falls below the scrap value. Hence, maximizing the value of equity is equivalent to maximizing the total social wealth created by the enterprise.

The Role of Specialized Human Capital

Now make the problem more complicated. Suppose that the widget machine needs a team of highly skilled workers to operate it and that a good worker would need about six months of training to learn the requisite skills. The entrepreneur now faces another set of decisions. At the same time that she is deciding whether to build the widget machine, she must also think about how to ensure that she will have a skilled work force in place and ready to go once the machine is built. Should she offer to pay the training costs for those workers, or should she count on them making the necessary investments on their own to acquire the relevant skills? Economists suggest that the answer depends on whether the skills the workers need are "generic" (meaning that the workers could use them many places in addition to the widget factory) or highly specific to the task of making widgets with her machine. If they are generic skills, the workers would reasonably expect that their investments in skills would have value in many other endeavors, and they should be well motivated to incur the expense of training themselves.

Suppose, however, that the skills the workers need are highly specific to the widget-making enterprise. Now the workers would have no incentive to incur the cost of training on their own unless they expect that, once they have acquired the skills, they would be paid more by WidgInc than they would earn at other jobs. So if the skills are firm-specific, the entrepreneur must essentially decide between paying the full cost of training or convincing the workers to share in that up-front cost by promising them a higher wage than they could earn in alternative employment once the business is up and running.

The addition of "firm-specific" skills changes the problem facing the entrepreneur in a variety of ways. First, it raises the hurdle on her initial decision to invest. Now, to invest, she must believe that the enterprise will generate enough in rents and quasi rents to pay not only for the cost of building the machine, but also for the cost of training the workers or of compensating them for their higher skills once they have the training (or some of both).[18]

Second, the addition of firm-specific skills introduces a bargaining problem between the entrepreneur and the workers. This second point requires some explanation, but it is important to the analysis. Suppose the entrepreneur proposes to pay the entire cost of training her employees, and once they have the specialized skills, she agrees to pay them only what they could earn in alternative employment (their "opportunity cost").[19] At first blush, it would appear that the

---

[18]This does not necessarily reduce the probability that the investment will be attractive to the entrepreneur, because production technologies that use highly specialized labor may, in general, be much more productive than technologies that use generic labor. Recall that the decision to organize production within a firm in the first place (rather than through a series of spot market transactions) is probably driven by the hope and belief that organizing production in a way that uses committed assets and long-term relationships will be more productive.

[19]In the short run, the employees' opportunity cost is what they could earn elsewhere without any specialized training. In the long run, however, their opportunity cost includes the fact that, by choosing to work for WidgInc, they may have to sacrifice an opportunity to learn special skills, and perhaps earn higher wages for doing so, at some other firm. Hence, if employees understand their long-term opportunity costs, this strategy by the entrepreneur might not be viable. As I soon show, this is just one of the reasons to believe this approach will not work, but assume for now that she tries it anyway.

entrepreneur would have an incentive to go forward with all of the investments (both the machine and the training) as long as she believed that the present value of the stream of operating profits would be greater than the sum of the cost of the machine and the cost of training. Under this plan, once the business was operating, all of the rents and quasi rents generated by the enterprise would, in effect, go to shareholders, and the value of the equity in WidgInc would be equal to the present value of that stream of rents and quasi rents.[20]

But, in fact, it is not so simple. Once the workers are trained, they are in possession of their specialized skills (or "knowledge capital"), and the firm is in possession of its machine. These assets—the machine, and the human capital—are "cospecialized." Neither has much value without the other. If, once the business is operating, the workers were paid only their (short-run) opportunity cost, they would have nothing to lose by threatening to walk out and take a different job. The workers are in a good bargaining position to try to capture some of the rents (and hence, some of the value of the enterprise) from the shareholders by threatening to quit if they are not paid more. Of course, the reverse is also true. If the workers had paid the cost of training (by, for example, accepting a wage that was below their opportunity cost while they were undergoing training) in exchange for a promise of higher wages once the business was up and running, the entrepreneur would then be in a position to expropriate some of the rents promised to workers by threatening to close down the business unless the workers agreed to work at a wage that was lower than what they had been promised. In the latter case, the workers would be at risk of losing the value of their investment.

---

[20]Recall that this analysis was simplified by assuming that the firm would not pay corporate income taxes.

Economists Paul Milgrom and John Roberts refer to this potential standoff as the "hold-up" problem.[21] Because they each control assets that are cospecialized with the other party's assets, the workers and the entrepreneur can, if they are inclined to do so, hold each other up to try to extract more of the total rents. Unless the parties have an agreement about the division of rents that will continue to be mutually satisfactory once the business is operating, some of the rents are likely to be dissipated over time in haggling and negotiating costs.

There are several important points here. First, because the machine and the specialized skills are cospecialized, the value of each cannot be determined without knowing the value of the other. The total expected rents and quasi rents (and hence the total value created and captured by the firm) from putting the machine and the trained workers together can be estimated. But external markets do not provide any guidance about how best to divide these rents between the equity holders and the workers.[22] The division of rents is, ultimately, a matter of negotiation, in which precedents, rules of thumb, bargaining skills, and other "noneconomic" factors may be very important.[23] Second, the entrepreneur must factor into her estimate of the value of the business, and therefore into her invest-

---

[21]Milgrom and Roberts (1992, p. 135.)

[22]Becker (1964, pp. 18-29) was the first to point out this problem. In the years since, a few attempts have been made to develop models in which the share of rents that go to labor and capital are determined as a function of the probability of labor turnover or the transactions costs of changing jobs. See, for example, Hashimoto (1981). To get a determinate solution in these models requires some heroic assumptions, however, and consequently, none have been considered very convincing by labor economists who have studied these models.

[23]"In practice," writes Hart (1989, p. 1762) about a related problem, "parties must negotiate many of the terms of the relationship as they go along." Such negotiations are costly in and of themselves and are subject to perverse ex ante incentives. "A party's bargaining power and resulting share of the ex post surplus may bear little relation to his ex ante investment." See also Hart and Moore (1990).

ment decision, some probability that she might be "held up" by the workers or that some of the value of the business will be dissipated in negotiations with workers. Likewise, if the workers were to undertake all or part of the investment in their specialized skills, they would also have to include in their investment decision some allowance for the fact that the employer might try to expropriate promised rents from them.

Oliver Williamson develops a similar argument about the bargaining problem between two firms, one a supplier to the other, when both parties must make investments in assets that are cospecialized to each other. Williamson argues that their relationship over time will be subject to severe governance problems because they will not generally be able to write contracts specifying the division of rents that are complete enough to cover all contingencies. Therefore, he says, most of the rents are likely to be dissipated in transactions costs. Where such cospecialized assets are important, he argues, the firms have an incentive to "integrate vertically." That is, one firm will probably acquire the other, so that all of the rents can be concentrated in one firm and the entire enterprise governed hierarchically rather than through a series of market transactions or long-term, arms-length contracts.[24] But, while the problem of cospecialized investments by a firm and its supplier is exactly analagous to the problem of cospecialized investments by employers and

---

[24]See Williamson (1981). Williamson's analysis may be applicable in the context of the litigious contracting environment in the United States. But several recent studies of Japanese corporate governance systems suggest that somehow the Japanese may have figured out ways to mitigate the tendency toward litigation and disputes between large corporations and their independent suppliers, so that both parties to the transactions routinely make relationship-specific investments, and the returns from these investments are not routinely dissipated in haggling between the parties. This suggests that vertical integration is not the only way to solve the problem caused by cospecialized assets.

employees, the vertical integration solution cannot be applied in the latter case.

The basic model most economists use to explain the distribution of rewards between employees and investors in a corporate enterprise assumes that workers (as well as suppliers and other input providers) contract with the firm for compensation equivalent to what they could earn in alternative employment and that equity holders in the firm get the rest. This is a reasonable assumption when the workers all bring only generic skills to the workplace, because what they could earn somewhere else is fairly easy to determine. But when employees acquire firm-specific skills, what they could earn in another firm becomes much harder to estimate because in another firm the workers would have acquired a different set of firm-specific skills. The opportunity cost to the workers is not just the value of their existing generic skills, but also the value of their lost opportunity to develop other firm-specific skills in a relationship with a different employer.

A growing body of empirical evidence supports the view that employees of large corporations are generally paid more than their short-run opportunity cost, which suggests that they are indeed being paid something for their firm-specific skills. One theory holds that higher wages improve worker morale, motivation, and stability and reduce recruiting costs, thereby increasing the productivity and reducing the costs of having a permanent work force. Economists refer collectively to theories explaining this pattern of wage determination as "efficiency wage theories."[25] Another explanation for wages that are persistently above market-determined rates is "rent

---

[25]See Akerlof and Yellen (1986). See also Krueger and Summers (1988) for a brief summary of various arguments about why wage payments above short-run opportunity cost may increase efficiency and for empirical evidence on persistent interindustry wage differentials that the authors argue can only be explained as evidence of "efficiency wages."

extraction" by unions.[26] In effect, these theories all postulate that employees share, to some degree at least, in the rents or quasi rents generated by their association with the firm. And because employees are promised a share in the rents, most economists believe that employees also share in the costs of firm-specific training, perhaps by accepting wages that are below what they might earn elsewhere during the early months and years that they work for a given employer and perhaps only by sacrificing the opportunity to learn special skills and share in the rents in some other enterprise.

What implications do these common labor relations practices have for corporate governance questions? To consider this question, return to the entrepreneur with the widget business. Suppose she decides to follow standard business practice by recruiting a team of employees who will accept a somewhat reduced wage during the period that they are learning how to operate the widget machine. In exchange, she promises them a wage that is above their short-term opportunity cost once the business is up and running.[27] Her hope is that this commitment to pay higher wages will mitigate the "hold-up" problem by making it more costly for workers to try to negotiate for a larger share of the rents later on by threatening to quit.

Now consider the choices faced by both the entrepreneur and the workers. If she is trying to maximize the value of the equity in her firm, the entrepreneur would decide to invest in building the widget machine and training the workers only if she believed the value of

---

[26]For a more general discussion of the evidence on "non-market clearing" wage patterns, see Katz and Summers (1989).

[27]This kind of agreement with the employees will produce what economists call a "rising wage-tenure profile." In other words, the compensation of employees will rise over time if they stay with the same firm (gaining tenure) by more than they would rise if the employees only gained generic experience. Rising wage-tenure profiles are commonly observed in studies by labor economists. See, for example, Hutchens (1989) for a discussion of the empirical evidence and theories about why wages rise with tenure.

the stream of profits from the enterprise would equal or exceed the up-front cost of those investments. Likewise, the employees would accept the jobs only if they believed that the value of the additional wages they would earn in the future would at least compensate them for the wages they would sacrifice during the training period and for their lost opportunity to work for a different company and learn a different set of firm-specific skills. So far so good. Both decision processes would lead to "efficient" investment decisions.[28] Both parties would invest only if their expected returns at least equaled their opportunity costs.

The problem comes once the business is up and running. The simple model of the corporation, on which this discussion has been based so far, assumes that the entrepreneur "controls" the enterprise in the sense that she is the one who decides whether to continue operating the business. This is a decision she must make repeatedly as business conditions (such as the purchase price of raw materials and energy or the sales price of widgets) change over time. To maximize the value of the equity in her business, the entrepreneur must continue operating only as long as the present value of the expected stream of profits from her business equals or exceeds the scrap value of the machine. The problem is that the "profits" of the business, as measured by the entrepreneur, no longer include all of the rents and quasi rents being generated by the business. Some of those rents have been promised to employees in the form of higher wages. These promised higher payments to workers—their compensation for their firm-specific investments—are viewed as a cost to

---

[28]Actually, it is not so simple. If the entrepreneur and the workers accurately anticipate and understand the incentive problems that may come up once the business is operating (and that are discussed in the following few paragraphs), the ex ante decisions they make will be affected by concerns about these problems and might not be so efficient. That is a second-order effect that would be taken into account in a full-blown model. I do not try to deal with it here except to acknowledge that it exists.

the enterprise and hence drive a wedge between what is optimal for shareholders and what is optimal for society as a whole. A socially optimal decision would require that the firm continue to operate as long as the present value of the total rents and quasi rents generated by the business is positive. By contrast, a decision that maximizes share values would require that the firm shut down whenever the present value of the profits (measured as the rents and quasi rents *minus the promised higher payments to workers*) of the business falls below zero. The actual rents and quasi rents generated could be positive and quite high, but if they are not high enough to at least cover the promised higher wages, the entrepreneur seeking to maximize share value has no incentive to keep the business going. From her point of view, the business would suffer losses in every period if she did so.

In a world in which firms reward the investments by workers in firm-specific human capital by sharing rents with them in the form of fixed higher wages, firms that fail to generate at least enough rents to pay those higher wages are considered failures by shareholders, who would prefer that the business shut down. The fact that the entrepreneur has control rights means that she may choose to shut down rather than pay the higher promised wages if doing so would mean a loss to the shareholders. Moreover, the fact that shareholders have limited liability means that, even if employees had a contract that required payment of higher wages, they could not force the firm to continue to employ them and pay these promised wages if doing so would require shareholders to make additional payments into the firm, over and above their initial equity contribution. In other words, the promised higher wages are, in fact, not "fixed," but contingent on the performance of the firm. Employees therefore are also "residual claimants," who share in the business risk associated with the enterprise.

Hence the empirical facts about the way risk and reward are actually shared in most large corporations run counter to the rather glib arguments made by Easterbrook and Fischel about who receives the residual return or bears the residual risk in corporations. These facts also make it clear that a whole set of issues normally thought of as "labor relations" matters must be considered in any analysis of the policy logic behind proposed corporate governance reforms.

In principle, the problems introduced by investments in firm-specific human capital could be resolved in several ways without necessarily changing the legal structure of control rights in firms or requiring that managers and directors be accountable to stakeholders other than shareholders. Some critics may argue, for example, that (using my example) if the rents generated by widget making fall below the level required to pay the promised higher wages to employees, those employees would have an incentive to renegotiate their agreement with the entrepreneur to keep her from shutting down the widget machine prematurely. A share-value-maximizing entrepreneur, in turn, would have an incentive to engage in such negotiations. Therefore, the argument would continue, the presence of firm-specific human capital should have no bearing on whether firms should be run in the interest of shareholders.

But labor economists commonly argue that workers resist such renegotiations and that wages are consequently downwardly rigid. The reason economists give is that, in large and complex businesses where firms are not required by law to share detailed, audited cost and revenue information with employees, employees may not be able to distinguish between a case in which rents truly are too low to support the promised higher wages and a case in which the entrepreneur (representing the interests of shareholders) is just trying to expropriate promised rents from employees. If wages are rigid and the entrepreneur wants to reduce the amount of rents paid out to employees, she must actually lay off employees rather than cut their wages. Rigid wages thereby serve to strengthen the bargaining position of employees by making it costly for the entrepreneur to try to expropriate rents. In any case, there is strong empirical evidence that wages are rigid and that employers adjust to declining rents by reducing employment rather than by cutting wages.[29]

Other critics may argue that firms do not actually promise "fixed" high wages. Instead, they make an implicit promise to share the rewards of the enterprise "fairly" and that this promise is credible to workers because the firm (meaning, in this case, management and shareholders) must maintain its reputation for fairness if it is to continue attracting skilled workers in the future. This supposed solution to the governance problem breaks down, however, if market conditions shift so that the firm has no need to hire new workers in the future. If a firm is in a declining market and needs to reduce, rather than expand, its work force, it no longer has the same incentive to play fair. Andrei Shleifer and Lawrence H. Summers argued that something like this happened in many of the hostile takeovers of the 1980s: the raiders took over firms in declining industries to extract the remaining rents from those firms by reneging on the "implicit" contracts those firms had with their employees.[30]

The reputation argument is also likely to break down if employees and potential employees lose confidence that reputation matters to firms. That could easily happen if firm identities (to which reputations are attached) are vulnerable to frequent or dramatic alterations. For that reason, the waves of takeovers, buyouts, spinoffs, corporate reorganizations, restructurings, and downsizings that have struck the corporate sector in the United States since the late 1970s have probably seriously undermined the usefulness of reputation as a mechanism for ensuring a "fair" allocation of rents from firm-specific investments.

---

[29]Keynes (1936, p. 9) first noted the downward inflexibility of wages and regarded it as an institutional characteristic that did not require theoretical justification. The idea has spawned a large literature to try to describe, model, and examine the implications of this feature of labor markets. See, for example, Okun (1981) and Hall (1995).

[30]Shleifer and Summers (1988, p. 41).

The Role of Competition and Innovation

Recall that in the widget examples, the original explanation offered
for why the entrepreneur might want to get into the widget business
is that she had designed a new widget-making machine that econo-
mized on the costs of raw materials. Suppose now that the entrepreneur somehow solves the problem of dividing the rents in a satisfactory way and that she and the employees make the necessary
investments, both in physical capital and in specialized skills, to get
into the widget business. Suppose too that, even though the market
for widgets is quite competitive, WidgInc initially earns positive
rents, because the new machine, together with its trained workers,
produces widgets at lower economic costs than do its competitors.

But competitors will eventually catch on. Suppose that, after a
few years, other widget manufacturers incorporate the essential elements of the entrepreneur's new technology into their operations.
As this happens, the price of widgets is competed down. As a result,
some of the wealth initially created by WidgInc can no longer be
captured by the firm and its employees, but instead must be passed
on to widget customers in the form of lower prices. In the extreme
case of perfect competition over the long run, consumers would
completely capture all of the wealth from the widget-making enterprise. On the other hand, because the new competition is using the
same widget-making technology, WidgInc's investment in the machine and the employees' investments in their knowledge capital,
which were both highly relationship-specific at the time they were
made, have become much less specific and much more marketable.
The loss of capturable rents means that the machine (and the specialized skills of the employees) has a lower value-in-use to WidgInc,
but the existence of competition means that it may have a resale
value (or, in the case of employees, an alternative wage) that is much
higher than its scrap value. In fact, the resale value of the machine
should be exactly equal to its value-in-use (which is the same as

saying that there are no capturable rents). The machine and the special skills of the employees are, in effect, no longer firm-specific investments. They could be readily redeployed to other firms in the competitive widget business.

All of this assumes, of course, that there has been no further innovation at WidgInc. The skilled workers at WidgInc, however, may have gained considerable experience that makes them more productive than the workers at competing widget-making firms. Suppose, for example, that the shop floor supervisor and other employees have developed procedures for rapid retooling and quick response to orders. They can now produce customized precision widgets in small batches with one-day notice, at no greater cost than their competitors require to do large batch jobs with long lead times. Customers are willing to pay extra for this service. Now, once again, the enterprise can create and capture new wealth, but the special input that makes this possible is not a new machine, but the organizational capabilities, the procedures, the routines, and the skills of the employees.[31]

In light of these new circumstances, let us reconsider the governance problems at WidgInc. Easterbrook and Fischel and, before them, Armen Alchian and Harold Demsetz argue that, to minimize the costs of haggling over returns in an uncertain world, a residual claimant should be assigned and control of the enterprise given to that residual claimant.[32] Williamson expanded on that idea by arguing that when two firms must make cospecialized investments, haggling costs will be reduced if one firm acquires the other.[33] But when the specialized asset is embodied in the organizational capabil-

[31]If the ability to provide better service derives from the specialized way that the workers interact with each other, those organizational skills are, by definition, firm-specific. No individual worker could take them to a job in another firm.

[32]Easterbrook and Fischel (1991) and Alchian and Demsetz (1972).

[33]Williamson (1981).

ities and skills of the employees, vertical integration is not a potential solution. And insulating those employees completely from the risks associated with the enterprise is probably not feasible. Nor can an employer write a complete contract with employees that will induce them to develop organizational innovations or guarantee that they will be appropriately rewarded if they do. One solution to this dilemma might be for employers to write contracts with skilled employees that explicitly share the residual gains (and losses) as well as the control rights and responsibilities. Or, to follow Williamson's logic to its rather radical implications in this case, since WidgInc cannot "acquire" the employees, the employees should perhaps form a worker's cooperative and acquire WidgInc. The machine that was the basis of the original equity investments is now more of a generic input, with a well-determined market value, and the specialized inputs are now the organizational capabilities and the employees' skills—both of which can be controlled only by the employees.

Governing Corporations When Firm-Specific Skills Are Important

This extended series of examples was obviously contrived to make certain points. The key point is that firm-specific investments create a governance problem that standard models for allocating risk, reward, and control in corporations do not explicitly acknowledge or address. The examples stress the special problems raised by investments in firm-specific human capital, but parallel arguments may apply to relationship-specific investments by suppliers of other inputs or by customers.[34] Policy arguments that rely on the old mod-

---

[34]A modest but rapidly growing literature in the management field discusses changes in relationships between large U.S. manufacturing companies, such as the

els—where shareholders are assumed to be the only parties making firm-specific investments—are unlikely to be sensitive to the way certain governance arrangements can alter the incentives for other participants in the corporate enterprise to make firm-specific investments, especially in human capital.

Measuring Human Capital's Contribution to Wealth Creation

How important are investments in firm-specific human capital to total wealth creation in corporations? No one knows for sure, of course, because the process of developing firm-specific skills and organizational capabilities and routines is not clearly distinguishable from the process of developing generic skills. Likewise, there are no ledger items in the "sources and uses of funds" statements of corporations that record investments in firm-specific human capital nor any item on the balance sheets showing the cumulative amount of such capital.

Labor economists who believe that firm-specific human capital may be quite important to wealth creation point to three kinds of evidence showing that employees accumulate valuable firm-specific skills if they stay with the same employer for an extended period. First, wages typically rise with job tenure by more than they would be expected to rise solely as a result of the employee's increased general experience. These higher wages are generally taken as evidence that the employee becomes more productive as he accumulates firm-specific human capital. Second, job turnover rates (both layoffs and quits) typically fall with job tenure. This is also con-

---

auto companies, and their suppliers, especially the trends toward long-term relationships with fewer suppliers and toward higher levels of relationship-specific investments on both sides. See Levine (1995).

strued as evidence that employees accumulate firm-specific human capital that makes them more valuable to the firm and the jobs more valuable to the workers.

Some labor economists say that there are other explanations for these two features of the labor market. Wages may appear to rise with tenure because, over time, workers tend to quit or be fired from jobs that are not good "fits" and to stay in the jobs where they are most productive and paid the most. Thus in any cross section of workers, those who have been in their jobs the longest are the ones who are most likely to have found a good fit and hence have higher wages. Likewise, because workers stay in jobs that are good fits, cross-sectional analysis indicates that workers who have been in their jobs longer are less likely to quit or be laid off than workers who have been in their jobs only a short time. Neither of these facts necessarily means that any given worker will get a higher wage or become less likely to separate from a job just by staying in the job she currently holds.[35] More important, neither of these arguments works against the point being made here: if a "good fit" is interpreted to mean that the worker has some innate skills or talents that are especially valuable to the firm where he or she is working, then these special skills or talents should still be regarded as "firm-specific human capital."[36]

[35]See Medoff and Abraham (1981). Abraham and Farber (1987) and Altonji and Shakotko (1987) present evidence that, when models control for the tendency of workers to move around until they find a good fit, wages do not rise with tenure.

[36]Lazear (1979) offers yet another explanation for wages rising with tenure. In situations where they cannot easily monitor workers, he argues, firms may offer workers "delayed-payment" contracts, with below-market wages in the early years and above-market wages in the later years. The point is to discourage workers from shirking, for fear that they would never get the payout of the higher wages in the future. This argument is not inconsistent with my arguments about firm-specific human capital, because no worker would agree to such a contract unless the total

The third piece of evidence is the fact that the costs of being laid off are typically larger for workers with more tenure.

If workers had only generic skills that they could easily take with them to the next job, labor markets would not be expected to exhibit any of these three features. Indeed, in industries such as general construction contracting, where workers can take all their relevant skills with them from job to job, they often do exactly that and do not accumulate tenure with any one employer. The most compelling evidence that firm-specific human capital is important is the simple fact that much economic activity is organized in ways that involve long-term stable employment relationships rather than a series of contracts and subcontracts.[37]

Robert C. Topel has studied two of these labor market features. He finds a very strong connection between job seniority and wages, with wages in the typical employment relationship rising by 25 percent for a worker with ten years of seniority, even after controlling for other factors.[38] As for the costs typically experienced by workers who are permanently laid off because a plant has closed or moved, Topel finds that "not only are costs large for the typical

---

wages paid over the life of the contract exceeded the amount the worker could get in a series of spot contracts at market wages in each period. Lazear's theory in fact buttresses my argument that, where firm-specific human capital is important, contractual arrangements within firms are very likely to reflect some sharing with employees of the rents or quasi rents arising from that relationship. See Hutchens (1989) for an accessible survey of the academic debate about the appropriate interpretation of the fact that wages usually rise with tenure.

[37]In the last five years, a growing body of anecdotal and statistical evidence suggests that workers are moving around from job to job much more now than they did ten or twenty years ago.

[38]Topel (1991, pp. 162, 172). Topel acknowledges the theoretical issues raised by Medoff and Abraham (1981), Abraham and Farber (1987), and Altonji and Shakotko (1987), but he takes issue with their econometric methodology, finding that wages do rise with seniority even after controlling for the job-shopping factors that concern these other authors.

worker, but they are higher for experienced workers . . . and . . . for workers with greater job seniority."[39] Topel reviewed a large sample of workers who had lost their jobs through business closings or layoffs in the mid-1980s and found that, on average, these workers earned about 14 percent less on their next jobs. The longer the worker had held his previous job, the greater the earnings loss. Workers who had eleven to twenty years of seniority earned 28 percent less on their next job, while workers with twenty-one years or more of seniority earned 44 percent less on their next job.[40]

The survey data Topel used covered men of prime working age only, but if his findings are generalizable to the entire labor force, they suggest that as much as 14 percent of total wages and benefits paid to employees of corporations in the United States may represent a return to firm-specific human capital. This actually should not be surprising, because, if the preceding arguments are correct, work is organized within firms rather than through market transactions precisely in those situations where firm-specific investments are important.[41] In 1993 corporations in the United States paid their employees a total of $2.26 trillion in total compensation. In that same year, corporations earned $293 billion in pretax profits.[42] If all of the accounting profits are counted as rents and quasi rents (a generous estimate), but only 10 percent of labor costs are treated as rents and quasi rents (a conservative estimate), then accounting profits represented only 57 percent of the total rents and quasi rents

[39]Topel (1990, p. 209).

[40]These estimates are based on weekly earnings rates for actual weeks worked, so they do not include losses due to time spent unemployed. But Topel (1990, table 1, p. 149) found that the number of weeks lost to unemployment also rose with tenure.

[41]If keeping employees on a corporate payroll does not significantly benefit the workers, the shareholders, or both, the workers presumably would be more likely to work as independent contractors.

[42]Council of Economic Advisers, *Economic Report of the President*, February 1994, Table B-88.

generated by corporate activity in the United States in that year. The rest of the rents went to employees as a return to specialized human capital. But, as such, they were treated as a cost to be reduced, rather than as one part of what the corporation as a whole should be trying to maximize.

Alternative Governance Structures

Before looking at alternative governance structures, let us review why firm-specific investments, particularly in human capital, create a problem for corporate governance. Such investments create wealth to the extent that they make it possible for employees to be more productive than they would be in alternative employment and thus to generate rents. But because the investments are firm-specific, competitive markets are of little use in determining how to allocate the rents and risk associated with those investments. Because the investments are costly to the firm, the employees, or both, a governance system that encourages such investments must provide some mechanism to assure those who make the investments that they will be compensated by sharing in the rents generated and be able to protect those rents from expropriation by the other participants in the firm.

Differences in corporate governance systems may be thought of as different approaches to solving the governance problem presented by firm-specific investments. Consider, for example, the different sets of incentives and protections for firm-specific investments in human capital provided by two stylized systems that I call the *kaisha* model, and the "U.S. Megacorp" model.[43]

---

[43]The word *kaisha* is Japanese for "business corporation." Although I borrowed the word from the title of a book (Abegglen and Stalk 1985), the following model was not taken from their book, but is my own stylized composite, based on various descriptions of Japanese corporations. These include Abegglen and Stalk (1985), Aoki (1988, 1993a), Gerlach (1992), Kester (1991, 1992b), and Sakakibara (1993).

In the *kaisha* model, employees are screened very carefully before they are hired to ensure a good fit. They are then guaranteed employment for life to encourage them to make investments in firm-specific skills. Strong cultural pressures on the firm's managers to operate the company for the benefit of employees support that commitment. Other stakeholders with significant firm-specific investments (including banks that make loans to the firm, major customers, and major suppliers), hold most of the firm's equity and are nominally entitled to select corporate directors. Ordinarily, however, top management and directors rise up through the ranks of employees, bringing with them strong cultural commitment to the perpetuation of the enterprise and the well-being of employees. Thus, in practice, the nominal right of equity holders to elect directors confers veto power only and is used only where severe problems have developed. Although employees are guaranteed lifetime employment (which protects each employee from a loss in value of the unique firm-specific skills of that individual), they nonetheless share significantly in the short-term risk of the enterprise as a whole because their compensation package includes a large component (an annual bonus, for example) that fluctuates with the performance of the firm as a whole.

This system thus explicitly allocates short-term risk of the enterprise among all the participants. It also tends to lock all of the parties into the enterprise, thereby compelling them all to share in the long-run risks as well. It is supported by a culture that strongly encourages cooperative behavior and discourages litigation. There appear to be well-established alternative mechanisms for dispute resolution, although these are not well understood, at least in the West. The *kaisha* system allocates a significant amount of control and risk to employees and treats them as important owners, along with equity holders.

This system has several strengths: it encourages all of the participants in the firm (investors, employees, managers, suppliers, and customers) to make committed, firm-specific investments, to share in the risks and returns, and to adjust the terms of their relationship to respond to a wide-range of business conditions. Its weakness may be that, as flexible as this system is in some ways, it is ultimately not flexible enough to permit massive layoffs and may thus not permit firms to move resources out of declining industries and into growing industries fast enough. This system may thus promote a tendency to overinvest in physical capital and to pursue growth and perpetuation of the enterprise at the expense of return for the providers of financial capital.[44]

In the U.S. Megacorp model, employees are promised a wage and benefit package that shares enough of the expected rents generated by the enterprise to discourage employees from quitting prematurely. Payments to employees are, in principle, independent of the performance of the firm, although that turns out to be true only in the short run. Even pensions are insulated to a great degree from risk associated with the firm by laws that set minimum funding and vesting requirements, insurance requirements, and diversification rules. In exchange for promises of a fixed return on their investments in human capital, employees cede control rights completely to shareholders, who bear all of the short-run risk and who have the right to select all directors.

Although they are protected from short-run fluctuations in returns to the enterprise, employees in this model are not given life-time job guarantees, so they do bear some of the long-run risks associated with the possibility that their special skills will cease

---

[44]Blaine (1993) shows that Japanese firms consistently had a lower return to equity capital throughout the 1980s than did U.S. firms, as well as a lower variability of returns across industries. He speculates that Japanese firms strive for revenue and market share, while U.S. firms seek profits and higher stock prices, and suggests that the lower variability of returns across industries may occur because Japanese firms spread risk among related companies through cross-shareholdings.

generating rents for shareholders. Cultural and reputational consid-
erations and, in some cases, union contracts help to reassure employees that firms will not casually dismiss them or attempt to
expropriate all of the rents. But other cultural and institutional
arrangements support the idea that shareholders are the owners of
the corporation and are free to sell the corporation or its assets,
merge it with another corporation, shut down plants, lay off employees, or otherwise reorganize the firm at will.

This system's strong point is its great flexibility for moving physical capital out of declining industries and into growing industries.
Its weakness manifests itself when industries are in decline or in
times of rapid technological change. If the total rents being generated
by the enterprise decline to the point where the fixed wages promised to employees absorb all of the rents generated and more, shareholders will have a strong incentive to pressure management to shut
down operations and lay off employees. Such a "downsizing" program may often be premature in the sense that the enterprise is still
generating substantial rents (or quasi rents) for some of the participants in the firm, even though the rents available to shareholders
have gone to zero or turned negative. Nonetheless, because the
control rights go to shareholders in this system, employees cannot
compel the firm to keep the enterprise going.[45]

Another weakness of this system occurs if shareholders frequently exercise their right to downsize, sell off, or restructure. Then
the promises made by firms to share rents may cease being credible,

---

[45]In such a situation, employees would obviously benefit if they accepted a wage
cut in order to give shareholders an incentive to keep the enterprise going. When and
if this sort of recontracting happens, it clearly undermines the premise that employees get a fixed wage and shareholders bear all the risk. Employees therefore would be
unlikely to make such a new contract without seeking some control rights in exchange. The recent buyout of United Airlines by employees is a good example of this
kind of recontracting.

and employees may eventually lose their willingness to continue making investments in firm-specific human capital. For the same reason, this system also creates a disincentive for employees to help develop labor saving innovations that may tend to make their own firm-specific capital obsolete.

Governance in the Workplace of the Future

The governance problem presented by firm-specific skills affects policy questions about the productivity of U.S. companies and their ability to create wealth for U.S. citizens for several reasons. First, advances in productivity depend not on any momentary or static advantage U.S companies may have in resource costs or technology, but on their ability to innovate constantly, to improve product quality and cut costs, and to provide customized services to their clients or customers. The ability to reconfigure a product on demand for a given customer, for example, may be the most important source of value added for the customer and therefore of wealth creation by the company.[46] If this assessment is correct, it implies significant changes in the way work must be organized.[47]

In an early academic account of these changes in the market and their implications for organizational form and political institutions, Michael J. Piore and Charles F. Sabel argue that a massive transition is taking place in industrial countries away from economies based

---

[46]See Dertouzos, Lester, and Solow (1989).

[47]These changes have been the subject of numerous books and articles in the popular business press lately. Webber (1993) reviews eight new books about managing in the "new economy." See also Walter Kiechel III, "How We Will Work in the Year 2000," Fortune, May 17, 1993, pp. 38–52; and a Wall Street Journal series entitled "Down the Up Escalator: Why Some Workers Are Falling Behind," March 10, p. A1; March 11, p. A1; March 16, p. A1; March 17, p. A1; and March 19, p. A1.

on mass production, which they defined as "the use of special-purpose (product-specific) machines and of semi-skilled workers to produce standardized goods." The new model of production more closely resembles the old craft systems, which used less rigid manufacturing technologies but relied on more highly skilled workers. Piore and Sabel describe the coming economy as one in which the predominant model of production uses flexible and general purpose machines or components (computers, for example), but in which the products and services offered are updated, customized, or specialized to the needs of each customer.[48] In this kind of environment, the input that is essential to wealth creation and that may need to be highly specialized to a given enterprise is more likely to be human capital—the organizational capabilities and the creative talents and skills of management and employees—than physical capital.[49]

In line with this assessment of the importance of human capital, numerous articles and studies of the problem of slow productivity growth and loss of world market share of U.S. firms in the 1980s and early 1990s stressed the need for improved education and training programs and for companies to focus on continuous innovation and process and product improvement.[50] But for the most part, these issues have been treated separately from the discussions about corporate governance. Corporate governance questions have been linked to the productivity and wealth creation largely through the effect they are believed to have on the direct and indirect costs of capital and thus on physical capital formation. This link is surely

[48]Piore and Sabel (1984, pp. 4-5).

[49]"Since all firms have access to the same machinery and nonhuman factors, a major source of differentiation, and opportunity to excel, becomes the quality of the work force and the way a firm organizes the work processes," writes Warren E. Farb (1993, p. 4).

[50]See, for example, Baily, Burtless, and Litan (1993, ch. 5); Dertouzos, Lester, and Solow (1989); and Competitiveness Policy Council (1993); and Council on Competitiveness (1995).

important, but it may not be the most important way that corporate governance arrangements affect productivity growth. Governance reforms aimed at increasing the power and control that shareholders exercise, for example, could reduce the cost of physical capital to U.S. companies but still drag down rates of productivity growth if they also impede the pace of innovation and investment in human capital.[51]

Corporate governance arrangements influence the ability of firms to create new wealth through their effects on the risks, rewards, prerogatives, and claims of stakeholders in addition to shareholders, and therefore on the incentives and motivations facing these other stakeholders. Governance systems, broadly defined, set the ground rules that determine who has what control rights under what circumstances, who receives what share of the wealth created, and who bears what associated risks. Governance systems thus help determine how priorities are set, how decisions are made about spending resources on building organizational capabilities, and how management and employees are evaluated and compensated. In industries and firms where human capital is critical, these factors are likely to affect wealth-creating behavior substantially. A firm's employees are much more likely to be motivated to find new ways to innovate or to cut costs, for example, if they have confidence that they will share in the wealth created by these activities—that it will not be expropriated from them by other participants in the enterprise—and if they believe that management will listen to them and devote resources to their ideas.

---

[51]Other scholars who have considered the problem of lagging productivity growth in the United States have noted that the cost of capital accounts for no more than about 30 percent of the total cost of production, so reducing the cost of capital by itself, cannot have as large an impact on productivity as improving the efficiency of labor. See, for example, Blinder (1990, p. 1).

In this context, corporate governance discussions that start from a premise that shareholders are the sole owners of corporations, that measure wealth creation only in terms of the share price of corporate stock, and that focus only on the power relationship between shareholders and managers may have the emphasis wrong. Reforms built on this premise may even destroy wealth-creating capacity. To be sure, the shareholder-management nexus is important. But it is not the only relationship within the corporation that is important to wealth creation. Corporate governance discussions need to acknowledge this reality explicitly.

Most of the participants in the corporate governance debates of the last few years have discredited the notion that corporations should be run in the interests of all of the stakeholders, rather than just for the shareholders. But if stakeholders are defined to mean all those participants who have substantial firm-specific investments at risk, then this idea is actually a reasonable and appropriate basis for thinking about corporate governance reforms. Far from abandoning the idea that firms should be run for all the stakeholders, contractual arrangements and governance systems should be devised to assign control rights, rewards, and responsibilities to the appropriate stakeholders—the parties that contribute specialized inputs.

8

GOVERNANCE STRUCTURES

DESIGNED FOR TOTAL

WEALTH CREATION

IN THE LAST TWO CHAPTERS, I argued that the goal of good corporate governance should be to maximize the wealth-creating potential of the corporation as a whole, rather than just to maximize value for shareholders. Most discussions of corporate governance tacitly assume that these two goals are the same, but, for the reasons outlined in chapter 7, that is not likely in modern corporations. These two goals differ whenever some participants in the enterprise other than shareholders make relationship-specific investments, that is, special investments in physical assets, organizational capabilities, or skills whose value is tied to the success of that enterprise.

Because it is difficult, if not impossible, to devise arrangements that insulate these other stakeholders from residual risk, governance systems that allocate appropriate decision and control rights to

275

those stakeholders may do a better job of encouraging wealth creation than do governance systems that assign too much control to shareholders.

This chapter considers what these abstract ideas may mean in practice. First, it examines several existing alternative governance structures that allocate important parts of the risk and return associated with the enterprise, as well as decision and control rights, away from shareholders and toward other participants in the enterprise. Some of these alternative systems are widely used in this country, some mainly in other countries, but all have been highly successful governance forms in certain situations. The chapter then reviews a variety of innovative governance structures and organizational forms with which many companies in the United States are experimenting. These new arrangements are being set up for many reasons, but some appear to reallocate risk and control rights in ways that may encourage employees to invest in firm-specific human capital. It is too early to tell for sure which will be successful. A comprehensive analysis of which organizational forms work and which do not under different circumstances is far beyond the scope of this book.[1] These two sections are intended only to provide some examples that suggest how governance systems can be devised to allocate risk and move decision and control rights closer to the parties that contribute or have de facto control over firm-specific assets.

The arguments to this point strongly suggest that, where firm-specific human capital is a critical component of wealth creation, one important solution to the governance problem is increased ownership and control of corporate equity by employees. The third

---

[1]A forthcoming book by law professor Henry B. Hansmann considers the economics rationales for and empirical evidence on the performance of a wide variety of organizational forms, including investor-owned, employee-owned, and customer-owned for-profit, as well as nonprofit, organizations. See also Hansmann (1988).

section looks at various ways that employee ownership of corporate equity is increasing in U.S. firms, factors that may be encouraging or discouraging this process, and empirical evidence on the effects of employee ownership on company performance.

Because U.S. corporation law, contract law, and securities law readily accommodate most experiments in new organizational forms, many new governance structures are emerging on their own. This is one of the strengths of the U.S. system. But in some areas tax and securities laws, pension fund regulations, and labor relations laws impose barriers to organizational innovation or create institutional biases in the allocation of risk and control that may discourage investments in human capital. The final chapter points out some of these potential problems and makes some suggestions about how the rules might be changed to facilitate innovation and foster efficient governance systems.

By far the most important reforms to be made are in the mindsets of business, finance, and labor leaders. All three of these groups—each for different reasons—have traditionally opposed (or, at best, been agnostic toward) employee ownership schemes and schemes that enhance employee control, with or without ownership. Many finance and business leaders have also strongly resisted the idea that managers and directors should be responsible to any stakeholders other than shareholders. Unless this culture changes, working people in the United States may grow increasingly unwilling to make career commitments and human capital investments in corporate enterprises. The economy would not come to a halt if that happened, but it is unlikely to be as productive as it could be if employees knew that their investments in firm-specific skills were explicitly protected.

Some Familiar Examples

Three familiar organizational forms and governance structures that appear to put risk, reward, and formal control rights much closer to those who supply or control the critical, firm-specific inputs have proved quite successful in certain circumstances. These organizational forms are entrepreneurial start-up companies, franchise systems, and partnerships.

Entrepreneurial Start-Up Companies

The unique, but essential assets at risk in an entrepreneurial company are the creative and organizational skills of the entrepreneur and the capital used to buy equipment or pay salaries before the project begins generating revenues. Entrepreneurial firms usually look like the basic model of the corporation, described in chapter 2. Typically, such firms are closely held and closely controlled by the entrepreneur, by the bankers or the venture capitalists who provide the start-up funding, and sometimes by a key supplier or customer. This same small circle of participants shares in the risk of failure and the rewards of success.

In the United States a special kind of financial intermediary—the venture capital investment firm—has emerged to identify and invest in the initial capital of start-up companies. Venture capital funds do not always succeed in picking winners. In fact, the failure rate among the companies they invest in is quite high. But these funds usually invest in twenty or thirty ventures at a time, enough to spread their risk effectively, but not so many that the fund managers lose their ability to be vigilant monitors. Fund managers are almost always close advisers to management, regularly serving on the board and often as chairman of the portfolio company. Many scholars and commentators regard the venture capital markets and associated governance systems as highly successful systems.[2]

---

[2]See, for example, Porter (1992, pp. 64–65); Sahlman (1992), and Florida and Smith (1993).

Many of the governance reform proposals advocated by Michael Porter and others are designed to imitate those features of this model that are thought to account for its success, such as commitment and close monitoring by suppliers of financial capital and representation on the boards by the venture capitalists as well as by key employees, suppliers, or customers.

Franchise Systems

The wealth-creating activity in, say, a fast-food restaurant chain, is the delivery of products of dependable quality to customers at convenient times and locations. Individual members of the chain rely heavily on its national or regional reputation to attract business; a well-established reputation assures customers that they will not have to spend time and energy shopping around to find a restaurant that meets their needs. This feature is particularly valuable to customers who are highly mobile. Thus the reputation of the franchiser is a critical input to wealth creation that the franchisee benefits from and that the managers and service workers at each individual location must maintain and enhance over the long run.

A national or regional restaurant chain would find it costly and difficult to direct and control individual store managers from central headquarters. Thus, the franchise system gives those managers a great deal of control over daily operations and assigns them much—but not all—of the risk and rewards associated with ownership. In other words, because franchisees have de facto control over location-specific assets (the individual stores) and have a significant influence on a critical corporate asset (the brand name and reputation), they are assigned a mix of the risks and rewards associated with the use of those assets. A large share of the profits (or losses) generated by each store goes directly to the franchisee. In exchange for the use of the brand name, franchisees typically pay a fee to the franchiser and are required to use standardized equipment and materials supplied by the franchiser. They may be subject to random inspections by the franchiser to ensure that recommended procedures and standards are being enforced. Franchise systems are classic examples of hybrid governance structures, designed to bundle together risk, reward, and control rights in ways conducive to encouraging and protecting investments in the corporation's reputation.[3]

Partnerships

Professional partnerships have long dominated certain professional and service businesses where the most important assets of the business are the creativity, intelligence, experience, and reputation for competence and integrity of the key individuals who work for the firms. In partnerships all of the control rights, as well as the claim to returns and responsibility for debts, are assigned to the partners individually and collectively. A partnership is thus a classic example of an employee-owned firm, but without the benefits of limited liability. In a partnership, the partners control the most important assets of the firm (their own human capital) and have an ownership interest in the firm—that is, they collectively receive the residual return and bear the residual risk. Professional partnerships have historically been the prevailing organizational form in law, accounting, medicine, architecture, advertising, public relations, consulting, and some financial services.

In recent years, a growing number of firms in these fields have been abandoning the partnership form, however. Goldman Sachs is the only major investment banking firm that continues to operate as a partnership, and many of the largest advertising agencies switched to the corporate form in the 1980s. Most large accounting firms and

---

[3]Economic arguments explaining franchising as an organizational form have been discussed and analyzed in Rubin (1978) and Brickley and Dark (1987).

law firms are changing their form, either to limited liability partnerships or to professional corporations, and physicians and other health care professionals are rapidly becoming employees of large corporations as the health care industry reorganizes itself. The rush to incorporate is not being driven by any fundamental problem arising from ownership and control by employees, but by the advantages of limited liability. In 1994 accounting firms in the United States faced some $30 billion in liability claims for what plaintiffs claimed were shoddy work practices and failure to discover and alert investors to problems brewing in hundreds of savings and loans and other failed firms. Law firms, too, have been sued over the savings-and-loan debacle. These lawsuits have caused indemnity insurance rates to soar and represent a significant threat to the personal assets of the partners in the target firms.[4]

The *Economist* identified three additional factors that are driving professional and service firms away from partnerships and toward the corporate form. These are the need to raise outside money for expansion; the sheer size and unwieldiness of the partnership governance structure in large firms (KPMG, an accounting firm, for example, employs nearly 50,000 people, of which 6,000 are partners); and the increased intensity of competition for clients and the end of client loyalty. Today a firm's revenues depend less on personal relationships between clients and individual partners, and more on the firm's general reputation for competence and integrity.

None of these factors in any way negates the importance of firm-specific human capital in these types of firms, however, nor do they diminish the benefits of employee ownership and control where firm-specific human capital is important. They simply imply that the mechanisms of employee ownership and control may need to be instituted within a corporate governance structure rather than

[4]"Partners in Pain," *Economist*, July 9, 1994, p. 61.

a partnership governance structure. But, as the *Economist* also notes, "many features of partnerships, such as profit-sharing, teamwork and devolved decision-making, have become increasingly fashionable in companies."[5]

Firm-specific skills may not always be important to professional service firms, however, and in those firms, ownership and control by all or most employees may also not be important. Although technically organized as partnerships, some law firms that do standard legal work have adopted organizational forms that resemble closely held corporations with many employees. Raymond Russell cites as examples Hyatt Legal Services, which in 1984 had 375 attorneys working as hired associates but only four partners, and Jacoby and Meyers, with 153 hired associates and only four partners. This structure became preferable, Russell wrote, once professionals were legally able to advertise their services. For standardized types of legal work, the advertising builds the reputational asset of the firm, not the special legal skills of individual lawyers or the personal relationships between clients and specific lawyers. "Advertising by professionals has led to the creation of a new type of group practice in which advertising and other entrepreneurial activities are highly centralized, and most professionals have little to do with attracting business to their firms. Under such circumstances, there is little need for more than a few key individuals to be owners," Russell argued.[6]

Japanese and German Governance Systems

A large literature has grown up around the idea that the Japanese and German economies have excelled in the last few decades because the

[5]"Partners in Pain," p. 62.
[6]Russell (1985, pp. 235–36).

financial institutions in those countries supposedly do a better job of monitoring management than do financial institutions in this country. The authors of these articles generally take the position that the important difference between the U.S. financial markets and governance systems and the systems in these other two countries is that shareholdings are much more concentrated in Germany and Japan and that financial institutions therefore have greater power to intervene in the affairs of corporations.

Many of these studies have ignored another key difference, however: corporate employees, key trading partners, and other stakeholders in Japan and Germany have a vastly greater role in monitoring and controlling management than either shareholders or other stakeholders of large companies typically do in the United States.[7] The corporate governance systems in Continental Europe and Japan have been called "insider" systems, in contrast to the "outsider" systems more typical of large, publicly traded firms in the United States and the United Kingdom. In the insider systems equity ownership is concentrated in banks, wealthy families, and other firms— often key suppliers or customers. Cross-shareholdings between firms are commonplace. In outsider systems cross-shareholdings are rare, and equity ownership is dispersed among a large number of individual and institutional investors.[8]

In the insider systems, shareholders are able to monitor a company not only by watching the share price, but by observing up close how the company performs in its key business relationships. Key stakeholders are also shareholders, so they have voting power that can be brought to bear to protect their relationship-specific investments. The make-up of boards of directors in insider systems tends

---

[7]Several scholars have begun to look at these differences. See especially Gilson and Roe (1992, 1993) and Kester (1992b).

[8]See Jenkinson and Mayer (1992) for a summary of the differences between insider and outsider systems, including citations to work by J. Franks and C. Mayer.

to mirror the make-up of the long-term stakeholder relationships. By contrast, companies in the United States have been moving toward boards of directors dominated by outsiders with little or no personal or business stake in the performance of the corporation, other than their stakes as shareholders.

According to W. Carl Kester, one of the benefits of insider systems such as the Japanese *keiretsu* is that "industrial group members may be more inclined to invest in specialized, efficient, customer-specific assets, and less inclined to undertake mergers and acquisitions as a means of reducing the hazards of such investment."[9] Kester notes, for example, that Nissan constructed a new, state-of-the-art assembly plant on the remote island of Kyushu with confidence that primary suppliers would construct plants nearby despite the risks inherent in investing in such location-specific assets. Suppliers, in fact, began constructing such facilities without formal purchase commitments from Nissan.[10] Similarly, Kester writes, German producers of automotive parts have been building new capacity in the United States at the behest of Daimler-Benz but without formal purchase contracts or guarantees from the auto maker.[11]

In large German companies, employees are long-term stakeholders in the companies where they work not only because of any investments in firm-specific human capital they may have made, but also because about two-thirds of their pension fund assets are invested in the employing company; only one-third is invested outside the company.[12] In firms that employ at least 2,000, employees have the right to elect half of the members of the "supervisory

---

[9]Kester (1992b, p. 38).

[10]Thus Kester suggests that the Japanese system may somehow help solve the hold-up problem discussed in chapter 7 without necessarily bringing all the relationship-specific assets under common ownership.

[11]Kester (1992b, p. 38).

[12]Schneider-Lenné (1992, p. 13).

boards." These boards select and oversee the activities of the "managing boards," which make day-to-day management decisions and represent companies externally. Shareholders elect the other half of the supervisory boards and control the chairman's position, however, and the chairman's vote is often tie breaking. By no means do employees have complete control, but they do have a significant mechanism of voice at the board level. Most German companies also have "works councils," made up of employees and union representatives, that management must consult about certain major business decisions. Other stakeholders, too, have significant mechanisms of voice. Typically, the lead bank controls enough of the shareholder votes to control the other half of the supervisory board, and it is not uncommon for a representative of this *hausbank* to serve as chairman. Trading partners and other industrial companies also frequently hold seats on the supervisory boards.[13]

Ellen Schneider-Lenné of Deutsche Bank claims that "German companies do not stop at maximization of the return on investment." Instead, "their philosophy is based on 'the concept of the interest of the company as a whole,' a key concept of German corporate culture. The company is seen as a combination of various interest groups whose goals have to be co-ordinated."[14]

In Japan, most of the stock of the typical large company is controlled by *keiretsu* members and the firm's other major trading partners. Employees also have a central role in the governance of firms, although it is more a cultural phenomenon than the result of

---

[13]Not all companies in Germany have two-tier boards, only the *Aktiengesellschaft* (joint-stock corporations), or AGs, and the *Gesellschaften mit Beschränkter Haftung* (limited liability companies), or GMBHs, who have at least 500 employees. Edwards and Fischer (1994, p. 95) estimate that firms with two-tier boards account for only 34 percent of the German economy. But the largest industrial companies are nearly always structured as AGs. See also Schneider-Lenné (1992, p. 20).

[14]Schneider-Lenné (1992, p. 13).

formal legal arrangements. Japanese executives and authorities on Japanese management report that corporations are run primarily in the interest of employees.[15] The common practices in Japan of lifetime employment, generous bonus plans, selection of executives from within the ranks of employees, and the low ratio of executive pay to average employee pay (relative to U.S. practice) all tend to support a culture that emphasizes the interests of the employees.[16]

Some Innovative New Examples

Major corporations all over the country are "downsizing," "outsourcing," and "reengineering"; focusing on "core competencies"; and implementing "total quality management" programs.[17] Although these management fads seem to mean something different to each company that engages in them, these programs share some important common themes. At the heart of the changes is a comprehensive rethinking of who should control which activities and who should earn the returns and bear the risks associated with those

[15]Matsumoto (1991) makes this point in detail. Abegglen (1984, p. 77) also notes that "especially good profits are generally not recognized in dividend payments but rather are recognized in terms of higher payments of bonuses to employees." See also Aoki (1987.)

[16]Fukao (1995) also supports this interpretation. Kester (1992b) argues that the practice of lifetime employment "raises the cost to individual managers of untrustworthy, opportunistic behavior." A growing number of reports in the popular press have noted that these practices may be weakening under the stress of extended recession in Japan. See, for example, Jacob M. Schlesinger, Michael Williams, and Craig Forman, "Soul-Searching: Japan Inc., Wracked By Recession, Takes Stock of Its Methods," *Wall Street Journal*, September 29, 1993, p. A1.

[17]In a survey of 497 large U.S. companies and 124 European companies by CSC Index, a consulting firm, 69 percent of the U.S. companies and 75 percent of the European ones reported that they were actively involved in a "reengineering" program, and half of the remaining companies reported that they were thinking about it. See "Re-engineering Reviewed," *Economist*, July 2, 1994, p. 66.

activities. Firms are reassessing what businesses they should be in, what activities they should do in-house, what they should contract out, and how responsibility and authority within the firm should be allocated. The thrust of many of these changes is to push authority, responsibility, risk, and reward—all the attributes associated with ownership—outward and downward, to employees, subcontractors, and, in some cases, former employees who are now subcontractors. In effect, new governance systems are being put into place, some haphazardly and without appreciation of the full consequences of the changes, and some quite self-consciously. Some of these new governance structures are described below.

Leveraged Buyouts

In the 1980s many firms (as well as subsidiaries or divisions of firms) were reorganized by means of leveraged buyouts. These controversial transactions, which were discussed at some length in previous chapters, were often defended and explained as mechanisms for realigning ownership and control rights in ways that supposedly better allocated risk-taking, reward, and responsibility.[18] In leveraged buyouts, a few key executives and a very tight circle of investors and creditors buy up the equity of a company so that little or none of it continues to trade publicly. The resulting company resembles a venture capital company in its allocation of ownership and control rights, but it is generally tightly constrained financially. Such companies have had mixed success as organizational forms, and, in fact, may be transitional forms rather than stable new forms. Steven Kaplan found, for example, that more than half of the 183 leveraged buyouts he studied were no longer privately owned seven years after they had been taken private in the buyout transaction.[19] If

[18]Jensen (1989).
[19]Kaplan (1991). See also Long and Ravenscraft (1993).

my arguments in the last chapter are right, closely held, highly leveraged firms would succeed as wealth-creating enterprises (as opposed to rent-expropriating organizational forms) only in businesses where the physical assets are fairly unspecialized and the source of wealth creation is the leadership and entrepreneurial skills of a few key people, rather than the specialized production, custom services, or innovation throughout the organization.

Redefining the Boundaries of Firms

A large body of anecdotal and casual empirical evidence indicates that two simultaneous trends are under way in the organization of corporations. Large firms are downsizing by selling off divisions, laying off workers who perform certain functions, and subcontracting out certain work rather than doing it in-house.[20] In some cases the companies hire back as subcontractors the same workers they just laid off. Companies are also redefining themselves in terms of their basic, or core, competencies, and then pursuing markets and projects that exploit these competencies.

These two trends can be interpreted as a rethinking of the management of firm-specific human capital. Corporate executives are reconfiguring their companies by deciding what kinds of skills are critical and specific to the firms' core competencies. In many cases

---

[20]Of 3,400 working people surveyed in 1992–93, 42 percent reported that their employers were downsizing or permanently reducing their work force; more than half of the workers at large companies reported that their employers were downsizing. See Barbara Presley Noble,"At Work: Dissecting the 90's Workplace," *New York Times,* Sept. 19, 1993, p. F21. Crawford (1991) reported that from 1970 to 1989, Fortune 500 industrial companies lost more than 2 million jobs, even as the U.S. economy as a whole created 37 million new jobs. Hamel and Prahalad (1994, p. 124) reported that in 1993 large U.S. companies announced nearly 600,000 layoffs, 25 percent more than in 1992, and 10 percent more than were announced in 1991, at the bottom of the recession.

managements are concluding that there are no compelling reasons why certain activities should be performed by company employees rather than by contractors. Companies now commonly turn to outsiders to provide building maintenance, payroll accounting, communication systems management, public relations, and other services that corporate employees once performed. As a consequence of these (and other) trends, employment in services has grown even as employment in manufacturing has declined. The temporary help industry, for example, has quadrupled as a share of total employment since the mid-1970s. Although still a small part of total employment (about 1.3 percent today), employment in the personnel supply industry grew by 687,000 workers from the bottom of the most recent recession in March 1991 through December 1993, representing 26 percent of all employment growth during this period.[21]

Meanwhile, employees seem to move from job to job more frequently now than they did in the past. In a study that documents the declining stability of employment in the United States since the mid-1970s, Dave E. Marcotte offered this explanation.

Rapid advances in communications and computer technologies over the past few decades may have lowered the relative cost of non-permanent employees, and increased the importance of general skills rather than firm-specific skills in many production processes. New technologies may have lowered the relative costs of using non-permanent employees by making information easier to transfer. As a result, having work done in remote locations by contracted or temporary workers is made easier. In addition, the increase in the applicability of the computer to many firms' operations has meant that firms are more likely to use common computing systems and software to accomplish tasks which in

[21]Council of Economic Advisers. *Economic Report of the President,* February 1994, p. 123.

the past may have required them to develop their own idiosyncratic processes. . . . This may have decreased the firm-specific knowledge necessary for some jobs, and made it easier for non-permanent workers to quickly fit in to some production processes.[22]

With respect to a firm's core competencies however, firm-specific human capital may be more important than ever before. Business consultants C. K. Prahalad and Gary Hamel have defined core competencies as "the collective learning in the organization, especially how to coordinate diverse production skills and integrate multiple streams of technologies." A company's core competencies, they add, must be unique to the firm in some way for the firm to deliver value to the customer and produce a profit for the firm. "A core competence should be difficult for competitors to imitate. And it will be difficult if it is a complex harmonization of individual technologies and production skills. A rival might acquire some of the technologies that comprise the core competence but it will find it more difficult to duplicate the more or less comprehensive pattern of internal coordination and learning," they write. Nor can "the embedded skills that give rise to the next generation of competitive products . . . be 'rented in' by outsourcing."[23]

Prahalad and Hamel contend that core competencies are the corporation's "critical resource" and refer to the employees who embody them as the "competence carriers." They stress the importance of managing core competencies and the people who embody them, just as firms must manage their physical assets.

Other authors have written about the complex arrangements that companies have developed as they reassess where their boundaries

---

[22]Marcotte (1994, pp. 4–5). Marcotte also cites Thompson (1990) for evidence on this last point in the banking industry.
[23]Prahalad and Hamel (1990, pp. 82, 84).

should be. "Consultants" may work for a company for years without ever technically being on the payroll, for example, and in some high technology industries, tiny companies form the nexus of "virtual corporations" that are really elaborate networks of companies brought together to create and market a particular product or service. Telepad Corp., a Reston, Virginia, company with only fourteen employees, for example, created and marketed a handheld, pen-based computer. But, according to *Business Week,*

> the computer was designed and co-developed with GVO Inc., a prominent industrial design company in Palo Alto, Calif. An Intel Corp. swat team was brought in to work out some enginering kinks. Several other companies have developed software for the product. A battery maker is collaborating with TelePad to develop the portable power supply. And to manufacture the computer, the company is using spare capacity at an IBM plant in Charlotte, N.C. [Even] the paychecks for its 14 employees are issued by an outside firm, Automatic Data Processing Inc.[24]

TelePad may be an extreme example, but it is not unique. "The point is," says Jeffrey H. Hudson, president of Visioneer, a Palo Alto-based "virtual" company in the document communications business, "there are things where we can add value and things where we can't. Where we can't, we let someone else do it."[25]

Richard Crawford refers to these new style organizations as "knowledge companies" and suggests that they are mechanisms for organizing and directing human capital rather than just bundles of physical assets. "Corporations are being formed and dissolved at a rapid rate as they are viewed increasingly as business conveniences

[24]See John A. Byrne, Richard Brandt, and Otis Port, "The Virtual Corporation," *Business Week*, February 8, 1993, pp. 98–102.

[25]Edward A. Gargan, "'Virtual' Companies Leave the Manufacturing to Others," *New York Times*, July 17, 1994, p. F5.

rather than permanent institutions," writes Crawford. "Replacing the traditional hierarchical or pyramidal organization of the industrial age is a new form of company—the entrepreneurial knowledge services company—operating in such fields as computer software, specialty manufacturing, law, consulting, specialty retailing and medical services. A knowledge company's primary resource and principal competitive advantage is the knowledge that its employees possess, which may or may not be captured in some form of intellectual property such as patented drugs, copyrighted books, or proprietary software."[26]

Where the critical resources are embodied in the employees and corporate boundaries are shifting rapidly, the traditional notion of remote and uninvolved shareholders as owners of corporations is an inherently unsuitable basis for thinking about how these institutions should be governed. In firms that fit the Prahalad and Hamel model, employees who embody the critical resources have important and inalienable control rights over the use of those resources. In such cases, those employees must be encouraged to make efficient decisions about how to use those resources. One way to achieve that is to give them sufficient claims on the returns and responsibility for the risks associated with their use—in other words, to give them ownership rights and responsibilities. If this were done well, the competence carriers in a corporation would look at least as much like owners as the shareholders would.

Internal Reorganizations to Imitate Ownership

Even where companies are not literally laying people off and hiring them back as subcontractors, they are experimenting with redesigning the way the work is done to give employees a greater sense of

---

[26]Crawford (1991, p. 113).

proprietorship over their tasks or projects and sometimes a share in the project's risks and rewards. The process Ford Motor Co. used to develop a new version of the Mustang is one example. A team of about four hundred people, cutting across functional lines, formed what the *Wall Street Journal* called a "skunk works" within the larger corporation. For three years—an exceptionally short period of time for new product development within the U.S. auto industry— this team acted as if it were a small development company funded by capital from Ford. The team decided "that the Mustang effort would need unprecedented freedom to make decisions without waiting for approval from headquarters or other departments," according to the *Journal.* "Team members wanted to think of themselves as independent stockholders of a 'Mustang Car Co.,' which happened to be financed by Ford."[27]

Richard Crawford provides a similar example at Merck, which he says "represents the emerging information-based organization of the future. . . composed largely of well-educated specialists who direct and discipline their own performance through organized feedback from colleagues, customers, and headquarters." These specialists, he says, "are not organized in a formal hierarchy of the traditional industrial model but instead according to twelve research disciplines and informal cross-discipline project teams. Each project is headed by a leader who must recruit team members from different disciplines to commit their own resources to the project based on its promise. In short, the project leader serves as an entrepreneur, and the research discipline as a venture capitalist."[28]

Some companies are transforming the workplace even in traditional manufacturing industries through the use of what David

---

[27]See Joseph B. White and Oscar Suris, "New Pony: How a 'Skunk Works' Kept Mustang Alive—On a Tight Budget," *Wall Street Journal,* September 21, 1993, p. A1.
    [28]Crawford (1991, p. 118).

Levine calls "high involvement workplaces." Levine's most extended example is NUMMI, the GM-Toyota joint venture set up in the former GM-Fremont plant in Fremont, California. GM-Fremont had been one of GM's worst-performing auto plants before it was shut down in 1982, but when it reopened as NUMMI in the fall of 1983, with largely the same work force, it "soon achieved productivity levels almost twice those of GM-Fremont in its best years, and 40 percent better than the typical GM assembly plant."[29] Levine and most of the other scholars who have examined NUMMI attribute the improvements to a massive transformation in shop-floor organization in which the firm invested much more heavily in training for workers, gave workers and the teams they worked in vastly more responsibility for decisionmaking, protected them with job security, and shared the returns with them, both through a formal bonus system and through collective bargaining, which tends to result in gainsharing.[30] The key feature of these high-involvement workplaces, according to Levine, is that employees as a group are recognized, along with shareholders, as constituents of the firm, and their interests are considered in the formation of managerial policy.[31]

Another example, in a much less glamorous industry, of a workplace transformed when employees were given responsibilities, rewards, and risks normally associated with ownership was related in *Fortune.*

Ten years ago, Robert Frey bought Cin-Made Corp., a manufacturer of paper packaging products in Cincinnati. It was losing as much as $30,000 a month on annual revenues of just $1.7 million. When Frey insisted that the 40 unionized hourly employees swallow a 25% pay cut, they went out on strike.

[29]Levine (1995, p. 13).
[30]Levine (1995).
[31]Levine (1995). See also Aoki (1987).

The workers stayed on the picket line until Frey threatened to hire permanent replacements. . . . When they capitulated, Frey told them he would never grant another pay raise. Instead, he offered to set aside 30% of all pretax earnings as a bonus pool and delegated to the workers—most of them high school dropouts—the authority to schedule production, control inventories, choose their own team leaders, and screen every new hire. Some were sent out to learn such techniques as statistical process control, which they then taught to teammates. Frey also began giving everyone detailed updates on Cin-Made's finances at monthly meetings. Says he: "Our goal was to learn to become worthy partners instead of being worthy adversaries." Since 1989, workers' bonuses have added an average of 30% to their annual compensation.[32]

In work he did jointly with Laura D'Andrea Tyson, Levine noted that several economists and organizational theorists argue that participatory management complicates the principal-agent problem by increasing the number of agents involved in each decision, thereby increasing transactions costs. Levine and Tyson counter, however, that "workers have information about the firm that the owner could never have and it is possible that a participatory structure with gain-sharing could induce workers to use their information." Noting that "workers must be motivated to share information as well as have opportunities to do so," Levine and Tyson claim that "participatory arrangements that offer workers no stake in returns have not been successful."[33]

Compensation Schemes that Share Risk and Rewards

If the analysis of the last two chapters is correct, managements of firms that singlemindedly pursue maximizing shareholder value

---

[32]See Louis S. Richman, "The New Work Force Builds Itself," *Fortune,* June 27, 1994, p. 68. Frey (1993, p. 70) tells his own story of the transformation at Cin-Made.
[33]Levine and Tyson (1990, p. 18).

may have trouble motivating employees to make productivity-enhancing changes in how they work or to make other investments in firm-specific skills. Could this problem be avoided by paying employees directly for acquiring skills? Motorola, for example, has experimented with paying workers for acquiring basic reading and math skills.[34] Likewise, Milwaukee Insurance has adopted skill-based pay, and Steelcase furniture shifted its white-collar work force to a skill-based pay system.[35] These systems have not generally been very successful, however. Motorola found that employees resented the fact that some team members were permitted to be absent for months at a time to get training and develop as individuals, while the other team members were expected to carry the load in their absence—and forgo the raises that would have accompanied the acquisition of the new skills. Motorola gave up on this system in 1992.[36] Implementing skill-based pay is also thought to be difficult because so many important skills—especially firm-specific skills that are likely to raise governance problems—are difficult to measure.[37]

Another, more common, approach to motivating employees to make firm-specific investments is to give them an ownership-like stake in the company by explicitly tying their compensation to the performance of the company. In profit-sharing arrangements a portion of employees' compensation fluctuates with the total profits of the whole corporation; under gain-sharing arrangements, a portion of compensation is tied to measurable improvements in certain perfor-

[34]Jaclyn Fierman, "The Perilous New World of Fair Pay," *Fortune,* June 13, 1994, p. 58.

[35]See Mary Rowland, "Your Own Account; For Each New Skill, More Money," *New York Times,* June 12, 1993, sec. 3, p. 16.

[36]Fierman, "The Perilous New World of Fair Pay," p. 58.

[37]Mary Rowland, "Your Own Account; For Each New Skill, More Money," sec. 3, p. 16.

mance measures at the unit or division level. It is estimated that profit-sharing or gain-sharing compensation plans now cover about a fifth of the private work force.[38]

A growing body of evidence suggests that profit-sharing schemes can increase productivity, although without other changes, the introduction of profit sharing seems to produce a one-shot increase in productivity and does not increase the rate of growth of productivity over time.[39] Other studies suggest that firms with profit sharing outperform firms without it on several performance indexes, and surveys of employers indicate that they think profit sharing is a good way to improve productivity and loyalty.[40]

Profit-sharing and gain-sharing arrangements are believed to induce better performance for the simple reason that they share some of the costs of bad performance and the returns from good performance with the employees. As one union employee said of such a system tried at Allied-Signal, "management asked us to be more productive, and we wanted to know what was in it for us."[41]

Employers also are adopting profit-sharing and gain-sharing arrangements because they understand that they cannot constantly monitor their employees, but must instead motivate them to think like owners.[42] Progressive Insurance Co., an auto insurer, has adopted a complex compensation system that pays its adjusters according to a gain-sharing formula tied to revenues, profits, and costs. The formula gives a typical adjuster the opportunity to increase his base salary by as much as 14 percent. But Progressive also

---

[38]Mitchell, Lewin, and Lawler (1990, p. 27).

[39]Kruse (1993).

[40]Weitzman and Kruse (1990).

[41]Fierman, "The Perilous New World of Fair Pay," p. 63.

[42]Stiglitz (1974) argues that where monitoring is difficult, profit-sharing, rather than fixed wage contracts, is a more efficient arrangement from the standpoint of both principal and agent.

helps to ensure that its adjusters have the skills they need by providing extensive training in insurance regulation, negotiation skills, and even grief counseling (for that part of their job that may involve dealing with relatives of crash victims). Explained Peter Lewis, Progressive's CEO: "To the extent that auto insurance is a commodity, our biggest differentiator is our people. We want the best people at every level of the company and we pay at the top of the market."[43]

Employee Ownership

The most direct way to tie employee pay to firm performance is to make sure that employees are also equity owners. Employees can be paid with restricted stock or restricted stock options, for example, or employee stock ownership plans (ESOPs) can be put in place to hold large blocks of the company's stock. In principle, at least, all the equity of a company could be owned by its employees.

Theoretical Objections

Employee-owned companies are the ultimate examples of governance structures that empower employees and protect investments in firm-specific human capital. But they have been viewed with great skepticism by some neoclassical economists and organizational theorists, who have argued that such firms are inefficient because employees do not have the incentive to maintain the physical capital properly. These theorists also have said that employees would prefer to maximize net revenues per worker rather than profits, which would result in inefficient levels of production and use of re-

[43]Ronald Henkoff, "Service Is Everybody's Business," *Fortune,* June 27, 1994, p. 50.

sources.[44] Furthermore, these economists have argued that hierarchies are necessary for efficient processing of large amounts of complex information and that democratically run firms would therefore be inefficient.[45]

Louis Putterman demonstrates that all of these supposed problems are consequences of the particular assumptions and modeling conventions used by the economists who make the arguments and do not necessarily apply to firms in which employees have a partial claim on the profits of the firm and exercise control through their ownership of securities such as common stock with voting rights. In short, two separate issues are at work here, and each should be analyzed separately. The first is whether the firm should be organized as a corporation; the second is whether employees should own or control the firm, however organized. All of the theoretical critiques of employee ownership turn out to be critiques of other organizational forms—the critiques do not apply if the firm is organized as a corporation, employees hold all or a significant part of the shares of the corporation, and these employee-owners are free to sell their stakes in the company.[46]

For example, some of the skeptics of employee ownership have equated it with participatory or democratic decisionmaking processes. But there is no particular reason why employee-owners could not agree to set up a hierarchical management structure. The argument that employees would use the physical capital inefficiently derives from the restrictive assumption that employee stakes in the

[44]For arguments that employee-owned firms would tend to "eat their seed corn," see Jensen and Meckling (1976), Furubotn and Pejovich (1974), and Vanek (1977). For arguments that employee-controlled firms would maximize net revenues per worker instead of maximizing profits, see Vanek (1977) and Meade (1972).

[45]See Williamson (1975, 1980).

[46]Putterman (1984).

firm are not marketable. If employees can sell their stakes in the company in a public market, the market price of those shares would reflect the full loss of value that would result from neglecting to maintain the physical capital. With marketable shares, employees would have the same incentive as other shareholders to see that the physical capital is efficiently maintained.[47]

Finally, the argument that employee-controlled firms would produce at inefficient levels turns out to be an artifact of a modeling convention in which physical capital is taken as the fixed, firm-specific input, and labor (or human capital) is taken as the generic and variable input. Gregory K. Dow has done some modeling that eliminates most of these peculiar assumptions and treats labor and capital symmetrically. In Dow's model, both human capital and physical capital can be fixed and firm-specific or generic and variable. Dow also assumes that the same financing mechanisms are available to both kinds of capital. Dow has used some formidable mathematical modeling building on these assumptions and has generated conclusions that closely resemble arguments I made in chapter 7. Where investments in specific physical capital are important and labor is unspecialized, Dow argues, traditional capitalist firms

[47]As long ago as the 1920s, Owen D. Young, then the CEO of General Electric Company, favored widespread employee ownership for precisely this reason: "Perhaps some day we may be able to organize the human beings engaged in a particular undertaking so that they truly will be the employer buying capital as a commodity in the market at the lowest price. It will be necessary for them to provide an adequate guarantee fund in order to buy their capital at all. If that is realized, the human beings will then be entitled to all the profits over the cost of capital. I hope the day may come when these great business organizations will truly belong to the men who are giving their lives and their efforts to them, I care not in what capacity. Then they will use capital truly as a tool and they will be all interested in working it to the highest economic advantage. Then an idle machine will mean to every man in the plant who sees it an unproductive charge against himself. Then every piece of material not in motion will mean to the man who sees it an unproductive charge against himself." See Monks and Minow (1995, pp. 385, 399).

will be most efficient; but where investments in firm-specific human capital are important and physical capital is unspecialized, labor-managed firms will be most efficient.[48]

Another class of objections to employee ownership comes from both finance specialists and labor leaders. This argument holds that worker ownership imposes the risk of fluctuating returns on employees, who may have relatively low incomes and may not be able to diversify their risks efficiently. According to this argument, employees are "risk-averse," but shareholders, who can generally invest in large, diversified portfolios are "risk-neutral." Therefore, it is efficient to provide employees with fixed wages and let shareholders bear all of the risk of fluctuating returns in the enterprise. For employees to hold shares would subvert this allocation of risk.

Putterman counters this argument by noting that workers may not necessarily prefer "fixed" wages if the ownership and governance structures that provide them with supposedly fixed wages also expose them to a significant chance of occasional layoff. Financial markets provide a wide variety of options for reallocating risk, Putterman notes, so it is not clear that workers could not insure themselves in secondary markets against the risks of fluctuating incomes. Of course, there are "inevitable trade-offs between insurance and incentives in any system," he continued, but there is no particular reason to believe that these trade-offs are any worse for systems with employee ownership of corporate equity than they are for systems with remote and uninvolved shareholders who insure themselves by diversifying their portfolios.[49]

---

[48]Dow (1993). Dow does not consider hybrid forms of management and does not say what should happen in situations where both physical capital and human capital must be highly specialized. Firms where control is shared in some way have rarely been modeled. Freeman and Lazear (1993) have developed the only model this author knows that attempts to study the effect of employee ownership on traditional capitalist firms.

[49]Putterman (1984, pp. 184–85).

If employees were given significant equity stakes in traditional capitalist companies, would they use their clout to prevent or impede plant closings and layoffs, even when these actions would increase efficiency? The answer depends on the proportion of the stock that employees hold, the share of the total rents earned by the enterprise that employees receive in fixed wages, and the share that they receive as a return on the stock they hold. Richard Freeman and Edward P. Lazear modeled this problem and concluded that giving employees shares in a company implies several things. Some shareholders who are also employees might occasionally vote against efficient layoff policies; but not all employees would because some of them would find that the gains in the value of their stock exceeded their losses from being laid off. Furthermore, the larger the share of stock in the hands of employees, the more likely that those employees would support efficient layoffs.[50] Freeman and Lazear further argued that workers could be induced to vote for efficiency-enhancing layoffs by providing them with "golden parachutes" that share some of the overall gains from the layoffs with the employees who lose their jobs.

But in the Freeman and Lazear model, employees would oppose efficient layoffs only if they are assumed to be receiving a wage that is higher than their (short-run) opportunity cost, as a way to compensate them for firm-specific investments. Losing their jobs would be costly to these employees because they would not be able to find employment that paid the same high wage. Other compensation schemes would not necessarily produce this result. Suppose employees were paid a fixed wage equal to their short-term opportunity cost and were compensated for their firm-specific investments with shares of stock. A layoff would not force these workers to take a lower base wage (because, by assumption, they could readily earn

[50]Freeman and Lazear (Forthcoming).

their base wage somewhere else), but an efficient layoff would cause the value of their stockholdings to rise. In theory, at least, if the mix of fixed wage and stock accurately reflected the mix of generic and firm-specific skills contributed by the employees, workers compensated in this way should never vote against an efficiency-enhancing layoff.

Employee Ownership in Practice

If theory fails to establish convincingly that employee ownership is a less efficient organizational form, why then are not more firms organized this way? Except for professional sectors discussed above, wholly owned employee cooperatives or corporations are indeed rare. But that situation may be changing. In a growing number of cases, employees have either bought out or traded wage and benefit concessions for significant equity stakes in their companies. In many more instances, workers own equity through holdings in employee stock ownership plans (ESOPs), pension funds, or other company benefit plans.

Equity ownership by employees is already much more important than most participants in the corporate governance debates realize. Joseph R. Blasi and Douglas L. Kruse identified 1,000 large, publicly traded companies where employees held more than 4 percent of the stock—an average of 12 percent of the voting shares—as of the end of the 1980s.[51] At the rate at which employee-ownership of corporate equity grew in the 1980s, Blasi, in a separate study, predicted that more than a quarter of all stock market companies would be more than 15 percent owned by their employees by the year 2000.[52]

---

[51]Blasi and Kruse (1991, p. 12).

[52]Joseph R. Blasi, "Employee Ownership and Participation: the Facts and the Trends, the Problems and the Policy Options; Analysis for the Clinton Transition Team," Memorandum, December 8, 1992.

According to Blasi and Kruse, employee ownership is widespread throughout the economy, not concentrated just in troubled sectors such as airlines and steel, where equity-for-wage-concession agreements by employees have made headlines. The four top employee ownership industries, they said, are utilities, oil and gas, consumer products, and financial services. As of 1990 employees owned 57 percent of Morgan Stanley's equity and 12 percent of the equity in the Paine-Webber Group, for example; Chevron employees held 16 percent of that company's equity, and Procter and Gamble's employees held 25 percent of P&G's stock. In utilities employees owned 11 percent of the shares of AT&T, 13 percent of Cincinnati Gas & Electric Co., 14 percent of Columbia Gas Systems Inc., and 13 percent of Pacific Gas & Electric Co. The aerospace and defense industry also has a high level of employee ownership: by 1990 employees held 43 percent of Grumman stock, 41 percent of Rockwell International stock, and 33 percent of McDonnell Douglas stock.[53] Health Trust of Nashville, Tennessee, EPIC Healthcare Group of Dallas, and Charter Medical of Macon, Georgia, are all majority-owned by their ESOPs.[54] Management and employees bought out Avis Car Rental, through an ESOP, in 1987, and employees throughout the company are now paid partially in stock. Avis has no nonmanagement employees on the board of directors, but employees participate in some 150 "employee participation groups" and send representatives to quarterly meetings of management.

Except for the steel industry, employee ownership has been somewhat rare in manufacturing, but a few such firms have been highly successful. For example, Herman Miller, a Grand Rapids, Michigan, office furniture maker with a long history of participative manage-

[53]Blasi and Kruse (1991, appendix A).

[54]Leslie Wayne, "Some Lessons from Avis for UAL Buyout," *New York Times*, September 24, 1989, p. 4.

ment and profit sharing, has 35 percent of its stock in the hands of employees.

By the early 1990s, according to Blasi, employees as a group held the single largest block of shares in more than 400 large companies, and in 250 of these, workers hold 20 percent or more of outstanding shares.[55] The National Center for Employee Ownership in Oakland, California, reported that in the early 1990s about 9,500 U.S. companies had ESOPs, and another 5,000 or so firms had share-option and other kinds of ownership plans.[56] In most cases employees own only a small share of the total company, but Blasi and Kruse estimated that, by the early 1990s, employees collectively held more than $150 billion worth of corporate equity.

Although no comparable data are available for the late 1970s, Blasi and Kruse showed that much of the employee ownership came about during the 1980s as result of stock buybacks, placement of stock in ESOPs to ward off unwanted raiders, and the restructuring of wage and benefit plans. Blasi and Kruse identified twenty-four companies that went private with the help of employee ownership and sixty units of larger companies that were spun off as private, employee-owned companies or partially bought out by employee-management groups during the 1980s. "Employee-held stock is starting to replace and restructure the system of fixed wages and benefits that have dominated the wage economy since World War II," Blasi and Kruse wrote.[57]

Recontracting at old troubled companies. One way that employees are expanding their equity ownership is through a process of recon-

---

[55]These data come from two different sources. See "A Firm of Their Own," *Economist,* June 11, 1994, pp. 59–61; and Blasi, "Employee Ownership and Participation."

[56]"A Firm of Their Own," p. 59–61.

[57]Blasi and Kruse (1991, p. 2).

tracting at old companies, where the rents being generated by the enterprise are no longer adequate to support high profits for shareholders as well as the high fixed wages employees had come to expect. Perhaps the most recent and well-published example of such recontracting is UAL: in the summer of 1994 the airline's employees traded wage and work-rule concessions for a controlling share of company stock. Just a year earlier, employees at Northwest Airlines accepted a 28 percent share in the equity of the company in exchange for $886 million in wage and other cost savings, and TWA employees swapped $660 million of concessions for 45 percent of that company's stock. Several similar agreements were reached in the steel and trucking industries in the 1980s. In 1984, for example, employees bought out the Weirton, West Virginia, steel plant from National Intergroup conglomerate (the parent company of National Steel). Weirton Steel is the tenth largest steel producer in the United States. Northwestern Steel and Wire and Republic Engineered Steel are also now majority-owned by employees for similar reasons.

In the trucking industry, unionized employees of Commercial Lovelace Motor Freight, Inc., agreed in 1983 to lower their wage and benefit levels substantially in response to intense competition from nonunion truckers. In return, workers received just over 50 percent of the stock and the right to elect three of the seven members of the board. At five other trucking firms, the union agreed to a similar package, but worker ownership was kept under 50 percent.[58]

Although it is too early to tell how employee ownership will affect the airlines, in the steel industry, some of the companies bought by employees have not only saved jobs, but have generated new profits for their employee-owners. The New York Times reported in July 1993 that Algoma Steel Inc. of Sault Ste. Marie, Ontario, had significant positive operating earnings in the second

---

[58]Weidenbaum (1994).

quarter of 1993 for the first time since an employee buyout two years earlier prevented the closing of the mill. The *Times* quoted several employees who said their approach to their jobs had changed since they had become equity owners. "Before, you left your brains at the gate," one said. "Now you take your brains through the gate and are allowed to use them. That's the big difference."[59]

The situation at Weirton Steel is still playing itself out. The company was profitable for the first six years after the buyout, but by 1989 it needed to raise new investment capital. The firm sold 4.5 million new common shares to the public, diluting the employee interest, a move which caused some rifts in relations between management and workers. In 1991 the firm had to take on $300 million in new debt to make the final payment to National Intergroup, while problems in the steel industry caused Weirton's stock price to fall by more than half. Sometime later the employee-owners got into a dispute with management over an investment plan to raise new capital by selling even more new shares of stock to the public. By May 1994, after three years of losses, employees finally approved another share sale, that diluted their ownership position to 51 percent.[60] It remains to be seen whether this dilution will weaken employee commitment.

Although the facts are different in each of these cases, a general pattern can be discerned. In each case, rents to the enterprise as a whole were declining under industrywide competitive pressures, and the old mechanisms (such as union contracts) that had been used to capture and protect some share in the enterprise rents for

---

[59]See Clyde H. Farnsworth, "Experiment in Worker Ownership Shows a Profit," *New York Times*, July 14, 1993, sec. 1, p. 33.

[60]Clare Ansberry and Dana Milbank, "Industry Focus: Small, Midsized Steelmakers Are Ripe for a Shakeout," *Wall Street Journal*, March 4, 1992, p. B4; Stephen Baker and Keith Alexander, "The Owners vs. The Boss at Weirton Steel," *Business Week*, November 15, 1993, p. 38; and "A Firm of Their Own," pp. 59–61.

employees were consequently under severe pressure. The old mechanisms simply were not flexible enough. Had they not given way to a new mechanism, the companies might have been forced to reduce employment drastically or to shut down altogether. Under the new mechanisms, employees accept a lower basic pay package and share in the risks associated with the total returns to the enterprise, but they also gain significant control rights through their ownership of stock and, occasionally, through having representatives on the boards of directors.

Creation of ESOPs. Another mechanism by which employee ownership has been expanding is through the creation or expansion of employee stock ownership plans. ESOPs are investment vehicles through which employer corporations can make tax deductible contributions of cash or stock into a trust, whose assets are allocated in some predetermined manner to the employee participants in the trust. ESOPs must be invested in the employer's stock and are regulated like pension funds, under the Employee Retirement Income Security Act of 1974 (ERISA).[61] As of 1992 ESOPs accounted for 43 percent of employee ownership of equity in public companies, according to Blasi.[62]

Small private companies began using ESOPs in the 1960s and 1970s to give employees a way to buy out the founding entrepreneur when he or she got ready to retire. As late as 1986, half of all existing ESOPs had been created for this reason.[63] Large corporations began to make significant use of ESOPs as part of their employee benefit

[61]Gaughan (1991, p. 399).

[62]Blasi, "Employee Ownership and Participation." The rest is accounted for by 401(k) and other pension plans (39 percent), employee share purchase plans (8 percent), and grantor trusts and other mechanisms (10 percent).

[63]General Accounting Office, "Employee Stock Ownership Plans: Little Evidence of Effects on Corporate Performance," GAO/PEMD-88-1, October, 1987.

packages in the late 1970s, in part as a result of a special tax credit provided in the Tax Reduction Act of 1975. Under this tax law, companies were permitted to take an additional 1 percent investment tax credit if the full amount of the credit were contributed to a special employee stock ownership plan (called a TRASOP for Tax Reduction Act Stock Ownership Plan). The General Accounting Office estimated that by 1983, 26 percent of all ESOPs were of the tax-credit type. But TRASOPs covered 90 percent of all ESOP participants, because the larger companies tended to use them. In 1983 this incentive was changed from a tax credit equal to 1 percent of investment to a tax credit equal to 1 percent of payroll. Congress then ended these so-called PAYSOP tax credits in 1986.[64]

Despite the elimination of the tax credit, interest in ESOPs increased dramatically in the late 1980s.[65] From 1974, when ERISA was passed, through 1987, U.S. corporations acquired a total of less than $20 billion of their own stock to put into ESOPs, but in the next three years, 1988 through 1990, they put something like $35 billion of their stock into ESOPs. By the end of the 1980s, more than 10 million employees of U.S. companies participated in ESOPs.[66]

[64]See Conte and Svejnar (1990) and accompanying appendix for details on the history of tax incentives to create ESOPs.

[65]Some analysts have argued that ESOPs continue to be tax-advantaged methods of financing for corporations because, if a corporation borrows funds to buy back its own stock and contribute it to an ESOP, both the interest and the principal on that loan are deductible. But the rationale for the deductibility of principal as well as interest is that the contribution to the ESOP is an employee benefit, so the full cost of the benefit is deductible, just as the full cost of a health care or retirement benefit would be deductible. The most careful analysis of ESOP financing concludes that since the tax credit was eliminated in 1986, financing through an ESOP does not continue to provide any net tax advantages for corporations. See Conte and Svejnar (1990) for details. The tax code has also provided minor tax incentives for lenders to provide funding for ESOPs, but these were greatly reduced in 1990.

[66]Data are from Gaughan (1991, p. 400), who reports that corporations bought back $5.6 billion worth of stock for ESOPs in 1988 and $19 billion in the first half of 1989 and Business Week, which cites Morgan Stanley as the source for its estimate that

An important reason for the rise in contributions to ESOPs was the discovery by corporations that putting a large block of stock in the hands of employees could serve as an effective takeover defense. Under a Delaware law passed in 1987, bidders holding more than 15 percent of a company must wait for three years to complete a takeover unless they acquire at least 85 percent of the target's shares, unless two-thirds of shareholders (excluding the bidder) approve the acquisition, or unless the board of directors and shareholders decide to exempt themselves from the law.[67] Setting up an ESOP can protect the target company by making it very difficult for a bidder to acquire the necessary 85 percent or to get the necessary two-thirds vote. Polaroid was the first large company to make use of this device under pressure from a hostile takeover attempt by Shamrock in 1988. Shamrock sued to stop Polaroid from setting up the ESOP, charging that it was just an attempt to entrench management. But the Delaware court upheld Polaroid and approved the ESOP despite its obvious antitakeover implications. In approving the ESOP, the court took into account the fact that Polaroid had been considering establishing an ESOP for about two years before the takeover attempt, that the ESOP would be funded by cuts in employees' other compensation, that the plan had simple "mirrored" voting rights (which meant that employees would control the votes of all shares in the ESOP) and no special features, and that it did not necessarily create strong incentives for employees to vote in favor of incumbent management.[68]

Thus the idea has been legally sanctioned that companies can set up institutional arrangements to protect employees' interests in the event of a takeover bid, even though those arrangements may some-

---

corporations put $18 billion in 1989 and $10 billion in 1990 in ESOPs. See Aaron Bernstein, "Joe Sixpack's Grip on Corporate America," *Business Week*, July 15, 1991, pp. 108–110.

[67]Gaughan (1991, p. 413).

[68]See Shamrock Holdings Inc. v. Polaroid Corp., 559 A.2d 257 (Delaware 1989). See also Blasi and Kruse (1991, p. 179), Barnatan (1992) and Lauerman (1990).

times prevent shareholders from cashing out at an immediate higher price. ESOPs and other employee-ownership schemes are particularly appealing mechanisms for achieving a balance between interests of shareholders and interests of employees because, if they are designed well, compensation systems that make employees into shareholders can reduce the potential for conflict by helping align the interests of employees with those of shareholders. But whether an ESOP serves to protect employees' firm-specific investments or just to entrench management depends on whether employees control the votes of the shares that are held by the ESOP. Employees do not always get this control, a point that is examined further in the sections that follow.

Restructuring of compensation schemes to emphasize equity ownership. A third important way that employee ownership is increasing is through the expanding use of wage and benefit programs that incorporate share ownership (of which ESOPs are only one variety). Employee-ownership plans come in numerous forms, ranging from investment of some portion of the portfolio of the conventional pension fund in company stock to companywide grants of stock options.[69] In a 401(k) plan, the company purchases its own stock with money deducted from employee salaries and holds the stock in a special account for the employee. If the company matches the employee contribution, such a plan is called a KSOP. In a deferred profit-sharing plan, the company invests a portion of company profits in a retirement fund that buys the company's stock. Companies may also set up employee stock purchase plans, in which the company matches the employee contributions or pays brokerage fees.[70]

---

[69]There are legal limits on the portion of a conventional pension fund that can be invested in the employer's own stock, however.

[70]See Blasi and Kruse (1991, pp. 24–28) for a brief overview of the most common types of employee ownership plans.

In most companies, stock option plans are still reserved for senior executives, but a growing number of companies are extending their stock option plans deep into the company. In 1991, for example, both DuPont and Merck began to grant options to nearly all employees. John W. Himes, human resources vice president at DuPont, told *Business Week*: "We want every individual to feel a higher level of personal responsibility for the company's success." The magazine reported that Imcera Group, Pepsico, Pfizer, Toys 'R' Us, Waste Management, and Wendy's also offered stock option plans to most employees.[71]

Only a handful of companies have tied compensation systems so tightly to share ownership and spread share ownership so widely and deeply in the companies that the companies can truly be regarded as employee-owned. The largest such company is Science Applications International Corp. (SAIC), a technical services contractor with more than 15,000 employees and $1.5 billion in revenues in 1993. SAIC has an ESOP and two profit-sharing retirement plans and awards stock bonuses and stock options to its employees for special achievements. Slightly more than half of the assets in its retirement funds were invested in SAIC stock as of the end of 1992, and, directly or indirectly through their retirement plans, nonmanagement employees owned 49 percent of the company. The company uses a variety of approaches to award stock to employees and to encourage them to buy stock; its goal is for key employees to hold two to two and a half times their annual salary in stock after five years of employment. It also uses "vesting stock bonuses" (which accrue to the employee in full over a specified number of years) to encourage employees to stay with the company. Because its stock is not traded publicly, the company has an in-house broker-dealer, and four times

---

[71]Joseph Weber, "Offering Employees Stock Options They Can't Refuse," *Business Week*, October 7, 1991, p. 34.

each year buyers are matched with sellers to give employees an opportunity to buy or sell shares. The stock price is determined by a formula incorporating net income, stockholders' equity, and a market factor that reflects outside market trends.[72]

SAIC is an excellent example of a firm whose critical assets consist almost entirely of human capital. The company is a service contractor to industry and government on technical problems in the environmental, energy, national security, health, and space fields. The company does not have a large base of physical plant and equipment and does not manufacture much, although it does assemble customized control and monitoring systems from components manufactured by others. The company's ability to generate wealth year after year is not a function of any physical resources it controls or any specialized factories it owns, but of its ability to assemble teams of specialists to work on specific projects, design specialized control systems, or solve specific problems for clients. Whether it does these things well depends, more than anything else, on the skills of its individual employees and managers, how adept they are at identifying client needs and solving problems, and, importantly, how well they work together.

How Does Employee Ownership Affect Performance?

The earliest empirical studies of employee ownership tended to be either isolated case studies or studies of companies that had set up ESOPs. The case studies often produced very optimistic results, suggesting that employee ownership would yield productivity improvements, but these studies were criticized because they were subject to "selection bias." Only the successful employee-owned companies survived to be studied, and the case studies tended to be

[72]Science Applications International Corporation, "Annual Report," 1993, San Diego.

of the most successful of those. The earliest systematic studies based on large samples provided little support for the idea that ESOPs improve company performance.[73] Subsequent research has tended to confirm that the presence of an ESOP does not, by itself, seem to improve corporate performance.[74]

But a growing number of studies suggest that performance is significantly enhanced when ownership of equity by employees is combined with other programs that enhance employee participation and control over the company. Michael A. Conte and Jan Svejnar conducted a comprehensive survey of the evidence on ESOPs and concluded that "it seems clear that participative institutions within firms lead to heightened performance levels when combined with employee ownership."[75] Moreover, Blasi observed that "most of what researchers call 'profit-sharing' plans are really deferred profit-sharing trusts that have sizeable amounts of employee ownership of employer securities."[76] If the results from studies of profit-sharing are treated as evidence for the effect of employee ownership, the case is much stronger that employee ownership enhances productivity. Kruse and Martin L. Weitzman conducted a "meta-analysis" of results from sixteen different studies of profit-sharing, examining forty-two different data sets. These studies produced a total of 226 different estimates of the effect of profit-sharing on company performance. Only 6 percent of these estimates were negative, while 60 percent were positive and statistically significant. Although each of these studies was flawed in its own way, Weitzman and Kruse concluded that the odds are "infinitesimal" that the true underlying

---

[73]Bloom (1985).

[74]See, for example, U.S. General Accounting Office, "Employee Stock Ownership Plans: Little Evidence of Effects on Corporate Performance," GAO/PEMD-88-1, October 1987.

[75]Conte and Svejnar (1990, p. 171).

[76]Blasi (1990, pp. 172–73).

effect of profit-sharing is zero or negative.[77] Kruse subsequently conducted a careful statistical analysis of 500 U.S. public companies and, after taking a variety of other potential influences on productivity into account, determined that the adoption of profit-sharing at a firm is associated with a one-time jump in productivity of 4 to 5 percent, with no subsequent decline or change in trend.[78]

What Effect Does Employee Ownership Have on Governance?

As employees become major owners of the equity in corporations, they may affect the way corporations are governed in a variety of ways, depending in part on how the employees become owners. Some of the equity-for-wage-concession deals in the steel, airline, and trucking industries, for example, have provided for employee or union representation on the board of directors. TWA, Northwest Airlines, and UAL all have nonmanagement employees on their boards, as do Weirton Steel and the other steel companies that were bought out by employees in the 1980s.[79]

But employees who have gained their ownership position through ESOPs or through other compensation and benefit plans have not,

---

[77]Weitzman and Kruse (1990, pp. 127, 137–38).

[78]Kruse (1993).

[79]In recent years, nearly all of the steel companies have agreed to major power- and profit-sharing arrangements with their employees, short of giving them a significant equity stake, as a result of union contract negotiations. Bethlehem Steel, Inland Steel, and National Steel all agreed during contract negotiations in 1993 to put union representatives on their boards, for example. All agreed to profit-sharing arrangements, too, and Bethlehem Steel further committed to giving the union "access to detailed business plans, involving 'products pricing, markets, capital spending, short- and long-term cash flow forecasts and the method and manner of funding or financing the business plan,' according to a memorandum of understanding between union and firm." See Alison Leigh Cowan, "Board Seat Is Promised to Steel Union," New York Times, August 2, 1993, p. D1.

typically, gained commensurate access to the boardroom. Of all the companies they studied, Blasi and Kruse identified only 4 that had put employee representatives on the board of directors. Less than half a percent of the companies Blasi and Kruse studied had nonsenior management employee representation of any kind, and, of 410 companies where the employees are the dominant shareholder, only 3 had any employee representation.[80] Why have these companies not taken this next step? The reason may simply be that no one has yet pushed to get employee representatives on the board. "We really haven't thought about issues like employee representation on the board. That's not a bridge we've crossed yet," Barbara Yatine told *Business Week* in 1991.[81] Yatine was the investor-relations director at Primerica Corp., which was 10 percent employee-owned.

Not only do employees not have board representation commensurate with their equity stakes, they may not even control the votes of the shares that are held in their interest, nor do they necessarily have the right to decide whether to tender these shares in the event of a takeover bid. Stock held in pension funds, profit-sharing trusts, and ESOPs are controlled by the trustees of these funds. According to Blasi and Kruse, employee stock plans usually call for "mirror voting" or other mechanisms for voting the shares held in such funds according to employees' wishes.

But the U.S. Department of Labor says that plan trustees can override the employee vote if the vote would violate the trustee's fiduciary responsibilities. The department has also made it clear that those duties require the trustees to consider the best interest of the beneficiaries as *shareholders only* and to ignore their interests as employees. "The Dept. of Labor has said, in effect, that if your mirror voting comes up with the same decision a trustee would have come

---

[80]Blasi and Kruse (1991, p. 232).
[81]Bernstein, "Joe Sixpack's Grip on Corporate America," pp. 108–100.

up with, it is legal," Washington attorney Steven Hester observed. "But in any case where it counts, it is illegal, so it is ok as long as it is irrelevant. They are saying that employees are too dumb, and the government must appoint a wise man to decide for them."[82]

Critics of employee ownership have argued that it has been used so far not to empower employees, but to dilute the interests of outside shareholders and to help to further entrench management. But employees may be waking up to their potential power as shareholders. In 1988, for example, Grand Metropolitan PLC bid to take over Pillsbury Co., and Pillsbury employees voted half the 1.9 million company shares in their pension plan in favor of the takeover because employees at Pillsbury's Burger King division were angry at Pillsbury management for planning to spin off that division. And in the spring of 1994, labor unions suddenly became shareholder activists at several companies, submitting seventy-one governance-related shareholders proposals and twenty-six proposals on social issues at more than fifty companies during the 1994 proxy season.[83] As the *Wall Street Journal* reported,

> The proposals come both from pension-fund trustees, who manage union members' retirement money, and from active or retired union members, who typically own shares through their companies' stock-purchase programs. While most of these proposals call for the same corporate governance reforms that public pension funds have long championed, a growing number seek to push controversial union agendas. That worries some shareholders-rights advocates, who fear that labor's new activism may subvert, not advance, their own goals. . . .

---

[82]Blasi and Kruse (1991, p. 190).

[83]Of the governance proposals, fifteen were later withdrawn, and eight were disallowed by the SEC. Of the forty-eight ultimately voted on, six passed. Only ten of the social issues were voted on, and none passed. Private communication with Virginia Rosenbaum, Investor Responsibility Research Center, Washington, D.C., March 16, 1995.

"These proposals have everything to do with labor relations and nothing to do with corporate governance," says James Allen, a vice president at Consolidated Freightways Inc., a Palo Alto, Calif., transport company that faces two such proxy initiatives. "These guys are the wolf in the sheep's clothing," he adds. "It's strictly a campaign of harassment."[84]

The SEC must rule on whether companies are required to accept these union proposals, and it has generally not been sympathetic to union-backed proxy proposals that appear to be more about labor relations than corporate governance. In particular, the SEC has ruled against union-sponsored proposals when it viewed them as part of campaigns to win higher wages or other contract improvements. But according to the *Wall Street Journal* story, shareholder activists, as well as unions,

> express discomfort with the SEC's making judgments about shareholders' motivations. "It's none of the SEC's business if I'm a union member . . . if it's a legitimate grievance," says Sara Teslik, executive director of the Council of Institutional Investors. . . . In any case, labor's new proxy initiatives aren't likely to die out soon. "We hope to see more of this," says Michael Calabrese, a lawyer with the AFL-CIO's Department of Employee Benefits. "Union activists do not view short-term portfolio returns as the sole criterion for taking positions on shareholder issues."[85]

Impediments to Employee Ownership

One of the impediments to successful employee ownership is union ambivalence, if not outright hostility.[86] Unions have opposed em-

---

[84]See Leslie Scism, "Labor Unions Increasingly Initiate Proxy Proposals," *Wall Street Journal*, March 1, 1994, p. C1.

[85]Scism, "Labor Unions Increasingly Initiate Proxy Proposals," p. C1.

[86]Stern and others (1983) discuss some of the reasons for union opposition to employee ownership.

ployee ownership in part because of legitimate concerns about the risks that ownership imposes on workers. If a pension plan is eliminated when the ownership plan is put in place, for example, employees' retirement savings become much more heavily dependent on the future performance of the company. And the associated risks are real. Employees of Carter Hawley Hale Stores were nearly wiped out, for example, after they had put thousands of dollars into a company-sponsored savings plan that was invested solely in Carter Hawley Hale stock, giving them more than a 40 percent stake in the company by 1991. The stock price collapsed that year, to less than $2 (from around $14 a share in 1989), when the recession forced the firm into bankruptcy. The bankruptcy settlement plan reduced the employees' share of the company to around 3 percent.[87]

The risks can be reduced if stock ownership plans are used not to replace regular, diversified, pension funds, but to substitute for some of the employees' cash salary. Another way to reduce the risks is to give employees convertible preferred shares, which have a higher priority than common shares in the event of bankruptcy. Perhaps insurance companies could develop some insurance products that would enable employees to insure, or hedge, against some of the risks they take on by investing in their companies' stock.

More important, the risks of ownership should be put in perspective. They should be weighed not against some idealized, perfectly secure pay and benefit package, which, in a world where even IBM lays off people with twenty-four years of seniority, probably does not exist any more (if it ever did). Instead, the risks should be weighed against the risk of not having a secure claim on the wealth created by investments in firm-specific skills, nor any voice in how those investments are to be administered.

---

[87]Bernstein, "Joe Sixpack's Grip on Corporate America," pp. 108–110; and Maggie Mahar, "Cracked Nest Egg," *Barrons*, April 8, 1991, pp. 14–24.

Unions also have resisted employee ownership for historical and cultural reasons. In the late nineteenth century, the earliest leaders of the American Federation of Labor endorsed collective bargaining as the main union strategy and rejected worker ownership.[88] Worker ownership was viewed as undermining collective bargaining and the whole union institution. There may be some truth to this. It is perhaps not coincidental that employee ownership and cooperative approaches to shop floor problem-solving in general have been increasing in recent years as union power and influence has declined. Nonetheless, unions are far from dead, and the long history of contentious labor-management relations in this country suggests that institutional and cultural barriers to employee ownership could be difficult to surmount in many companies and industries.

On the corporate side too, one of the biggest obstacles to employee ownership may be cultural. Blasi and Kruse classified five ways that public corporations approach employee ownership. In "feudal cultures," senior management tightly controls employee ownership, which is seen solely as a means to a financial end. Firms that set up ESOPs as a tax-advantaged way to fund acquisitions would be examples. Firms with "investor cultures" are proud of employee ownership and promote it as an incentive to work hard but do not empower the employees by giving them a role in corporate governance. Firms with "participatory cultures" believe the greatest benefits of employee ownership come from the increased information flows to and from employees and the corresponding increase in their involvement in problem-solving and other company issues. Firms with "shareholder cultures" treat the employees collectively

[88]Worker cooperatives were sometimes formed as part of strategies to end strikes, but those were rarely, if ever, successful business enterprises. See Stern and others (1983, pp. 82–83). Samuel Gompers, first president of the federation, also opposed government pension schemes and employer pensions for fear they would reduce worker and union autonomy. See Ghilarducci (1992, p. 17).

as significant shareholders, who have certain leverage over the management, as they would any other investors holding 10 or 15 percent of the company. Finally, firms with "entrepreneurial cultures" want employees to be activist entrepreneurial workers and concerned, aggressive shareholders.

Blasi and Kruse estimate that 20 to 30 percent of the 1,000 publicly traded firms they studied had feudal ownership cultures; 60 to 75 percent had investor cultures; and about 5 percent had participatory cultures. "An estimated zero percent espouses an entrepreneurial culture," they claim.[89]

Conclusions

This chapter does not argue for employee ownership of corporate equity as the only way to encourage and protect firm-specific investments by employees. It simply takes issue with a large body of analysis that tries to rule out employee ownership as a feasible system on theoretical grounds or on the basis of old or outdated empirical evidence. The view that employee ownership will always be inefficient is based on a model of production in which the specialized asset is the physical plant and equipment and labor is relatively unskilled, doing routine work that can be effectively monitored. The share of total economic activity for which these assumptions are reasonable is rapidly shrinking.

Nor does this chapter call for a focus on employees to the neglect of other stakeholders. Such a distorted focus, combined with generous lifetime employment contracts, may, in fact, have contributed to the adjustment difficulties Japanese and German companies seemed to have had in the recession of the early 1990s. I do not

[89]Blasi and Kruse (1991, chap. 4).

advocate governance changes that are intended to disenfranchise shareholders or give total control to employees or to any other stakeholder. Instead, I stress that the goals of directors and management should be maximizing total wealth creation by the firm. The key to achieving this is to enhance the voice of and provide owner-ship-like incentives to those participants in the firm who contribute or control critical, specialized inputs and to align the interests of these critical stakeholders with the interests of outside, passive shareholders. Ownership of shares by employees and other stake-holders will, I suspect, prove to be an important way to achieve this. Compared with lifetime employment and generous wage and benefit contracts, for example, employee ownership should give firms more flexibility, not less, because the total compensation of employees will be more explicitly tied to the wealth-creating activity of the firm. I stress the role of employees in this process (rather than other stakeholders) because I believe investments in firm-specific human capital to be crucial to wealth creation in the U.S. economy. Moreover, the contracting problems that arise from these investments are especially widespread and severe.

9

CONCLUSIONS AND

RECOMMENDATIONS

FLEXIBILITY, RESILIENCE, AND RESPONSIVENESS have always been important strengths of the U.S. economy. These strengths are becoming more important every day. Thus any reforms in the rules and institutions of corporate governance should encourage, not inhibit, experimentation in contractual design, organizational form, and labor relations. They should provide a reasonably level playing field and should not unduly bias the choices about organizational form or contractual terms between firms and their employees, suppliers, or customers.

In a legal and institutional environment that is open and flexible, in which property rights can be protected and contracts can be enforced, there is good reason to believe that individuals who are free to do so will devise efficient contractual arrangements, organizational forms, and governance structures. I have argued in this book that such arrangements will, among other features, allocate ownership rights and responsibilities toward those who control the critical assets and that they will provide some protection for the parties whose investments in those assets are at risk. The last chapter cited numerous examples of companies that have already implemented a variety of governance arrangements that seem to be designed, at least in part, to achieve these goals.

Nonetheless, such arrangements will not be adopted automatically nor quickly, especially in times of rapid change when the development of governance structures that are responsive to the problems of today and tomorrow may be stymied by a tendency for all the parties involved to fight yesterday's war. In this regard, the greatest impediment to the development of new, more effective corporate governance arrangements may be the mindsets of many leaders among corporate management, labor, boards of directors, executives of financial institutions, and their lawyers. They, to a great degree, are stuck in an old model, in which shareholders put up risk capital that is used to build the factory, workers are hired at their opportunity cost and paid fixed wages, and the job of management is to maximize profits for shareholders. The typical business corporation of the 1990s does not look like this model, and the business corporation of the next century will be different yet again. All the different forms the corporation may take are not apparent yet, but it is a good bet that human capital will be at least as important to the wealth-creation process in the coming century as it is today, and probably more so. The struggle is to design systems that simultaneously foster and protect such investments and attempt to maximize the returns to both human capital and physical capital.

Because this process is iterative and experimental, there is no need for radical changes in the law or the tax code, or in the structure of existing regulatory institutions. This book does, however, suggest a fairly radical new way of thinking about the problem.

Following are several specific ways that corporate governance should be reformed in line with this new thinking.

Ultimately, It's Up to the Boards of Directors

A system that is flexible and responsive is also a system that is subject to abuses. The first and most important line of defense against abuses must be effective and responsible boards of directors. Each firm is engaged in a unique and complex balancing act to encourage and reward innovation and wealth creation, to satisfy providers of capital, and to discourage waste and empire-building. Only management and directors who understand the business intimately, who are willing to devote the time and energy necessary, and who are properly motivated can be expected to accomplish this balancing act.

Directors must have wide latitude to set strategy and decide how to use the company's resources. Nonetheless, they must be guided by clear standards for what constitutes success. The goal of wealth creation by the enterprise as a whole can provide that standard. This standard should be taught in management schools and supported by the law and by the culture of the boardroom. Measurement tools should be developed to provide information to the board about how well the company is doing at creating wealth.

Directors and management should carefully examine the businesses their companies are in to identify the true sources of wealth creation. What are the critical assets, who currently controls them, and how well do the existing management and governance systems align risk and reward with control over these critical assets? What incentive structures and organizational designs are likely to elicit and support good leadership by management and responsible, informed oversight by directors? These questions should guide companies in designing governance systems that better foster wealth creation.

Boards must understand that they are the representatives of *all* the important stakeholders in the firm—all those whose investments in physical or human capital are at risk. Thus, individuals who explicitly represent critical stakeholders should be put on boards, to give those stakeholders some assurance that their interests will be taken into account. Shareholder rights advocates object to the idea that directors should represent any stakeholders other than shareholders because, they argue, such "constituency" directors are tainted by conflicts of interest. Wherever there are relationship-specific investments in an enterprise, however, there is no way to avoid conflicts of interest. Shareholder representatives are just as conflicted—they advocate maximizing share value, even at the expense of total wealth creation—as employee representatives would be.

A valid objection to constituency directors is that this practice would tend to foster an adversarial atmosphere, rather than a cooperative one, on boards. Conflicts would be mitigated, however, if all of the participants in the firm who have made firm-specific investments also had an equity stake in the firm proportional to their firm-specific investments. In this way, all of the stakeholders would also be shareholders, and all would have an interest in maximizing share value. These shareholder-stakeholders must be given access to the nominating process, however, so that they can collectively choose the board that they feel best represents their total interest.

Most U.S. corporations are a long way from such an ownership structure. In the absence of such a structure, directors should represent all of the constituencies or stakeholders who have made relationship-specific investments so that the conflicts are explicitly acknowledged and dealt with in ways that give all of the relevant interests access to the decisionmaking process.

Directors should have a major personal stake in the long-run success of the enterprise. For example, they should be required to hold some significant amount of their company's stock (significant, at least, relative to their own net worth), should be compensated in restricted stock or at least in indexed stock options that mature over a long period of time, and should be allowed to serve on the boards of only a few corporations, so that their professional reputations are more strongly tied to the well-being of each company. Boards should also be able to hire outside consultants to help them gather and assess independent information about the performance of their company.

As appendix 5-2 illustrated, other reform advocates have put forward a long list of specific proposals to improve the incentives and functioning of boards and special board committees. Although many of these proposals may have much to recommend them, in general, reforms of this sort should probably not be imposed from outside because boards need the flexibility to design systems that are responsive to their own special circumstances Indeed, many companies are experimenting with these sorts of board reforms, and research should continue into how these structural reforms affect board performance.

Learn to Measure and Monitor Total Wealth Creation

The accounting system that U.S. corporations use tallies returns on equipment, inventories, and other physical assets but provides no information about the return a company can earn on other kinds of investments, such as investments in the skills of its employees or in organizational capabilities. The system also fails to measure and count as wealth creation the share of the rents generated by the firm that are captured by employees (or other stakeholders). Instead, the system "treats investment in people as a cost, biasing managers away from human capital," as David Levine has argued.[1] Thus even directors and managers who understand their jobs to be maximizing

---

[1]Levine (1995, p. 123).

total wealth creation and who are well motivated to pursue that goal, are generally receiving partial and misleading information about the sources of wealth in their firms.

Developing new measures of investment and wealth creation is not an easy task, and I am not qualified to suggest specific changes to accounting rules. But clearly this is an area where extensive research is needed.[2]

Encourage Employee Ownership and Stewardship

Employees who acquire firm-specific skills obviously have an interest in maximizing the return to those skills. But, the goal of total wealth maximization is better served if employees focus on the success of the enterprise as a whole, not just on the perpetuation of their own jobs. An important way to reduce the potential conflict between these two goals would be to compensate employees for their firm-specific investments with shares of common stock. Such compensation can be

[2] Henry P. Hill, a scholar and practitioner of accounting and formerly the national director of accounting and auditing services for Price Waterhouse & Co., has written a readable and persuasive book (Hill 1987) that sharply criticizes standard corporate accounting practice in this country because it is based on the illogical and unsustainable premise that shareholders are the only owners of corporations and that all other contributors of capital are outsiders. He proposes, instead, that the basic logic of accounting methods for publicly traded corporations be revised to follow what he calls an "entity" concept. Under entity accounting, all sources of capital, whether they be long-term debt, deferred compensation in the form of pension fund credits, capital leases negotiated, or common or preferred stock, would be treated in a parallel fashion, and income generated by the enterprise would be measured as the total return to all sources of capital, not just that portion of such return that is currently reported as "profits." Hill's entity concept seems a good starting place to rethink the way wealth creation is measured in publicly traded corporations. Hill argues that it would also provide a more rational way to resolve several major disputes in the accounting profession about how to account for such complex transactions as mergers and pension fund accruals.

handled in several different ways, and each company will have to develop a system that works best for its situation.

In general, however, a significant portion of the compensation of both executives and rank-and-file employees should consist of restricted stock that cannot be sold immediately but must be held for some minimum period, such as five years. Unlike stock options, grants of restricted stock expose employees to the downside risks of ownership, as well as to the upside potential. The stock grants should replace some of the cash compensation that would have otherwise been paid, not just be added on top—and this rule must apply to top executives as well as to lower-level employees. Employees should be required to hold the stock for at least five years, unless they are laid off (but not if they quit on their own initiative or are fired for cause). Such stock grants should be treated as a cost to the company at the time of the grant (valued at the market price of the stock at that time) and as income to the employee. But employees should be allowed to defer paying income taxes on such grants until they sell the stock, at which time the total sales price of the stock would be taxed at the employee's marginal rate.[3]

Ideally, all employees should be paid a base wage or salary that represents a return to their generic human capital. This level of compensation is not really at risk because, by assumption, employees could take their particular mix of skills numerous other places and get paid that much. Shares in the equity of the corporation should then be given as compensation for their investments in firm-specific skills. Obviously, there is no way to measure precisely the value of such investments, but there is surely room for a significant shift in compensation patterns toward a much larger share of

---

[3]Under the "entity" concept method of accounting discussed in note 2, stock awarded to employees would be treated as an investment of capital funds, exactly as a new stock issue is treated under most accounting systems now.

payment to be in the form of restricted stock. To the extent that the split between fixed wages and benefits and shares in equity accurately reflects the split between generic and firm-specific human capital, maximizing shareholder return will be a much better proxy for total wealth creation.

Employees should also be given full control rights over shares held for them in ESOPs or profit-sharing plans. Thus the regulations governing the fiduciary responsibilities of the trustees of such plans should be changed to ensure that voting rights on these shares are passed through to employees. In companies where employees hold a large share of equity, employee owners should have access to the nomination process for board members.

Several labor laws on the books that tend to discourage employee participation in management should be revised. The National Labor Relations Act, for example, makes it illegal for employers to discuss "conditions of employment" with company-sponsored committees of employees, because such committees are regarded as illegal company unions. U.S. labor law also defines workers as managers if they make or help make decisions about hiring, promotion, upgrading machinery, and pay raise allocations. But members of management are barred from being union members. The effect of these laws is that employees who want to maintain their union membership cannot particpate in important managerial decisions.[4]

Remove Barriers to Organizational Innovation by Providing Mobile Benefits

In a rapidly changing economy, companies and their employees need to be able to react quickly, to reorganize themselves in response to

---

[4]Levine (1995, pp. 154–55) discusses these problematic labor laws and provides more detailed suggestions about how they should be amended.

market changes, and to retrain and retool. But in the short run, such restructurings are extremely threatening and destabilizing to many employees who are ill prepared to start over—who have no way to pay for retraining, no alternative source of income, little in the way of savings, and no protection of basic benefits such as health care and pension funds.

In some large, old-line companies, decisions about reorganizing work are being distorted by the companies' efforts to get out from under commitments to costly benefits for full-time permanent employees. Clearly, some companies in this country overpromised and must rewrite their implicit and explicit contracts with employees. But decisions about whether work should be done by employees or contracted out to subcontractors, or whether employees should be paid a fixed wage or share in the profits of the enterprise, should be made for other reasons, such as utilizing resources more fully, enhancing flexibility, or improving incentives. Requiring all employers to provide a minimum level of mandated portable benefits would level the playing field, soften the impact of restructuring on individual working people, reduce the risk for working people associated with leaving big companies to work for small contractors, and thereby reduce the resistance to necessary and healthy restructuring.

Such programs could be paid for with payroll taxes applied across the board to large and small employers, the same way unemployment benefits and social security are already provided. Many small employers will resist this proposal (as they have resisted the prospect of having to provide health care coverage for their employees), but, in the long run, such policies would facilitate organizational innovation, which should help to make the economy more productive and more responsive to economic change.

Do Not Legislate the Terms of Financial Contracts

Companies should be free to experiment with alternative securities and contracts with their suppliers of financial capital that allocate risk, reward, and control in new ways. Firms should be able to issue securities with voting rights that vest over a period of time, for example, or provide for more than one vote per share if held by employees or other stakeholders.[5] Once issued, such securities, as well as more ordinary securities, should not be subject to unilateral or arbitrary changes in voting rights or other claims unless the initial registration statement explicitly notes that voting rights could be changed unilaterally. In other words, voting rights should be clear and contracts honored, but there should be no prohibitions against particular contract terms. If outside investors are leery of these securities, companies may find that they are a higher-cost source of capital and avoid them. But companies might also find that the motivational effects of giving certain stakeholders special voting strength outweigh the negative effects of a higher cost of capital. Investors might even find that investing in companies where employees act like owners and exercise considerable control entails less risk than investing in firms whose managers have no monitors other than anonymous financial markets.[6]

Freedom of contracting should not be feared because most new financial capital for firms, whether debt or equity, is provided by large, sophisticated financial institutions, which are in a good position to protect themselves. If they are lenders, they can protect their position through loan covenants. If they are shareholders, and if they are given adequate information, they can protect their interests by

[5]Such securities are not currently prohibited by law, but the New York Stock Exchange requires that securities of listed companies have only one vote per share, and several "reformers" have suggested that firms should be prohibited from issuing common stock that does not have one vote per share.

[6]Investors have not shied away, for example, from investing in companies in which Warren Buffet's Berkshire Hathaway has cut a special deal in exchange for injecting some "patient capital."

selling out (or never buying into) their positions.[7] If all else fails, investors also have recourse to the courts to litigate gross abuses.

Continue to Emphasize Disclosure

Securities regulation in this country has always stressed full and timely disclosure by issuers rather than attempting to regulate the terms of securities or rule individually on their soundness as investments. This policy has fostered a lively and fairly efficient capital market widely acknowledged to be among the fairest, most honest, and most liquid in the world. This policy has permitted a vast expansion in the terms and types of securities available, and the ability of financial analysts to evaluate various risk structures and contractual terms has expanded just as fast.[8] If disclosure is adequate, there is no reason to believe that issuers of publicly traded securities will systematically exploit investors.

Changes in disclosure rules regarding executive compensation implemented in the fall of 1992 were appropriate and consistent with the spirit of this recommendation. Other areas where disclosure should be enhanced include providing audited information about the market value (rather than just the book value) of underlying assets; providing more detailed information about the risks associated with investment programs, as well as the risks of failing to make those investments; providing more information about invest-

---

[7]Although small, individual investors are probably less well-situated to protect their own interests, they are not generally the ones who are clamoring for one-share, one-vote rules.

[8]Peter Tufano (1989, 1993) has written extensively about financial innovation. Bronwyn Hall (1993) has argued that financial innovation has been hastened by the widespread use of computer spreadsheets and other computer tools that make it very easy to evaluate and compare different promised return streams.

ments in human capital; and providing actuarially sound estimates of the present value of compensation and benefit commitments. The latter would be especially important in any firms where employees exercise significant control to help offset any tendency employees of such companies might have to loot the company for their own benefit.

One impediment to firms that would like to provide additional information in their public documents is the fear of lawsuit by shareholders who feel they were mislead. Attempts to forecast performance currently make firms especially vulnerable to such lawsuits if the forecasts are not borne out. The SEC could encourage firms to disclose more information than they currently do by providing certain "safe harbors" in the law to protect firms from suit over certain kinds of information. Such information must be provided by the firm in good faith, however.

Reconsider Regulations that Inhibit Investment by 'Patient Capital'

Individual and institutional investors who are willing to take large positions and sacrifice some liquidity to provide committed capital may be in a very good position to monitor management in a productive way. The idea of creating investment vehicles through which individuals and institutions can take sizable and committed positions in corporations and engage in the governance process should therefore be pursued. The problem has been that institutional investors are unwilling to give up the benefits and protection of diversification and liquidity, in some cases because regulatory and tax requirements unnecessarily restrict or discourage them from doing so.

Several individual scholars, commissions, and working groups are systematically reviewing these regulations to see if any of them could be revised to make patient investing strategies a more viable option for more institutional investors, without unduly risking the safety, liquidity, and transparency of the financial system. Some of the proposals under review are listed in appendix 5-1. Specifically, I favor proposals that make voice more attractive to institutional investors but that tie enhanced voice to restrictions on their ability to sell. An investment company should be able to take larger positions in a portfolio company—say, up to 25 percent—and should be able to put a representative on the board of that company without being subjected to the unrelated business income tax, for example, or without being considered a controlling person for the purpose of assessing liability. Such investors should continue to be regarded as insiders, however, with restrictions on their ability to trade their shares. Some of the regulatory and reporting burden on investors who are communicating with other investors about corporate policies but not seeking to control the company could also be eased. The Subcouncil on Capital Allocation of the Competitiveness Policy Council has proposed, among other things, that an attempt by a group of institutional investors to elect a single board member or a clear minority of members should not be considered an effort to seek control and should be exempt from the reporting burden imposed on control groups.[9]

Manage Pension Funds for Total Wealth Creation

The idea that pension funds should be tapped for various "socially targeted investments" is extremely controversial for good reason, and I do not suggest it. Pension funds, both public employee funds and private funds, should be treated as the property of the employees and retirees and invested for their benefit. In fact, pension funds

[9]Competitiveness Policy Council Subcouncil on Capital Allocation (forthcoming).

should be governed by boards of trustees that include representation by current employees and retirees.[10] Thus the primary concern of pension fund managers should be to earn the highest return they can on the assets they manage.

The well-being of current employees and retirees, however, may depend on factors in addition to the return on the financial assets already in the pension portfolio. Current employees benefit from the continued ability of their companies to generate wealth in the form of high-paying jobs, for example. And current employees and retirees benefit from the presence of viable businesses in the communities where they live. Thus in some cases it may be appropriate for pension fund managers to consider other wealth effects of their investment decisions. The recent decision by the California Public Employees Retirement System to use measures of employee relations as part of its investment criteria is consistent with this approach.[11] Where the right to vote shares held in a pension fund flows through to the beneficiaries (as in many defined-contribution plans), the beneficiaries can be counted on to vote their own interests. For ERISA funds and others in which trustees retain the voting rights, fiduciary responsibilities should be clarified so that trustees have some discretion to consider the total well-being of their beneficiaries.

In general, retirement plans are a good way to tie the long-run well-being of employees to the long-run health of the companies they work for and, within limits, should be used that way. Under ERISA, private defined-benefit plans are permitted to invest as much as 10 percent of their portfolios in the stock of the sponsoring

---

[10]Peter Drucker (1976) was among the first to advocate this step.

[11]CalPERS claims that firms that treat their employees well perform better in the long run; it has stated that, in choosing investment prospects, it considers "whether companies offer employees training programs and give more responsibility to lower-level workers." See Asra Q. Nomani, "CalPERS Says Its Investment Decisions Will Reflect How Firms Treat Workers," *Wall Street Journal*, June 16, 1994, p. A5.

company. Unless employees also have a significant proportion of their retirement savings in an ESOP, or unless there are other compelling reasons not to do so in a particular case, pension funds should invest in the sponsoring company up to this limit.

Private defined-contribution plans are not legally so limited. Nonetheless, if employees of the sponsoring company already have an ESOP in addition to their pension fund, then the assets in the pension fund should be diversified away from the sponsoring company. If no ESOP exists, then defined-contribution plans, like defined-benefit plans, should also put up to 10 percent of their assets into the sponsoring company. Employees should be given voting control over this block of stock, however, because, in defined-contribution plans, they bear the investment risk.

Managers of both kinds of pension funds may also want to set aside a portion of their portfolios to invest in patient capital funds that monitor companies, for example, or to provide partnership capital for worker-owned firms. These kinds of investments could improve the economies in the communities where the fund beneficiaries live and therefore have important indirect benefits for them. Beneficiaries should be given a chance to vote on such investment policies, however.

Monitor the Results and Be Prepared to Reform Again

The reforms suggested here are intended to encourage organizational innovation, while providing for a more formal role for stakeholders (especially employees) in corporate governance. But no corporate governance arrangement will be ideal for all situations, and many individual experiments will fail. It is important that the legal and institutional system be flexible enough to accommodate a variety of governance arrangements so that the private sector can adjust on its own if a given experiment does not succeed. Furthermore, any reform may have unintended and possibly perverse effects on incentives and on the kinds of governance structures that survive. Thus the results of any reform should be monitored by scholars, policymakers, and the companies themselves, and further research should be encouraged into what kinds of organizational forms promote wealth creation, and why. Individual companies experimenting with new organizational forms and new divisions of responsibilities will want to know, for their own purposes, how these experiments are working out, and they will also want to track changes taking place in other organizations. And policymakers and scholars will be interested in the effect of systemic reforms.

To reiterate, whether one is monitoring the effects of corporate governance reforms or considering further changes, the standard of performance should be total wealth creation by the organization. The effect of governance changes on share prices should be regarded as one element of wealth creation. Changes in share prices may be the easiest component of wealth creation to measure, but it is still only one element. It is also important to know whether the corporations in question are providing goods and services of value to consumers and jobs that enable their workers to be more productive than they could be in alternative employment. These three types of wealth creation are all important to maintaining and enhancing the standard of living of U.S. citizens.

Final Thoughts

Early in the twentieth century, the prevailing organizational form for controlling and managing large business enterprises in the United States shifted from the closely held company to the publicly traded corporation. The potential weaknesses of that form, which separated certain risk-bearing functions from certain critical control functions, have been known for decades. One of the key advantages of the form, however, may not have been appreciated enough. When shareholders, who have nominal but indirect, control over management through their ability to elect boards of directors, are scattered and individually weak, management is freer to build organizational forms, develop corporate cultures, and enter into implicit contracts that foster and protect firm-specific investments by other stakeholders. Thus, over the course of last century, and especially in the years from World War II through the end of the 1970s, employees of large corporations grew to believe that if they devoted their careers to a major company, the company would take care of them. That confidence, however well- or ill-founded, encouraged them to make significant personal commitments to building their organizations.

The system worked because the rents available in many industries were large enough and secure enough in the prosperous postwar years to support secure, high, and growing wages and benefits for employees and still provide attractive returns for shareholders. Since the 1970s, however, the pace of wealth creation by the corporate sector in the U.S. economy has slowed considerably, and, many would argue, the pace of change has accelerated. It is probably no longer reasonable to promise employees a lifetime of secure wages and benefits to encourage them to make investments in special skills or organizational capabilities. Yet, it seems likely that such investments will grow more, not less, important during the decades ahead. If so, the governance systems that do the best job of creating wealth will be those that provide the best alternative ways of encouraging and rewarding those investments.

REFERENCES

Abegglen, James C. 1984. *The Strategy of Japanese Business.* Cambridge, Mass.: Ballinger Publishing Co.

Abegglen, James C., and George Stalk, Jr. 1985. *Kaisha, The Japanese Corporation.* Basic Books.

Abraham, Katherine, and Henry S. Farber. 1987. "Job Duration, Seniority, and Earnings." *American Economic Review* 77 (June): 278–97.

Aghion, Philippe, Oliver Hart, and John Moore. 1992. "The Economics of Bankruptcy Reform." *Journal of Law, Economics and Organization* 8 (October): 523–46.

AICPA Special Committee on Financial Reporting. 1994. "Improving Business Reporting—A Customer Focus: Meeting the Information Needs of Investors and Creditors." Jersey City, N.J.

Akerlof, George A., and Janet L. Yellen, eds. 1986. *Efficiency Wage Models of the Labor Market.* Cambridge University Press.

341

Alchian, Armen A., and Harold Demsetz. 1972. "Production, Information Costs, and Economic Organization." *American Economic Review* 62 (December): 777–95.

Allen, William T. 1992. "Our Schizophrenic Conception of the Business Corporation." Cardozo Law Review 14 (2): 261–81.

Altonji, Joseph G., and Robert A. Shakotko. 1987. "Do Wages Rise with Job Seniority?" *Review of Economic Studies* 54 (July): 437–59.

American Bar Association. 1985. *Revised Model Business Corporation Act.* Harcourt Brace Jovanovich.

"The American Corporation and the Institutional Investor: Are There Lessons from Abroad?" 1988. *Columbia Business Law Review.* 3 (Fall): entire issue.

American Law Institute. 1994. *Principles of Corporate Governance: Analysis and Recommendations: Accepted Final Draft.* Philadelphia.

American Society of Corporate Secretaries. "Report on Shareholder Proposals July 1, 1990–June 30, 1991." New York.

Aoki, Masahiko. 1987. "The Japanese Firm in Transition." In *The Political Economy of Japan.* Vol. 1, *The Domestic Transformation,* edited by Kozo Yamamura and Yasukichi Yasuba. Stanford University Press.

———. 1988. *Information, Incentives, and Bargaining in the Japanese Economy.* Cambridge University Press.

———. 1993a. "The Contingent Governance of Team Production: Analysis of Institutional Complementarity." Working Paper 358. Center for Economic Policy Research, Stanford University. August.

———. 1993b. "Monitoring Characteristics of the Main Bank System: An Analytical and Historical View." Working Paper 352. Center for Economic Policy Research, Stanford University. June.

Baily, Martin N., Gary Burtless, and Robert E. Litan. 1993. *Growth with Equity: Economic Policymaking for the Next Century.* Brookings.

Baldwin, Carliss Y., and Kim B. Clark. 1992. "Capabilities and Capital Investment: New Perspectives on Capital Budgeting." *Journal of Applied Corporate Finance* 5 (Summer): 67–81.

Barnatan, Timothea Marie. 1992. "ESOPs as a Defensive Weapon When a Hostile Takeover Rears Its Ugly Head." *Wayne Law Review* 38 (Summer): 1877–96.

Basu, Sanjay. 1983. "The Relationship between Earning's Yield, Market Value and Return for NYSE Common Stocks: Further Evidence." *Journal of Financial Economics* 12 (June): 129–56.

Becker, Gary S. 1964. *Human Capital: A Theoretical and Empirical Analysis, with Special Reference to Education.* New York: National Bureau of Economic Research.

Berle, Adolph A., Jr. 1932. "For Whom Corporate Managers Are Trustees: A Note." *Harvard Law Review* 45: 1365–72.

Berle, Adolf A., Jr., and Gardiner C. Means. 1932. *The Modern Corporation and Private Property*. New York: Commerce Clearing House, Inc.

Bhagat, Sanjai, Andrei Shleifer, and Robert W. Vishny. 1990. "The Hostile Takeovers in the 1980s: The Return to Corporate Specialization." *Brookings Papers on Economic Activity: Microeconomics*: 1–72.

Black, Bernard S. 1990. "Shareholder Passivity Reexamined." *Michigan Law Review* 89 (December): 520–608.

———. 1992a. "Agents Watching Agents: The Promise of Institutional Investor Voice." *UCLA Law Review* 39 (April): 811–93.

———. 1992b. "The Value of Institutional Investor Monitoring: The Empirical Evidence." *UCLA Law Review* 39 (4): 895–939.

Blaine, Michael J. 1993. "Profitability and Competitiveness: Lessons from Japanese and American Firms in the 1980s." *California Management Review* 36: 1 (Fall): 48–74.

Blair, Margaret M. 1991. "Who's in Charge Here? How Changes in Corporate Finance Are Shaping Corporate Governance." *Brookings Review* 9 (Fall): 8–13.

———, ed. 1993. *The Deal Decade: What Takeovers and Leveraged Buyouts Mean for Corporate Governance*. Brookings.

———. 1994. "CEO Pay: Why It Has Become So Controversial." *Brookings Review* 12 (Winter): 22–27.

———. 1995. "Corporate Governance Schemes When Firm-Specific Human Capital Is Important." Working paper. Brookings. January.

Blair, Margaret M., and Robert E. Litan. 1990. "Corporate Leverage and Leveraged Buyouts in the Eighties." In *Debt, Taxes, and Corporate Restructuring*, edited by John B. Shoven and Joel Waldfogel, 43–80. Brookings.

Blair, Margaret M., and Martha A. Schary. 1993. "Industry-Level Indicators of Free Cash Flow." In *The Deal Decade*, edited by Margaret Blair, 99–135. Brookings.

Blair, Margaret M., and Girish Uppal. 1993. *The Deal Decade Handbook*. Brookings.

Blasi, Joseph R. 1990. "Comment by Joseph Rafael Blasi." In *Paying for Productivity*, edited by Alan S. Blinder, 172–81. Brookings.

Blasi, Joseph R., and Douglas L. Kruse. 1991. *The New Owners: The Mass Emergence of Employee Ownership in Public Companies and What It Means to American Business*. HarperCollins.

Blinder, Alan S., ed. 1990. *Paying for Productivity: A Look at the Evidence*. Brookings.

Bloom, Steven Marc. 1985. "Employee Ownership and Firm Performance." Ph.D. dissertation. Harvard University.

Board of Governors of the Federal Reserve System. 1994. "Flow of Funds Accounts: Flows and Outstandings." Washington. September 20.

Bradley, Michael, and Michael Rosenzweig. 1992. "The Untenable Case for Chapter 11." *Yale Law Journal* (March): 1043–96.

Brancato, Carolyn Kay. 1991. "Institutional Investor Concentration of Economic Power: A Study of Institutional Holdings and Voting Authority in U.S. Publicly Held Corporations, Part I: Top 25 U.S. Corporations as of December 31, 1990." Columbia University School of Law, New York. October.

Brealey, Richard, and Stewart C. Myers. 1991. *Principles of Corporate Finance.* 4th ed. McGraw-Hill Book Co

Brickley, James A., and Frederick H. Dark. 1987. "The Choice of Organizational Form: The Case of Franchising." *Journal of Financial Economics* 18 (June): 401–20.

Business Roundtable. 1992. "Executive Compensation/Share Ownership." New York.

Cadbury, Sir Adrian. 1993. "Thoughts on Corporate Governance." *International Review* 1 (January): 5–10.

Cadbury Commission. "Code of Best Practice: Report of the Committee on the Financial Aspects of Corporate Governance." London: Gee and Co., Ltd.

Campbell Soup Board of Directors. 1994. "Campbell Soup Corporate Governance Standards." Reprinted in *Director's Monthly* 18 (December): 11.

Carosso, Vincent P. 1970. *Investment Banking in America: A History.* Harvard University Press.

Cary, William L. 1974. "Federalism and Corporate Law: Reflections upon Delaware." *Yale Law Review* 83 (March): 663–705.

Chan, S. H., J. D. Martin, and J. W. Kensinger. 1990. "Corporate Research and Development Expenditures and Share Value." *Journal of Financial Economics* 26 (August): 255–76.

Chandler, Alfred D., Jr. 1977. *The Visible Hand: The Managerial Revolution in American Business.* Harvard University Press (Belknap).

———. 1990. *Scale and Scope: The Dynamics of Industrial Capitalism.* Harvard University Press.

Chaney, P. K., T. M. Devinney, and R. S. Winer. 1989. "The Impact of New Product Introductions on the Market Value of Firms." Report 89-105. Marketing Science Institute, Cambridge, Mass.

Clark, Robert L. 1992. "Increasing Use of Defined Contribution Pension Plans." U. S. Department of Labor. Unpublished paper.

Coase, R. H. 1960. "The Problem of Social Cost." *Journal of Law and Economics* 3 (October): 1–44.

Coffee, John C., Jr. 1991. "Liquidity Versus Control: The Institutional Investor as Corporate Monitor." *Columbia Law Review* 91 (October): 1277–1368.

Competitiveness Policy Council. 1993. *A Competitiveness Strategy for America*. Second report to the President & Congress. Washington. March.

Competitiveness Policy Council, Subcouncil on Corporate Governance and the Financial Markets. 1992. "The Will to Act." Washington. December 7, 1992.

Competitiveness Policy Council, Subcouncil on Capital Allocation. Forthcoming. "Lifting All Boats: Improving America's Return on Private Investment in the Information Economy." Washington.

Conte, Michael A., and Jan Svejnar. 1990. "Employee Ownership Plans." In *Paying for Productivity*, edited by Alan S. Blinder, 143–82. Brookings.

Council of Institutional Investors. 1989. "Shareholder Bill of Rights." Washington.

Council on Competitiveness. 1995. *Human Resources Competitiveness Profile*. Washington. April.

Crawford, Richard. 1991. *In the Era of Human Capital*. HarperCollins.

Crystal, Graef S. 1992. *In Search of Excess: The Overcompensation of American Executives*. W. W. Norton.

De Long, J. Bradford. 1991. "Did J. P. Morgan's Men Add Value? An Economist's Perspective on Financial Capitalism." In *Inside the Business Enterprise: Historical Perspectives on the Use of Information*, edited by Peter Temin. University of Chicago Press.

Dertouzos, Michael L., Richard K. Lester, and Robert Solow, eds. 1989. *Made in America: Regaining the Productive Edge*. MIT Press.

Dodd, Jr., E. Merrick. 1932. "For Whom Are Corporate Managers Trustees?" *Harvard Law Review* 45: 1145–63.

Donaldson, Thomas, and Lee E. Preston. 1995. "The Stakeholder Theory of the Corporation: Concepts, Evidence, Implications." *Academy of Management Review* 20 (January): 65–91.

Dow, Gregory K. 1993. "Why Capital Hires Labor: A Bargaining Perspective." *American Economic Review* 83 (March): 118–34.

Drucker, Peter F. 1976. *The Unseen Revolution: How Pension Fund Socialism Came to America*. Harper and Row.

———. 1991a. "Reckoning with the Pension Fund Revolution." *Harvard Business Review* 69 (March-April): 106–14.

———. 1991b. "Debate: Can Pension Funds Lead the Ownership Revolution?" *Harvard Business Review* 69 (May-June): 166–83.

Dunlop, John T. 1988. "Labor Markets and Wage Determination: Then and Now." In *How Labor Markets Work: Reflections on Theory and Practice*, edited by Bruce Kaufman, 47–88. Lexington, Mass.: Lexington Books.

Easterbrook, Frank H., and Daniel R. Fischel. 1983. "Voting in Corporate Law." *Journal of Law and Economics* 26 (June): 395–427.

———. 1991. *The Economic Structure of Corporate Law*. Harvard University Press.

Edwards, Franklin R., and Robert A. Eisenbies. 1991. "Financial Institutions and Corporate Investment Horizons: An International Perspective." Unpublished manuscript.

Edwards, Jeremy, and Klaus Fischer. 1994. *Banks, Finance, and Investment in Germany*. Cambridge University Press.

Epstein, David G. 1991. *Debtor-Creditor Law*. St. Paul: West Publishing Co.

Epstein, Edward Jay. 1986. *Who Owns the Corporation?—Management vs. Shareholders*. New York: Twentieth Century Fund-Priority Press Publications.

Fama, Eugene F. 1980. "Agency Problems and the Theory of the Firm." *Journal of Political Economy* 88 (April): 288-307.

Fama, Eugene F., and Michael C. Jensen. 1983. "Separation of Ownership and Control." *Journal of Law and Economics* 26 (June): 301–25.

Farb, Warren E. 1993. "Competitiveness Studies and Worker-Management Relations: A Review of Common Themes." Draft paper for the U. S. Department of Commerce. August.

Fischel, Daniel R. 1985. "The Business Judgment Rule and the Trans-Union Case." *Business Lawyer* 40 (August): 1437–55.

Fleming, Michael J. 1994. "Large-Stake Investors and Corporate Performance." Ph.D. dissertation. Harvard University, Department of Economics and Harvard Business School. August.

Florida, Richard, and Donald F. Smith, Jr. 1993. "Keep the Government Out of Venture Capital." *Issues in Science and Technology* 9 (Summer): 61–68.

Frankel, Jeffrey A. 1991. "The Cost of Capital in Japan: Update." *Business Economics* 26 (April): 25–31.

Freeman, Richard, and Edward P. Lazear. Forthcoming. "Relational Investing: The Worker's Perspective." In *Meaningful Relationships: Institutional Investors, Relational Investing, and the Future of Corporate Governance?* edited by Ronald J. Gilson, John C. Coffee, and Louis Lowenstein. Oxford University Press.

Frey, Robert. 1993. "Empowerment or Else." *Harvard Business Review* 71 (September-October): 70–71.

Friedland, John H. 1994. *The Law and Structure of the International Financial System: Regulation in the United States, EEC, and Japan.* Westport, Conn.: Quorum Books.

Froot, Kenneth A., André F. Perold, and Jeremy C. Stein. 1992. "Shareholder Trading Practices and Corporate Investment Horizons." *Journal of Applied Corporate Finance* 5 (Summer): 42–58.

Fukao, Mitsuhiro. 1995. *Financial Integration, Corporate Governance, and the Performance of Multinational Companies.* Brookings.

Furubotn, Erik G., and Svetozar Pejovich. 1974. "Property Rights and the Behavior of the Firm in a Socialist State: The Example of Yugoslavia." In *The Economics of Property Rights*, edited by Furubotn and Pejovich. Cambridge, Mass.: Ballinger Publishing Co.

Galambos, Louis, and Joseph Pratt. 1988. *The Rise of the Corporate Commonwealth: United States Business and Public Policy in the 20th Century.* Basic Books.

Gaughan, Patrick A. 1991. *Mergers and Acquisitions.* HarperCollins.

Gavis, Alexander C. 1990. "A Framework for Satisfying Corporate Directors Responsibilities Under State Nonshareholder Constituency Statutes: The Use of Explicit Contracts." *University of Pennsylvania Law Review* 138: 1456–97.

General Motors Board of Directors. 1994. "GM Board Guidelines on Significant Corporate Governance Issues." Detroit. March 17.

Gerlach, Michael L. 1992. *Alliance Capitalism: The Social Organization of Japanese Business.* University of California Press.

Ghilarducci, Teresa. 1992. *Labor's Capital: The Economics and Politics of Private Pensions.* MIT Press.

Gilson, Ronald J. 1981. "A Structural Approach to Corporations: The Case against Defensive Tactics in Tender Offers." *Stanford Law Review* 33 (5): 819–91.

Gilson, Ronald J., and Reinier Kraakman. 1993. "The Case for Professional Directors." *Harvard Business Review* 71 (January-February): 82.

Gilson, Ronald J., and Mark J. Roe. 1992. "Comparative Corporate Governance: Focusing the United States-Japan Inquiry." Memorandum prepared for Center for Economic Policy and Research conference. Stanford University.

———. 1993. "Understanding the Japanese Keiretsu: Overlaps between Corporate Governance and Industrial Organization." *Yale Law Journal* 102 (4, January): 871–906.

Gordon, Lilli A., and John Pound. 1992. "Active Investing in the U.S. Equity Market: Past Performance and Future Prospects." Report prepared for the California Public Employees' Retirement System by the Gordon Group, Newton, Mass. December.

———. 1993. "Governance Matters: An Empirical Study of the Relationship between Corporate Governance and Corporate Performance." Paper presented at the Wharton School of Business, University of Pennsylvania; the Columbia University Law School; and the annual meetings of the American Finance Association.

Greenwald, Bruce, and Jeremy Stein. 1988. "The Task Force Report: The Reasoning Behind the Recommendations." *Journal of Economic Perspectives* 2 (Summer): 3–23.

Grundfest, Joseph A. 1990. "Subordination of American Capital." *Journal of Financial Economics* 27 (September): 89–114.

———. 1992. "Just Vote No: A Minimalist Strategy for Dealing with Barbarians *Inside* the Gates." *Stanford Law Review* 45 (April): 857–937.

Hall, Bronwyn H. 1990. "The Impact of Corporate Restructuring on Industrial Research and Development." *Brookings Papers on Economic Activity: Microeconomics:* 85–135.

———. 1993. "General Discussion." In *The Deal Decade,* edited by Margaret M. Blair, 314–15. Brookings.

Hall, Bronwyn H., and Robert E. Hall. 1993. "The Value and Performance of U.S. Corporations." *Brookings Papers on Economic Activity* 3:1–34.

Hall, Robert E. Forthcoming. "Lost Jobs." *Brookings Papers on Economic Activity* 1.

Hamel, Gary, and C. K. Prahalad. 1994. "Competing for the Future." *Harvard Business Review* 72 (July-August): 122–28.

Hamilton, Robert W. 1987. *The Law of Corporations in a Nutshell.* St. Paul: West Publishing Co.

Hansmann, Henry. 1988. "Ownership of the Firm." *Journal of Law, Economics, and Organization* 4(2): 267–304.

———. Forthcoming. *The Ownership of Enterprise.* Harvard University Press.

Hanson, Dale. 1992. "The Long-Term Perspective: One Institutional Investor's Point of View." *Corporate Governance Today—and Tomorrow; The Thoughts of Seven Leading Players.* Washington: Investor Responsibility Research Center.

Hanson, Lord. 1991. "Shareholder Value: Touchstone of Managerial Capitalism." *Harvard Business Review* (November-December): 141–43.

Hart, Oliver. 1989. "An Economist's Perspective on the Theory of the Firm." *Columbia Law Review* 89: 1757–73.

———. 1993. "Theories of Optimal Capital Structure: A Managerial Discretion Perspective." In *The Deal Decade,* edited by Margaret M. Blair, 19–43. Brookings.

Hart, Oliver, and John Moore. 1990. "Property Rights and the Nature of the Firm." *Journal of Political Economy* 98 (December): 1119–58.

Hashimoto, Masanori. 1981. "Firm-Specific Human Capital as a Shared Investment." *American Economic Review* 71 (3): 475–82.

Hatsopoulos, George N. 1983. "High Cost of Capital: Handicap of American Industry." Paper presented at the American Business Conference, Waltham, Mass., sponsored by Thermo Electron Corporation.

Hayek, Friedrich A. 1985. "The Corporation in a Democratic Society: In Whose Interest Ought It and Will It Be Run?" In *Management and Corporations,* edited by Melvin Anshen and George Leland Bach, 99–117. Westport, Conn.: Greenwood Press.

Hayes, Robert H., and William J. Abernathy. 1980. "Managing Our Way to Economic Decline." *Harvard Business Review* 58 (July-August): 67–77.

Hazen, Thomas Lee. 1990. *The Law of Securities Regulation.* 2d ed. St. Paul: West Publishing Co.

Herman, Edward S. 1981. *Corporate Control, Corporate Power.* Cambridge University Press.

Hill, Henry P. 1987. *Accounting Principles for the Autonomous Corporate Entity.* New York: Quorum Books.

Hirschman, Albert O. 1970. *Exit, Voice, and Loyalty: Responses to Decline in Firms, Organizations, and States.* Harvard University Press.

Hutchens, Robert M. 1989. "Seniority, Wages and Productivity: A Turbulent Decade." *Journal of Economic Perspectives* 3 (Fall): 49–64.

International Monetary Fund. 1994. *World Economic Outlook.* Washington.

Investor Responsibility Research Center. 1991. *Takeover Defense Directory.* Washington.

Jacobs, Michael T. 1991. *Short-Term America: The Causes and Cures of Our Business Myopia.* Harvard Business School Press.

———. 1993. *Break the Wall Street Rule: Outperform the Stock Market by Investing as an Owner.* Reading, Mass.: Addison-Wesley.

James, Christopher. 1994. "When Do Banks Take Equity in Debt Restructuring?" Working paper. University of Florida, Department of Finance.

Jenkins, Edmund L. 1994. "Letter from the Chairman of the American Institute of CPAs Special Committee on Financial Reporting." *Journal of Accounting* (October): 39–40.

Jenkinson, Tim, and Colin Mayer. 1992. "The Assessment: Corporate Governance and Corporate Control." *Oxford Review of Economic Policy* 8 (Autumn): 1–10.

Jensen, Michael C. 1986. "Agency Costs of Free Cash Flow, Corporate Finance, and Takeovers." *American Economic Review* 76 (May: *Papers and Proceedings 1985*): 323–29.

———. 1989. "Eclipse of the Public Corporation." *Harvard Business Review* 67 (September-October): 61–74.

———. 1991. "Corporate Control and the Politics of Finance." *Journal of Applied Corporate Finance* 4 (Summer): 13–33.

———. 1993. "The Modern Industrial Revolution, Exit, and the Failure of Internal Control Systems." *Journal of Finance* 48 (July): 831–80.

Jensen, Michael C., and William H. Meckling. 1976. "Theory of the Firm: Managerial Behavior, Agency Costs and Ownership Structure." *Journal of Financial Economics* 3 (October): 305–60.

Jensen, Michael C., and Richard S. Ruback. 1983. "The Market for Corporate Control: The Scientific Evidence." *Journal of Financial Economics* 11 (April): 5–50.

Johnson, H. Thomas, and Robert S. Kaplan. 1991. *Relevance Lost: The Rise and Fall of Management Accounting.* Harvard Business School Press.

Jones, Thomas M. 1986. "Corporate Board Structure and Performance: Variations in the Incidence of Shareholder Suits." *Research in Corporate Social Performance and Policy* 8: 45–59.

Kaplan, Steven N. 1989. "The Effects of Management Buyouts on Operating Performance and Value." *Journal of Financial Economics* 24 (October): 217–54.

———. 1991. "The Staying Power of Leveraged Buyouts." *Journal of Financial Economics* 29 (October): 287–313.

Kaplan, Steven N., and Jeremy C. Stein. 1993. "The Evolution of Buyout Pricing and Financial Structure in the 1980s." *Quarterly Journal of Economics* 108 (May): 313–57.

Katz, Lawrence F., and Lawrence H. Summers. 1989. "Industry Rents: Evidence and Implications." *Brookings Papers on Economic Activity: Microeconomics:* 209–75.

Kester, W. Carl. 1991. *Japanese Takeovers: The Global Contest for Corporate Control.* Harvard Business School Press.

———. 1992a. "Governance, Contracting, and Investment Time Horizons." Working paper 92-003. Harvard Business School. Boston.

———. 1992b. "Industrial Groups as Systems of Contractual Governance." *Oxford Review of Economic Policy* 8 (Autumn): 24–44.

Keynes, John M. 1936. *The General Theory of Employment, Interest and Money.* Harcourt Brace & Co.

Kleiman, Robert, Kevin Nathan, and Joel Shulman. 1994. "Are There Pay-offs for Patient Corporate Investors?" *Mergers and Acquisitions* 28 (March-April): 34–41.

Kopcke, Richard W., and Eric S. Rosengren, eds. 1990. *Are the Distinctions between Debt and Equity Disappearing?* Federal Reserve Bank of Boston Conference Series 33.

Koppes, Richard H. 1992. "Acting like a 'Real' Owner." *Corporate Governance Today—and Tomorrow: The Thoughts of Seven Leading Players,* 77–84. Washington: Investor Responsibility Research Center.

Krueger, Alan B., and Lawrence H. Summers. 1988. "Efficiency Wages and Inter-Industry Wages Structure." *Econometrica* 56 (March): 259–93.

Kruse, Douglas L. 1993. "Does Profit Sharing Affect Productivity?" Working Paper 4542. Cambridge, Mass.: National Bureau of Economic Research. November.

Lakonishok, Josef, Andrei Shleifer, and Robert W. Vishny. 1992. "The Structure and Performance of the Money Management Industry." *Brookings Papers on Economic Activity: Microeconomics:* 339–91.

Lang, Robert Todd. 1995. "Shareholder Voting Rights." *Insights: The Corporate and Securities Advisors* 9: 2 (February): 4–8.

Lauerman, Anthony E. 1990. "Comment." *Journal of Corporation Law* 16 (Fall): 143–72.

Lazear, Edward P. 1979. "Why Is There Mandatory Retirement?" *Journal of Political Economy* 87 (December): 1261–84.

Lazonick, William. 1992. "Controlling the Market for Corporate Control: The Historical Significance of Managerial Capitalism." *Industrial and Corporate Change*, vol. 1. Oxford University Press.

Lee, Joe 1990. *Bankruptcy Service, Lawyers Edition.* vol. 10. Rochester, N.Y.: Lawyers Cooperative Publishing.

Leibenstein, Harvey. 1976. *Beyond Economic Man: A New Foundation for Microeconomics.* Harvard University Press.

Levine, David I. 1995. *Reinventing the Workplace: How Business and Employees Can Both Win.* Brookings.

Levine, David I., and Laura D'Andrea Tyson. 1990. "Participation, Productivity, and the Firm's Environment." In *Paying for Productivity*, edited by Alan S. Blinder, 183–237. Brookings.

Lichtenberg, Frank R., and Donald Siegel. 1987. "Productivity and Changes in Ownership of Manufacturing Plants." *Brookings Papers on Economic Activity: Special Issue on Microeconomics* 3: 643–73.

Lipton, Martin, and Jay W. Lorsch. 1992. "A Modest Proposal for Improved Corporate Governance." *Business Lawyer* 48 (November): 59–77.

Lipton, Martin, and Steven A. Rosenblum. 1991. "A New System of Corporate Governance: The Quinquennial Election of Directors." *University of Chicago Law Review* 58 (Winter): 187–253.

Long, M., and I. Malitz. 1985. "The Investment-Financing Nexus: Some Empirical Evidence." *Midland Corporate Finanance Journal* 3 (Fall): 53–59.

Long, William F., and David J. Ravenscraft. 1993. "Decade of Debt: Lessons from LBOs in the 1980s." In *The Deal Decade,* edited by Margaret M. Blair, 205–24. Brookings.

Lorsch, Jay W., and Elizabeth MacIver. 1989. *Pawns or Potentates: The Reality of America's Corporate Boards.* Harvard Business School Press.

———. 1991. "Corporate Governance and Investment Time Horizons." Working paper. Harvard Business School, Boston. October.

Lowenstein, Louis. 1991. *Sense and Nonsense in Corporate Finance.* Reading, Mass.: Addison-Wesley.

McCauley, Robert N., and Steven A. Zimmer. 1989. "Explaining International Differences in the Cost of Capital." *Federal Reserve Bank of New York Quarterly Review* 14 (Summer): 7–28.

McConnell, John J., and Chris J. Muscarella. 1985. "Corporate Capital Expenditure Decisions and the Market Value of the Firm." *Journal of Financial Economics* 14 (September): 399–422.

McVea, Harry. 1993. *Financial Conglomerates and the Chinese Wall: Regulating Conflicts of Interest.* New York: Clarendon Press.

Manne, Henry G. 1965. "Mergers and the Market for Corporate Control." *Journal of Political Economy* 73 (April): 110–20.

———. 1966. *Insider Trading and the Stock Market.* Free Press.

Marcotte, Dave E. 1994. "The Declining Stability of Employment in the U.S.: 1976–1988." University of Maryland School of Public Affairs. April.

Marris, Robin. 1964. *The Economic Theory of Managerial Capitalism.* Glencoe, Ill.: Free Press.

Marsh, Paul. 1992. "Short-Termism." In *The New Palgrave: A Dictionary of Economics,* edited by John Eatwell, Murray Milgate, and Peter Newman, vol. 3, 446–53. New York: Stockton Press.

Mason, Edward S. 1960. *The Corporation in Modern Society.* Harvard University Press.

Matsumoto, Koji. 1991. *The Rise of the Japanese Corporate System: The Inside View of a MITI Official.* London: Kegan Paul International.

Mattione, Richard F. 1992. "A Capital Cost Disadvantage for Japan?" Morgan Guaranty Trust Co., advisory, April 6. New York.

Meade, J. E. 1972. "The Theory of Labor-Managed Firms and of Profit Sharing." *Economic Journal* 82 (March supplement): 402–28

Medoff, James, and Katherine Abraham. 1981. "Are Those Paid More Really More Productive?: The Case of Experience." *Journal of Human Resources* 16 (Spring): 186–216.

Miles, David. 1993. "Testing for Short Termism in the UK Stock Market." *Economic Journal* 103 (November): 1379–96.

Milgrom, Paul, and John Roberts. 1992. *Economics, Organization, and Management.* Prentice Hall.

Millstein, Ira M. 1991. "Can Pension Funds Lead the Ownership Revolution?" *Harvard Business Review* (May-June): 166–70.

———. 1992. "The Evolving Role of Institutional Investors in Corporate Governance." *Corporate Governance Today—and Tomorrow: The Thoughts of Seven Leading Players,* 35-66. Washington: Investor Responsibility Research Center.

Minow, Nell. 1991. "Proxy Reform: The Case for Increased Shareholder Communication." *The Journal of Corporation Law* 17 (Fall): 149–62.

———. 1992. "Revolt of the Corporate Boards." *Legal Times.* May 18, 22–27.

Minow, Nell, and Kit Bingham. 1993. "The Ideal Board." *The Corporate Board* (July-August): 11–14.

Mishkin, Frederic S. 1992. *The Economics of Money, Banking, and Financial Markets.* 3d ed. HarperCollins.

Mitchell, Daniel J. B., David Lewin, and Edward E. Lawler, III. 1990. "Alternative Pay Systems, Firm Performance, and Productivity." In *Paying for Productivity,* edited by Alan S. Blinder, 15–94. Brookings.

Modigliani, Franco, and Merton H. Miller. 1958. "The Cost of Capital, Corporation Finance, and the Theory of Investment." *American Economic Review* 48 (June): 261–97.

Monks, Robert A. G. 1993. "Tomorrow's Corporation: Corporate Constituencies and Structure." Speech to Aspen Institute, Aspen, Colorado. July.

Monks, Robert A. G., and Nell Minow. 1991. *Power and Accountability.* HarperCollins.

———. 1995. *Corporate Governance.* Cambridge: Blackwell Business.

Myers, Stewart C. 1984a. "The Capital Structure Puzzle." *Journal of Finance* 39 (July): 575–92.

———. 1984b. "Finance Theory and Financial Strategy." *Interfaces* 14 (January-February): 126–37.

Nader, Ralph, Mark Green, and Joel Seligman. 1976. *Taming the Giant Corporation.* W. W. Norton.

National Association of Corporate Directors. 1992. *1992 Corporate Governance Survey*. Washington. February.

Nelson, Richard R., and Sidney G. Winter. 1982. *An Evolutionary Theory of Economic Change*. Harvard University Press (Belknap).

Nesbitt, Stephen L. 1994. "Long-Term Rewards from Corporate Governance." Wilshire Associates, Santa Monica, Calif. January.

Netter, Jeffry M., Annette B. Poulsen, and Philip L. Hersch. 1988. "Insider Trading: The Law, the Theory, the Evidence." *Contemporary Policy Issues* 6 (July): 1–13.

Neumark, David, and Steven A. Sharpe. Forthcoming. "Rents and Quasi Rents in the Wage Structure: Evidence from Hostile Takeovers." *Industrial Relations*.

O'Barr, William M., and John M. Conley. 1992. *Fortune and Folly: The Wealth and Power of Institutional Investing*. Homewood, Ill.: Business One Irwin.

O'Cleireacain, Carol. 1992. "Zero-Based Compensation—Design from the Institutional Investor's Point of View." In *Corporate Governancee Today—and Tomorrow: The Thoughts of Seven Leading Players*, 85–96. Washington: Investor Responsbility Research Center.

Okun, Arthur M. 1981. *Prices and Quantities: A Macroeconomic Analysis*. Brookings.

Oxford Analytica Limited. 1992. "Boards of Directors and Corporate Governance, Trends in the G7 Countries over the Next Ten Years." Executive report prepared for Russell Reynolds Associates, Price Waterhouse, Goldman Sachs International Ltd., and Gibson, Dunn & Crutcher. August.

Palmiter, Alan R. 1989. "Reshaping the Corporate Fiduciary Model: A Director's Duty of Independence." *Texas Law Reveiw* 67 (June): 1351–1464.

Piore, Michael J., and Charles F. Sabel. 1984. *The Second Industrial Divide: Possibilities for Prosperity*. Basic Books.

Pontiff, Jeffrey, Andrei Shleifer, and Michael S. Weisbach. 1990. "Reversions of Excess Pension Assets after Takeovers." *Rand Journal of Economics* 21 (Winter): 600–13.

Porter, Michael E. 1980. *Competitive Strategy: Techniques for Analyzing Industries and Competitors*. Free Press.

———. 1992. *Capital Choices: Changing the Way America Invests in Industry*. Research report presented by the Council on Competitiveness and cosponsored by Harvard Business School. Washington.

Poterba, James M., and Lawrence H. Summers. 1991. "Time Horizons of American Firms: New Evidence from a Survey of CEOs." Unpublished manuscript.

Pound, John. 1992a. "Beyond Takeovers: Politics Comes to Corporate Control." *Harvard Business Review* (March-April): 83–93.

———. 1992b. "The Rise of the Political Model of Corporate Governance and Corporate Control." In "The Will to Act," Final Report of the Competitiveness Policy Council Subcouncil on Corporate Governance and Financial Markets. Washington. December.

———. 1993. "Institutional Monitoring: A Proposal to Restore Balance in Governance." *Director's Monthly* 17 (November): 1–10.

Prahalad, C. K., and Gary Hamel. 1990. "The Core Competence of the Corporation." *Harvard Business Review* 68 (May-June): 79–91.

President's Commission on Industrial Competitiveness. 1985. *Global Competition: The New Reality*. Washington. January.

Putterman, Louis. 1984. "On Some Recent Explanations of Why Capital Hires Labor." *Economic Inquiry* 22 (April): 171–87.

Rappaport, Alfred. 1986. *Creating Shareholder Value*. Free Press.

———. 1990. "The Staying Power of the Public Corporation." *Harvard Business Review* 68 (January-February): 96–104.

Ravenscraft, David J., and F. M. Scherer. 1987. *Mergers, Sell-Offs, and Economic Efficiency*. Brookings.

Regan, Edward V. 1992. "Comments on Proposed Amendment to Rule 14A-8." Letter from the Office of the State Comptroller, New York, New York, to Johnathan G. Katz, Office of the Secretary, Securities and Exchange Commission. March 18.

Reinganum, Marc R. 1981. "Misspecification of Capital Asset Pricing: Empirical Anomalies Based on Earnings' Yields and Market Value." *Journal of Financial Economics* 9 (March): 19–46.

Roe, Mark J. 1983. "Bankruptcy and Debt: A New Model for Corporate Reorganization." *Columbia Law Review* 83 (April): 527–602.

———. 1990. "Political and Legal Restraints on Ownership and Control of Public Companies." *Journal of Financial Economics* 27 (July): 7–41.

———. 1991a. "Political Elements in the Creation of a Mutual Fund Industry." *University of Pennsylvania Law Review* 139 (June): 1469–1511.

———. 1991b. "A Political Theory of American Corporate Finance." *Columbia Law Review* 91 (January): 10–67.

———. 1993a. "Foundations of Corporate Finance: The 1906 Pacification of the Insurance Industry." *Columbia Law Review* 93 (April): 639–84.

————. 1993b. "The Modern Corporation and Private Pensions." *UCLA Law Review* 41 (October): 75–116.

————. 1993c. "Some Differences in Corporate Structure in Germany, Japan, and the United States." *Yale Law Journal* 102 (June): 1927–2003.

————. 1993d. "Takeover Politics." In *The Deal Decade*, edited by Margaret M. Blair, 321–80. Brookings.

————. 1994. *Strong Managers, Weak Owners: The Political Roots of American Corporate Finance.* Princeton University Press.

Romano, Roberta. 1993. *The Genius of American Corporate Law.* Washington: AEI Press.

Ross, Stephen A. 1973. "The Economic Theory of Agency: The Principal's Problem." *American Economic Review* 63 (May): 134–39.

Rostow, Eugene V. 1960. "To Whom and for What Ends Is Corporate Management Responsible?" In *The Corporation in Modern Society*, edited by Edward S. Mason, 47–71. Harvard University Press..

Rubin, Paul H. 1978. "The Theory of the Firm and the Structure of the Franchise Contract." *Journal of Law and Economics* 21 (April): 223–33.

Russell, Raymond. 1985. "Employee Ownership and Internal Governance." *Journal of Economic Behavior and Organization* 6 (September): 217–41.

Sahlman, William A. 1992. "Insights from the American Venture Capital Organization." Washington: Council on Competitiveness, draft of July 16, 1992.

Sakakibara, Eisuke. 1993. *Beyond Capitalism: The Japanese Model of Market Economies.* University Press of America and the Economic Strategy Institute.

Scanlon, Kevin, Jack Trifts, and Richard Pettway. 1989. "Impacts of Relative Size and Industrial Relatedness on Returns to Shareholders of Acquiring Firms." *Journal of Financial Research* 12 (Summer): 103–12.

Schneider-Lenné, Ellen R. 1992. "Corporate Control in Germany." *Oxford Review of Economic Policy* 8 (Autumn): 11–23.

Securities and Exchange Commission. 1992. "Regulatory Reform of Communications among Shareholders, Fact Sheet." October 15.

Shiller, Robert J. 1989. "Do Stock Prices Move Too Much to be Justified by Subsequent Changes in Dividends?" In *Market Volatility*, edited by Shiller, 105–30. MIT Press.

————. 1992. *The Report of the Twentieth Century Fund Task Force on Market Speculation and Corporate Governance* with background paper *Who's Minding the Store?* New York: The Twentieth Century Fund Press.

Shleifer, Andrei, and Lawrence H. Summers. 1988. "Breach of Trust in Hostile Takeovers." In *Corporate Takeovers: Causes and Conse-*

quences, edited by Alan J. Auerbach, 33–56. University of Chicago Press.

Singer, Joseph W. 1988. "The Reliance Interest in Property." *Stanford Law Review* 40 (February): 615–751.

Smith, Adam. 1922. *An Inquiry into the Nature and Cause of the Wealth of Nations.* London: Methuen and Co., Ltd.

Snipes, William J. 1983. "Corporate Battles for Control: Edgar v. MITE and the Constitutionality of State Takeover Legislation—The Continuing Saga." *Howard Law Journal* 26 (Fall): 1425–84.

Sommer, A. A., Jr. 1991. "Whom Should the Corporation Serve? The Berle-Dodd Debate Revisited Sixty Years Later." *Delaware Journal of Corporate Law* 16 (1): 33–56.

Stern, Paul G. 1993. "The Power and the Process." *Directors & Boards* 17 (Spring): 6–9.

Stern, Robert N., and others. 1983. "The Union and the Transition to Employee Ownership." In *Worker Participation and Ownership: Cooperative Strategies for Strengthening Local Economies,* edited by William Foot Whyte and others. Ithaca, N.Y.: ILR Press.

Stiglitz, Joseph E. 1974. "Incentives and Risk Sharing in Sharecropping." *Review of Economic Studies* 64: 219–56.

Taylor, William. 1990a. "The Business of Innovation: An Interview with Paul Cook." *Harvard Business Review* 68 (March-April): 96–106.

———. 1990b. "Can Big Owners Make a Big Difference." *Harvard Business Review* 68 (September-October): 70–82.

Teslik, Sarah. 1993. "Do You Know a Pension Purpose When You See One?" *Council of Institutional Investors Central* 6 (July): 1–6.

Thompson, J. V. 1990. "Human Resources in Banking's Brave New World." In *The New Frontier in Bank Strategy: Managing People for Results in Turbulent Times,* edited by William J. Korsvik and Hervey A. Juris. Homewood, Ill.: Dow Jones-Irwin.

Thurow, Lester C. 1988. "Let's Put Capitalists Back into Capitalism." *Sloan Management Review* 30 (Fall): 67–71.

Tobin, James. 1992. "Dissent." In Twentieth Century Fund, *Report on the Task Force on Market Speculation and Corporate Governance.* New York.

Topel, Robert C. 1990. "Specific Capital and Unemployment: Measuring the Costs and Consequences of Job Loss." In *Studies in Labor Economics in Honor of Walter Y. Oi,* edited by Allan H. Meltzer and Charles I. Plosser, 181–214. Amsterdam: North Holland.

———. 1991. "Specific Capital, Mobility, and Wages: Wages Rise with Job Security." *Journal of Political Economy* 99 (February): 145–76.

Tufano, Peter. 1989. "Financial Innovation and the First-Mover Advantage." *Journal of Financial Economics* 25 (December): 213–40.

———. 1993. "Financing Acquisitions in the Late 1980s." In *The Deal Decade*, edited by Margaret M. Blair, 289–320. Brookings.

Turnbull, Shann. 1993. "Improving Corporate Structure and Ethics: A Case for Corporate 'Senates'." *Director's Monthly* 17 (May): 1–4.

Twentieth Century Fund. 1992. *Report of the Task Force on Market Speculation and Corporate Governance.* New York: Twentieth Century Fund Press.

United Shareholders Association. 1990. "Proposing Amendments to Proxy Regulations." Letter to Johnathan G. Katz, Office of the Secretary, Securities and Exchange Commission. Washington. March 20.

U.S. Senate, Committee on Government Operations. Subcommittee on Reports, Accounting and Management. 1977. *The Accounting Establishment: A Staff Study.* Government Printing Office.

Vanek, Jaroslav. 1977. "The Basic Theory of Financing of Participatory Firms." In *The Labor-Managed Economy: Essays by Jaroslav Vanek*, edited by Vanek, 186–98. Cornell University Press.

Votaw, Dow. 1965. *Modern Corporations.* Prentice-Hall.

Wallman, Steven M. H. 1991. "The Proper Interpretation of Corporate Constituency Statutes and Formulation of Director Duties." *Stetson Law Review* 21: 163–92.

———. 1993. "Corporate Constituency Laws." In *The Deal Decade Handbook*, edited by Margaret M. Blair and Girish Uppal, 31–33. Brookings.

Webber, Alan M. 1993. "What's So New About the New Economy?" *Harvard Business Review* 71 (January-February): 24–42.

Weidenbaum, Murray. 1994. *The Evolving Corporate Board.* St. Louis: Washington University, Center for the Study of American Business.

Weitzman, Martin L., and Douglas L. Kruse. 1990. "Profit Sharing and Productivity." In *Paying for Productivity*, edited by Alan S. Blinder, 95–141. Brookings.

Wharton, Clifton R., Jr. 1991. "Just Say No." *Harvard Business Review* 69 (November-December): 137–39.

Wigmore, Barrie. 1995. "Securities Markets in the 1980s: The Volatile Years, 1979–1984." Goldman Sachs, New York, New York. Unpublished manuscript.

Williamson, Oliver E. 1964. "Organizational Behavior." In *The Economics of Discretionary Behavior: Managerial Objectives in a Theory of the Firm.* Prentice Hall.

———. 1975. *Markets and Hierarchies: Analysis and Antitrust Implications.* Free Press.

————. 1979a. "Transaction-Cost Economics: The Governance of Contractual Relations." *Journal of Law and Economics* 22 (October): 233–61.

————. 1979b. "On the Governance of the Modern Corporation." *Hofstra Law Review* 8 (Fall): 63–98.

————. 1980. "The Organization of Work: A Comparative Institutional Assessment." *Journal of Economic Behavior and Organization* 1 (March): 5–38.

————. 1981. "The Modern Corporation: Origins, Evolution, Attributes." *Journal of Economic Literature* 19 (December): 1537–68.

Wohlstetter, Charles, 1993. "Pension Fund Socialism: Can Bureaucrats Run the Blue Chips?" *Harvard Business Review* 71 (January-February): 78.

Woolridge, J. Randall. 1988. "Competitive Decline and Corporate Restructuring: Is a Myopic Stock Market to Blame?" *Journal of Applied Corporate Finance* 1 (Spring): 26–36.

The Working Group on Corporate Governance. 1991. "A New Compact for Owners and Directors." *Harvard Business Review* 69 (July-August): 141–43.

Wruck, Karen Hopper. 1991. "What Really Went Wrong at REVCO?" *Journal of Applied Corporate Finance* 4 (Summer): 79–92.

INDEX

Abernathy, William, 124
Accountability: duty of, 165; executive, 3, 10, 109; to investors, 19
Accounting profession: and disclosure, 84; and securities regulations, 49
Accounting systems, U.S., 327–28
Advisors, financial, 191
AFL-CIO Department of Employee Benefits, 318
Agency costs, 97–98
Alchian, Armen A. 261
Algoma Steel, 306–07
Allen, James, 318
Allen, William T., 209, 211–12, 215
Allied Investment Partners, 155, 181
Allied Signal, 297
American Express, 10, 172, 180–81
American Federation of Labor, 320

American Institute of Certified Public Accountants (AICPA), 85
American Law Institute, 217
American Society of Corporate Secretaries, 74
America Stock Exchange (Amex), 112
Anders, W.A., 9
Antifraud provisions, 52
Antitakeover measures. See Takeover defenses
Antonini, Joseph E., 163
Apple Computer, 52
Assets: claims to, 34; disposal rights, 5
At&T, 304
Audit, annual, 49, 85; and market values, 333
Audit committees, 82
Automatic Data Processing Inc., 291

Avis Car Rental, 304

Balance sheet, 50
Bank holding companies, 185
Bankruptcy Reform Act of 1978, 24
Bankruptcy rules, 3, 23–26;
   restructuring of, 113–14
Banks: as investors, 149–52;
   prohibitions on, 30
Basic model of the corporation, 20–22,
   26–28
Benefits, mandated portable, 331
Berkshire Hathaway, 185
Berle, Adolf A., 12, 29, 61, 204–06,
   211–12
Berle-Means model of the corporation,
   30, 33, 43–45, 95
Biggs, John H., 162
Black, Bernard S., 71, 174, 176–77
Blasi, Joseph R., 303, 305, 314, 316,
   320–21
Bloomingdales, 41
Board of directors, 21, 56, 77–79, 229;
   commitment of, 190–92; as
   fiduciaries, 56–61; independence of,
   80–81, 171; nonmanagement
   employees on, 315–16; power and
   responsibility of, 2, 325–27; terms of
   office, 66, 74; and total wealth
   creation, 219
Boesky, Ivan, 53, 176
Bonus plans, 286
Borden, 10, 90, 172
Broker-dealer, in-house, 312–13
Brown Brothers Harriman, 155
Brown-Forman Distillers Corp., 65
Buffet, Warren, 182, 185
Burger King, 317
Business conditions, response to, 107,
   268–69
Business judgment, 98
Business judgment rule, 58–60, 219
Business Roundtable, 72, 112
Business Week, 89, 291, 312, 316
Bylaws, 23

Calabrese, Michael, 318

California Public Employees
   Retirement System (CalPERS),
   164–67, 170–71; and corporate
   behavior, 48, 74–75, 179; investment
   criteria of, 336
Campbell's Soup Co., 158–59
Campeau Corp., 41–42
Capital: committed, 334–35; cost of, 7,
   125–28, 216; knowledge, 251; optimal
   structure, 37; patient, 155, 337. See
   also Human capital
Capital budgeting systems, 83, 87
Capital gains, 21; taxation of, 38
Career commitments, 277
Carter Hawley Hale Stores, 319
Cash offers, 63
CEO (chief executive officer), 21, 78
Champion International Corp., 103, 171
Chandler, Alfred D., Jr., 209
Chapter 11, 24–25
Charitable support, 214–15
Charter Medical, 304
Charters, corporate, 2, 23, 207
Chevron, 304
Chicago Rivet and Machine Co., 64
Chicago School, 210
Chrysler, 180
Churning, portfolio, 47
Cincinnati Gas & Electric Co., 304
Cin-Made Corp., 294–95
Claims. See Residual claims
Closely held corporations, 28, 32, 76,
   338
Coase, Ronald, 225
Coffee, John C., Jr., 76, 185
Collective action, 173
Columbia Gas Systems Inc., 304
Commercial Lovelace Motor Freight,
   Inc., 306
Commercial paper markets, 150
Communicate with management, duty
   to, 164
Compensation, 90, 110, 295–98, 334;
   combined wages/stock, 329–30;
   committees, 82, 91; fixed, 98–99;
   restructuring, 305, 311–13; of
   stakeholders, 240; systems, 7, 87–92,
   327–28; variable, 268–70

Compensation, executive, 2, 9–10, 88–89, 91, 114–15, 286; justification of, 82; and proxy process, 74
Competence carriers, 290, 292
Competition, 260–62; global, 2, 7–8, 103, 145, 216
Competitive myopia, 124–25
Competitiveness Policy Council, 140–41; Subcouncil on Capital Allocation, 335
Concession theory, 208
Confidential voting, 74, 114
Conflicts of interest, 173–74; and relationship investing, 187–88, 326
Congress, U.S.: and executive compensation, 82, 91
Consolidated Freightways Inc., 318
Constitution, U.S., 24
Consultants, 291
Consumer surplus, 240
Conte, Michael A., 314–15
Contracts, complete, 230, 237, 262
Control share laws, 66
Core competencies, 286, 288, 290
Corporate constituency laws, 219–20
Corporate democracy, 68, 76
Corporate ethics committees, 82
Corporate governance committees, 82
Corporate Partners, 181
Corporation, 1–2, 17, 211; closely held, 32, 76; evolution of, 207–08; formation of, 22; perpetual existence of, 22, 248; as private property, 209–10, 223–24; publicly traded, 338–39; virtual, 291
Cospecialized assets, 251–52
Cospecialized investments, 261–62
Council of Institutional Investors, 159, 165, 169, 318
Council on Competitiveness, 137
Cram down, 25
Crawford, Richard, 291–93
Creditors, 24; veto power of, 26
CREF (College Retirement Equity Fund), 162, 169
Critical resources, 290, 292, 313, 325
Cross-discipline project teams, 293
Cross-shareholdings, 283
Crown jewel sales, 166

Cumulative voting, 74
Cuomo, Governor Mario, 164

Daimler-Benz, 284
D'Amato, Anthony, 90
Davis, Martin, 78, 221
Debentures, convertible subordinated, 43
Debt, 26–27, 33–35; as control, 40, 102; high levels of, 113; taxation and, 36–37
Debt-equity ratio, 36–37, 248; and corporate governance, 39
Debtor in possession, 25
Decisionmaking, residual, 244–45
Declining industries, 259, 269–70, 305–08
Dedicated capital systems, 138–39, 142, 243–44
Deferred payment instruments, 43
Deferred profit-sharing plan, 311, 314–15
Defined-benefit plans, 156–60
Defined-contribution plans, 160–64, 337
Delaware, incorporation in, 22–23, 220–23
Delaware Chancery Court, 78
Delaware Supreme Court, 23, 60, 66, 220–23
Demsetz, Harold 261
Department of Labor, U.S., 316
Depression, Great, 1, 37, 69, 95; and legitimacy of corporations, 213; and securities markets, 48; and subsequent securities laws, 123–24
Derivative suits, 69–70
Dillon, Read, 155
Directors. See Boards of directors
Directors and officers (D&O) liability insurance, 60
Disclosure rules, 49–56, 63, 83–88, 333–34
Disinterested trustee, 25
Diversified mutual funds, 153–55
Diversifying risks, 96–97, 188–89, 229
Dividends, 20, 34; taxation of, 38
Dodge v. Ford Motor Co., 209
Donaldson, Thomas, 224–25

Dow, Gregory K., 300
Downsizing, 10, 270, 286
Drexel Burnham Lambert, 53, 65,
    108–09
Drucker, Peter, 183
DuPont, 312
Duty of care, 57, 60
Dysner-Kissner-Moran (DKM), 59

Easterbrook, Frank H., 57, 236–37,
    244–45, 258, 261
Economic profits, 241–42
Economist, The, 281–82
Edgar v. MITE, 64
Education and training, 272
Efficiency wage theories, 254–55
Efficient markets model, 107
8-K report, 51
1818 Fund, 155
Empire building, 99–106
Employee ownership, 16, 239, 298–322;
    and financial investment risk, 332
Employee Retirement Income Security
    Act of 1974 (ERISA), 156–61, 164–65,
    308–09; investing limits of, 336–37
Employees, 191, 330; and basic model,
    26–28; benefits of, 230–31; and
    company downturn, 189, 258; as
    owners, 239; as residual claimants,
    256–57. *See also* Human capital;
    Stakeholders
Employee stock ownership plans
    (ESOPs): creation of, 308–11; and
    performance, 314–15; as takeover
    defense, 305, 310
Entrepreneurial cultures, 321
Entrepreneurial start-ups, 278–79
Environmental committees, 82
EPIC Healthcare Group, 304
Epstein, Edward Jay, 68–69, 76
Equitable subordination, 149–51
Equity, 20; and high-risk debt, 102;
    maximizing the value of, 249,
    256–57; taxation of, 36–37
ERISA. *See* Employee Retirement
    Income Security Act of 1974
ESB Inc., 102

ESOPs. *See* Employee stock ownership
    plans
European Community (EC), 152
European securities regulations, 54
Exchanges, market, 243
Executive rewards, 89
Executive selection, 286
Exit, shareholder, 68, 175, 229
*Exit, Voice, and Loyalty: Responses to
    Declines in Firms, Organizations,
    and States*, 68
Expenditures, actual, 86–87
Externalities, 19
Exxon, 10

Fairness, legal test of, 57
Federal Reserve Bank of New York, 176
Federal Trade Commission, 49–50
Federated Department Stores, 41
Feudal cultures, 320
Fidelity Investments, 154–55, 169
Fiduciary duties, 56–61, 158, 186, 316
Fiduciary principle, 56–58
Finance model, 12–13, 94–121, 231–32
Financial Accounting Standards Board
    (FASB), 84; and stock options, 91–92
Financial institutions, 14, 147–48. *See
    also* Institutional investors
Financial markets: distrust of, 123–24;
    internationalization of, 216
Financial restructuring, 42
Financial system, increased security of,
    29–30
Firm-specific investments, 188, 269,
    327–28; and governance, 262–63; and
    stakeholders, 142. *See also* Human
    capital
Fischel, Daniel R., 57, 236–37, 244–45,
    258, 261
Fleming, Michael, 176
Fluid capital system, 137–38
FMC Corp., 40
Ford, Henry, 209
Ford Motor Co., 10, 293
Fortune, 102, 294
401(k) plans, 161, 311
Franchise systems, 279–80

Freeman, Richard, 302–03
Free rider problems, 173, 185
Frey, Robert, 294–95

Gains, residual, 3, 43, 227–29, 231–32, 325
Gatekeeping authority, 69
Gavis, Alexander C., 219
General Dynamics, 9
General Electric, 10
General Motors, 10, 165, 170, 172
General Motors-Toyota (Fremont, CA), 294
German capitalism, 138–39. 187–88
German competition, 6–7, 127
Gilson, Ronald J. 227–28
Glass-Steagall Act of 1933, 149
Goals, corporate, 79, 84, 206; and social responsibility, 216–23
Golden parachutes, 166, 302
Goldman Sachs, 280
Gordon, Lilli, 177–79
Government intervention, 69
Grace, J. Peter, 163
Grand Metropolitan PLC, 317
Greenmail, 166
Group psychology model, 129
Grumman, 304
Grundfest, Joseph, 75
Gulf Oil Co., 65, 102
GVO Inc., 291

Hamel, Gary, 290, 292
Hanson, Dale, 165
Hartley, Fred, 103
Hart-Scott-Rodino Act of 1976, 154
Harvard Business School, 137
Hausbank, 152, 285
Hayek, Friedrich A., 226
Hayes, Robert, 124
Health Trust of Nashville, TN, 304
Herman, Edward S., 30
Herman Miller, 304–05
Hester, Steven, 317
Himes, John W., 312
Hirschman, Albert O., 68, 175

Hold-up problem, 251–53, 255
Hostile takeovers, 62, 65, 101, 105, 216–17; in Germany or Japan, 145–46; as value to shareholders, 105
Household International, 59
Houston Natural Gas, 53
Hudson, Jeffrey H., 291
Human capital, 238–40, 289–90, 300; and customized goods, 272; discouraging investment in, 277; firm-specific, 15, 249–59, 322; generic, 289–90, 329–30; management of, 16, 288; return of investment in, 327–28, 333–34
Hyatt Legal Services, 282

IBM, 10, 172, 181, 184, 291
Imcera Group, 312
Income statement, 50
Incorporation, 22–23, 207; as federal right, 110–11
Indemnity insurance, 281
Independents, 80–81
Indexed funds, 162
Information, financial: disclosure of, 33, 44, 49, 135; insider, 51; and making money, 133–34
Information assymetries, 19
Informed business judgment standard, 60
Innovation, 260–62, 271–72; barriers to, 103, 277
Inputs, specialized, 261–62, 274
Insiders, 51; in Japan and Europe, 283
Insider trading, 53–54
Institutional investors, 2, 45, 145–201, 334–35; and communication, 72; increased role in governance, 139–40; and insider trading, 55
Institutional Investors Service, 166
Insurance companies, 30, 45, 152–53
Intel Corp., 291
Interest payments and control, 39
Interest rates, real, 108–09, 127
Interests served by corporations, 202–34
Internal measurements and controls, 83–88, 110, 136, 327–28

International Nickel Company, 102
In the long run device, 216–17
Inventory control, 83
Investment companies, 153–55
Investment Company Act of 1940,
    153–55
Investments: incentive for, 94;
    measures of, 327–28; relationship,
    244–45, 262–63, 275
Investor cultures, 320
Investors. *See* Institutional investors;
    Shareholders
Irrelevancy of stock prices, 128–29, 133

Jacobs, Michael, 112, 130, 172, 183
Jacoby and Meyers, 282
Japanese capitalism, 138–39, 187–88
Japanese competition, 6–7, 127
Japanese industrial trading groups, 151,
    187, 284–85
Japanese securities regulations, 54
Jensen, Michael, 41–42, 76, 107
Johnson, H. Thomas, 86
Joint stock companies, 207
Jones, Thomas, 90
Junk bonds, 40, 43, 45, 65, 102
Justice, distributive, 224–25

Kaisha model, 267–69
Kaplan, Robert S., 86
Kaplan, Steven, 287
Keiretsu, 151, 187, 284–85
Kester, W. Carl, 284
Keynes, John Maynard, 123–24
Kmart, 163
Knowledge companies, 291–92
Kodak, Eastman, 10, 163, 172
Korn/Ferry International, 79
KPMG, 281
Kruse, Douglas L., 303, 305, 314–16,
    320–21
KSOP, 311

Laboı Department, U.S., 158
Labor laws, 330
Labor relations, 258

Labor unions, 18, 318–20
Lawsuits, corporate, 52
Layoffs, 301–02; costs and seniority,
    264–66
Lazard Freres & Co., 181
Lazear, Edward P., 302–03
Lenders, 20, 26–28
Lenox Corp., 65
Lens Fund, The, 180–81
Leveraged buyouts (LBOs), 40, 42, 62,
    99–106, 287–88; and institutional
    investors, 45
Levin, Gerald, 171
Levine, David, 293–95, 327
Levine, Dennis, 53
Lewis, Peter, 298
Liability, limited, 22, 26–27, 229, 248
Lifetime employment, 268, 286, 339
Liquidity, 35, 55, 76, 167; cost of,
    136–37; increased, 96–97
Lockheed, 171
Long-term v. short-term profit
    maximization, 215–20; goals, 84
Lorsch, Jay W., 79

McDonnell Douglas, 304
Machold, Roland, 165
Magellan Fund, 154–55
Management: accountability, 69,
    212–15, 225–34; control, 30; new
    orthodoxy of, 124–25; restrictions,
    110; vulnerability, 103
Management team, 20–21
Managers, 56–57, 96, 98–99;
    accountability of, 227; as board
    members, 78; and control, 226;
    discretion of, 39; professional, 3, 211
Managing boards, German, 285
Manhattan, U.S. Attorney, 108
Manne, Henry, 61, 100, 102
Marcotte, Dave E., 289
Market for corporate control, 61–62,
    100–01
Market myopia model, 12, 122–44; and
    long-term profits, 215
Market pressure, 18, 76
Marris, Robin, 61, 100, 102
Marsh, Paul, 132

Mason, Edward S., 98
Maximizing value, 216; monitoring and, 176–79, 231–32; and societal interest, 14, 202
Means, Gardiner C., 12, 29, 61, 203–06, 212
Measurements, performance, 7, 83–88, 110, 327–28
Median pay growth, 89
Medical Care America, 72
Merck, 293, 312
Mergers, 99, 104–05
Mesa Petroleum, 59
Michigan Supreme Court, 209–10
Milgrom, Paul, 252
Milken, Michael, 108
Miller, Merton H., 36
Millstein, Ira, 168, 172
Milwaukee Insurance, 296
Minow, Nell, 80, 165–66, 174, 183, 186
Mirror voting, 316
Misconduct, 81
MITE Corp., 64
Mobil, 10
Modern Corporation and Private Property, The, 211
Modigliani, Franco, 36
Monitor, 141; duty to, 164; and residual risk/gain, 227–29, 231–32
Monitoring, 44, 182–85; adequate, 89, 190; by institutional investors, 176–79, 187; managers, 33, 94
Monks, Robert, 165, 174, 180–81, 186
Monopolies, 18–19; and rents, 242
Moran, John A., 59
Moran v. Household International, 59, 66
Morgan Stanley, 101–02, 304
Motorola, 296
Mustang, 293
Mutual funds, 14, 45, 153–55; tax penalties and, 30

Nabisco Brands, 53
National Bank Act of 1863, 149
National Center for Employee Ownership, 305
National Intergroup, 306–07

National Labor Relations Act, 159–60, 330
Nesbitt, Stephen L., 179
Net negative transactions, 168
New York City Employees Retirement System, 164, 171
New York Stock Exchange (NYSE), 22, 56, 82, 111
New York Times, 103, 181, 306–07
Niches, market, 242–43
Nissan, 284
Nominating committees, 82, 326
Northern Telecom Ltd., 77
Northrup, 81, 90
Northwest Airlines, 306, 315
Northwestern Steel and Wire, 306
NUMMI, 294

O'Connell, Philip R., 103
Officers and directors. *See* Boards of directors.
Oligopoly power, 2
Opportunity cost, 86; calculating, 254; to investors, 108; social, 230; of workers, 250–51
Option value, 138
Organizational capabilities, 261–62
Organization for Economic Cooperation and Development (OECD), 146–47
Outside investors, trust of, 123
Outsiders, 61, 78, 80–81
Outsourcing, 286
Owners as shareholders, 5, 223–25

Pacific Gas & Electric Co., 304
Paine-Webber Group, 304
Paramount Communications, 67, 78
Paramount Communications v. Time Inc., 220–23
Participatory cultures, 320
Participatory management, 295
Partnerships, 280–86
Passive owners, 109, 157–58, 162, 204–05
Patient investing strategies, 140, 334–35
Payments, flexible: and residual returns, 244–45

Payroll Stock Ownership Plan
    (PAYSOP), 309
Pennsylvania Railroad Co., 29
Pension Benefit Guaranty Corp., 161
Pension funds, 14, 45, 155–72;
    governance of, 335–37; invested in
    employing company, 284;
    multiemployer, 159–60; private,
    156–64, 337; public employee,
    164–65, 186
Pepsico, 312
Performance, 13, 83–88, 110, 327–28;
    analysis and decisionmaking, 130–32;
    declines in, 107; and ESOPs, 314–15;
    short-term, 42, 47, 122–44; and
    societal interest, 215–16
Perkins, Donald S., 37
Perpetuities, 43
Personnel evaluation, 83, 87
Pfizer, 312
Phar-Mor, Inc., 181
Phillips Petroleum, 81
Physical capital, 272, 298–300
Pickens, T. Boone, 59, 65, 73, 102
Pillsbury Co., 317
Piore, Michael J., 271–72
Poison pills, 58, 65, 73–74, 108, 110,
    166, 172
Polaroid, 310
Pollution, 18, 174
Porter, Michael, 137–39, 174, 191–92,
    279; on corporate goals, 206
Portfolio traders and stock prices,
    129–30
Posner, Victor, 176
Poterba, James M., 138
Pound, John, 75, 172, 177–79
Power: of creditors, 26; of large
    corporations, 213; of liquidity, 76; of
    officers and directors, 325–27; private
    uses of, 226; of shareholders, 45, 110,
    191
Pozen, Robert, 155
Prahalad, C.K., 290, 292
Preferred shares, 43, 65; convertible, 319
Preston, Lee E., 224–25
Price volatility, 47
Primerica Corp., 316
Privatized industries, newly, 11

Process inefficiencies, 86
Procter and Gamble, 10, 304
Production management, 86
Productivity growth, U.S., 7–8
Profits. See rents
Profit-sharing plans, 314–15
Progressive Insurance Co., 297–98
Prospectus, 50
Proxy fight, 62–63
Proxy process, 56, 70–73, 75, 114, 170
Pujo Committee, 209
Putterman, Louis, 299, 301

Quality control systems, 83, 87
Quarterly statement, elimination of, 134
Quasi rents, 241–42
QVC Network, 67, 78, 221

Raiders, 101
Ratio of pay, executive/employee, 286
Ravenscraft, David J., 99
Reagan, President Ronald, 125
Reasonable man standard, 57
Recapitalizations, debt-based, 166
Reengineering, 286
Reform, evaluation costs of, 173
Reform proposals: finance model, 110,
    116–21; market myopia model,
    134–44; relationship investing,
    193–201
Reich, Robert, 159
Relationship investing, 14, 140, 172–86.
    See also Institutional investors
Rents, 241–42, 251–53, 256–57;
    extraction by unions, 254–55; as
    return on human capital, 267
Reorganization plan, 25
Reporting systems, 83–88
Republic Engineered Steel, 306
Reputation, 259; professional, 211
Residual claims, 20, 27, 227–29,
    237–38; assigned, 261–62; and
    creditors, 26; and employees, 256–57
Resolutions: shareholder, 170
Restructuring, 10, 270, 330–31;
    debt-driven, 40
Retained earnings, 38–39

Retraining, 174
Returns, 27, 217, 301; residual, 15, 244–45
Revised Model Business Corporation Act (RMBCA), 34
Risk, residual, 15, 26, 43, 186, 231–32, 277; allocation of, 3, 227–29, 308, 325
R.J. Reynolds, 53
RJR Nabisco, 40
Roberts, John, 252
Rockwell International, 304
Roe, Mark, 64, 113–14, 123, 227
Romano, Roberta, 111
Russell, Raymond, 282

Sabel, Charles F., 271–72
Salomon Brothers, 180, 185
Savings and loans, 84
Scandals, 81
Scherer, F.M., 99
Schneider-Lenné, Ellen, 285
Science Applications International Corp. (SAIC), 312–13
Scientific approach to organization, 98
Screening, employee, 268
Sears, 10, 180
Securities Act of 1933, 49
Securities and Exchange Act of 1934, 49, 63, 70
Securities and Exchange Commission (SEC), 49–51, 108, 112; and compensation, 74, 82; and proxy process, 56, 318; and reporting requirements, 69–70, 85
Securities dealers, 56
Securities markets, 18, 28–30, 48–56
Self-dealing transactions, 154, 157
Senate Banking Committee, 52
Service industries, 238–40, 289
Shamrock, 310
Shareholder cultures, 320
Shareholder democracy, 68, 76
Shareholders, 20–22, 30–34, 69–70, 204–05; activist, 140, 158–60, 182, 317; and closely held companies, 28; communication with, 71–72, 130–31; and control, 41, 95–96, 103, 226; as owners, 5, 223–25, 237–38; passive, 109, 162; power of, 45, 110, 191

Shareholder votes, solicitation of, 50, 112, 114
Shiller, Robert J., 129
Shleifer, Andrei, 259
Short-term performance, 42, 47, 122–24
Simmons, Harold, 171
Singer, Joseph William, 224
Size of boards, 82
Skill-based pay, 296
Skilled work force, 249–59, 261–62, 272
Skills, 289–90; firm-specific, 15, 249–59, 322. *See also* Human capital
Small investors, 96, 115
Smith, Adam, 18, 95
Smith, Roger, 165
Smith v. Van Gorkom, 59
Social entity conception, 211–15
Social purpose, corporate, 13, 14, 174, 202–03
Social responsibility, 2, 73, 82, 203, 226
Sommer, A.A., Jr., 42
Special committees within boards, 82
Stakeholders, 142, 191–92, 210, 226, 326; compensation of, 240; and corporate constituency laws, 222–23; corporate responsiveness to, 214–15, 337–38; in Germany and Japan, 282–86; as owners, 238–40; and property rights, 225; and residual risk, 275; and state laws, 218–20; v. shareholders, 188, 226
Standardized accounting and reporting, 99
State legislatures, 108
State of Wisconsin Investment Board, 164
Steelcase, 296
Stempel, Robert C., 170
Stern, Paul G., 77
Stock: as employee compensation, 114–15, 311–12, 328–30; options for executives, 89–92
Stock buybacks, 305
Stock exchanges, 56
Stockholders, 20–21
Stock market collapse, 216
Stock options, 89–92
Stock prices, 128–33
Stock repurchase plans, selective, 58–59

Strike price, option, 90
Subcouncil on Corporate Governance
    and Financial Markets, 140–41
Sullivan principles, 73
Summers, Lawrence H., 138, 259
Supermajorities, 66
Supervisory boards, German, 284–85
Suppliers, 26–28, 189, 191
Supreme Court, 64
Surgical Care Affiliates, 72
Svejnar, Jan, 314–15

Taft-Hartley Act of 1947, 159–60
Takeover defenses, 58, 64, 66, 73; and
    employee interests, 310; in
    Pennsylvania, 166, 219–20
Takeovers, 42, 45, 100–10, 166; and
    efficiency gains, 103–04, 106. See also
    Hostile takeovers, Takeover defenses
Tax liabilities, 105–06
Tax Reduction Act of 1975, 309
Tax Reduction Act Stock Ownership
    Plan (TRASOP), 309
Taylor, William, 186
Teamsters Union, 160
Technology-intensive enterprise, 238–40
Telepad Corp., 291
Temporary help industry, 289
Tender offers, 42, 56, 62, 64
10-K statements, 50
10-Q statements, 51
Teslik, Sara, 318
Thurow, Lester C., 134, 174–75
TIAA-CREF, 48, 160–64, 171
TIAA (Teachers Insurance and Annuity
    Association), 162
Time horizon problem, 7, 126
Time Inc., 67–68
Time Warner, 171, 180
Tokyo Stock Exchange, 128
Topel, Robert C., 265–66
Total quality management, 286
Toys 'R' Us, 312
Trading flexibility, 174–75
Training, 294
Transactions costs, 19
Transactions tax, 135
Trans Union Corp., 59–60

Trust funds, private, 149–50
Trusts, 207
Turnover costs and seniority, 263–66
TWA, 306, 315
Tyson, Laura D'Andrea, 295

UAL, 9, 306, 315
Underperforming companies, 169
United Shareholders Association, 73
Unocal, 59, 103
Unruh, Jesse, 165
U.S. system: corporate model, 269–71;
    strengths of, 115, 277
USX, 10

Value created, organizational, 86–87
Value-in-use, 246, 260–61
Value proxies, 138
Van Gorkom, Jerome W., 60
Venture capital companies, 278–79, 287
Vertical integration, 253–54, 260–61
Vesting: stock bonuses, 312–13; voting
    rights on securities, 332
Viacom, 67, 78, 221–22
Visioneer, 291
Vocational education, 174
Voice, employee, 285
Voice, shareholder, 68, 76, 110, 175;
    and institutional investors, 164,
    168–69
Volatility of stock prices, 128–30, 133
Votaw, Dow, 96, 211, 213, 224
Voting rights, 34, 166, 330
Voting stock, multiple classes, 111

Wages, 263–65; fixed, 259, 301;
    variable, 268
Wallman, Steven M.H., 219
Wall Street Journal, 54, 78, 293, 317–18
Wall Street Walk, 35
Warner Communications, 67–68, 220
Washington Post Co., 111
Waste Management, 312
Wealth-creation, 3–4, 233–34, 241,
    245–49; and human capital, 273,
    327–28; incentives to, 19, 232–34;

maximizing total, 12–13, 16, 219,
    275–322, 338; potential, 275; and
    resource use, 94
Wealth for society, 93, 203–04
Wealth of Nations, The, 18, 95
Weirton Steel, 306–07, 315
Weitzman, Martin L., 314–15
Wendy's, 312
Westinghouse, 10, 172, 181
White knights, 112
Williams Act, 63–64
Williamson, Oliver, 100, 244, 253,
    261–62
Winans, R. Foster, 54

Wolf, Stephen M., 9
Workplaces, high involvement, 294
Works councils, German, 285
W.R. Grace & Co., 163, 180

Xerox, 10

Yatine, Barbara, 316

Zero-sum transactions, 168